gateway science

FOUNDATION

OCR
Additional
Science
for GCSE

Ian Honeysett

David Lees

Averil Macdonald

Steven Bibby

Series Editor: Bob McDuell

www.heinemann.co.uk
✓ Free online support
✓ Useful weblinks
✓ 24 hour online ordering

01865 888058

Heinemann

Inspiring generations

Heinemann Educational Publishers
Halley Court, Jordan Hill, Oxford OX2 8EJ
Part of Harcourt Education

Heinemann is the registered trademark of Harcourt Education Limited

First published 2006

10 09 08 07
10 9 8 7 6 5 4 3 2

ISBN: 978 0 435 67525 7

Edited by Bob McDuell
Designed by Wooden Ark
Typeset by Kamae Design, Cassington, Oxford
copy edited by Sharon Jordan

Original illustrations © Harcourt Education Limited, 2006

Illustrated by HL Studios
Printed in China by South China Printing Co.
Cover photo: © Getty Images
Picture research by Natalie Gray

Acknowledgements
The authors and publisher would like to thank the following individuals and organisations for permission to reproduce photographs:
Page 2, Roslin Institute / Phototake Inc / OSF; 3, T Eric Grave / Phototake Inc / OSF; M Getty Images / PhotoDisc; B Digital Vision; 6, Getty Images / PhotoDisc; 7, Harcourt Education Ltd (×2); 10, Getty Images / PhotoDisc; 11, Getty Images / PhotoDisc; 14, Brad Nelson / Phototake Inc / OSF; 15, Harcourt Education / Tudor Photography; 16, Pascal Goetgheluck / SPL; 18, T Digital Vision; B Getty Images News; 19, T Harcourt Education / Jules Selmes; B britishcolumbiaphotos.com / Alamy; 20, Jose Luis Pelaez, Inc. / Corbis; 23, T Holt Studios International Ltd / Alamy; B Getty Images / PhotoDisc; 26, T Corbis; 27, T Getty Images / PhotoDisc; B Stone / Getty; 28, Chris Rogers / Corbis; 29, AJ / IRRI / Corbis; 30, T George Bernard / SPL; B Getty Images / PhotoDisc; 31, T Getty Images / PhotoDisc; B Roslin Institute / Phototake Inc / OSF; 34, Papilio / Alamy; 38, Kevin Schafer / Corbis; 39, T Harcourt Education Ltd; B Getty Images / PhotoDisc; 42, Getty Images / PhotoDisc; 43, Holt Studios International Ltd / Alamy; 44, Steve Gschmeissner / SPL; 46, Getty Images / PhotoDisc (×2); 47, T Robert Harding; B Holt Studios International Ltd / Alamy; 50, Wim Wiskerke / Alamy; 51, T Getty Images / PhotoDisc; M Getty Images / PhotoDisc; B Mary Ellen Baker / Botanica / OSF; 52, Martyn F. Chillmaid / SPL; 53, Rothampstead Research Station; 54, Doug Allen / naturepl.com; 55, T Richard Smith; B Harcourt Education; 58, TL unknown; ML Prof. David Hall / SPL; BR At a Scandinavian site, a truck collects chipped wood residue left after forest harvest for use as bio-fuel in electricity generation. (Texas Cooperative Extension photo by Dr. C.T. Smith); 59, T Harcourt Education / Debbie Rowe; B Stone / Getty; 61, Mary Clark / Alamy; 62, Bill Waldman / Alamy; 63, T Peter Johnson / Corbis; B Corbis / Corbis Sygma; 64, T Hybrid Medical Animation / SPL; B Robert Pickett / Corbis; 66, The Garden Picture Library / Alamy; 67, T John Wilkinson; Ecoscene / Corbis; B Gary Braasch / Corbis; 68, Getty Images / PhotoDisc; 69, John Howard / SPL; 70, L Dr Jeremy Burgess / SPL; R Corbis; 74, Getty Images / PhotoDisc; 75, T Corbis; B Getty Images / PhotoDisc; 78, WorldFoto / Alamy; 79, Kim Myung Jung Kim / PA / Empics; 80, Harcourt Education / Gareth Boden; 82, Andrew Lambert Photography / SPL; 83, Digital Vision; 86, Hulton Archive / Getty; 87, T Corbis; B Harcourt Education; 88, T Andrew Lambert Photography / SPL (×2); B Harcourt Education / Trevor Clifford (×3); 90, Digital Vision; 91, The Image Bank / Getty; 92, TL Charles D. Winters / SPL; Andrew Lambert Photography / SPL (×3); 94, imagebroker / Alamy; 95, Corbis; 96, Science and Society; 97, Adam Hart-Davis / SPL; 98, TL SPL; BR Bettmann / Corbis; 99, Harcourt Education Ltd; 100, SPL; 101, Andrew Lambert Photography / SPL (×3); 102, Glasses Direct; 103, TR Corbis; BR Honda; BL Harcourt Education / Gareth Boden; 104, Reed International Books, Australia; 105, T Getty Images / PhotoDisc; B Leslie Garland Picture Library / Alamy; 106, Hillcreek Pictures Bv / OSF; 110, Harcourt Education Ltd; 111, T Corbis; BL Getty Images / PhotoDisc; BR Greenshoots Communications / Alamy; 113, Martyn F. Chillmaid / SPL; 114, T Agripicture Images / Alamy; B Martyn F. Chillmaid / SPL; 115, The Image Bank / Getty; 118, Andrew Lambert Photography / SPL; 119, Getty Images / PhotoDisc; 120, Leslie Garland Picture Library / Alamy; 121, Harcourt Education / Trevor Clifford; 122, T Chris Howes / Wild Places Photography / Alamy; B geogphotos / Alamy; 123, T Getty Images / PhotoDisc; B Harcourt Education Ltd; 126, Photo Courtesy of Terra Nitrogen (UK) Limited; 127, Corbis; 128, Corbis; 129, Harcourt Education Ltd; 130, Peter Turnley / Corbis; 131, Getty Images / PhotoDisc; 133, Scott T. Smith / Corbis; 134, Erich Schrempp / SPL; 135, Frank Trapper / Corbis; 137, Dr Peter Harris / SPL; 138, Edwige / BSF / OSF; 139, T Digital Vision; B DK / Getty; 141, WaterAid / Jon Spaull; 142, Getty Images / PhotoDisc; 146, Harcourt Education / Debbie Rowe; 147, T Corbis; B NASA; 148, Dominic Burke / Alamy; 150, Reportage / Getty; 151, picturesbyrob / Alamy; 153, Getty Images / PhotoDisc; 154, Gabe Palmer / Corbis; 155, Getty Images / PhotoDisc; 157, Photofusion Picture Library / Alamy; 158, Digital Vision; 159, T Corbis; M1 Corbis, M2 Getty Images / PhotoDisc; B Realimage / Alamy; 162, Ian Miles-Flashpoint Pictures / Alamy; 163, Corbis; 164, T Motoring Picture Library; B Getty Images / PhotoDisc; 166, David Hancock / Handout / epa / Corbis; 167, T David Woods / Corbis; B Corbis; 169, Joe Fox / Alamy; 170, Janine Wiedel Photolibrary / Alamy; 171, T Dennis Galante / Corbis; B NASA Headquarters – Greatest Images of NASA (NASA-HQ-GRIN); 172, Corbis; 173, Schlegelmilch / Corbis; 174, Photos.com; 175, T Corbis; B Harcourt Education / Tudor Photography; 177, Corbis; 178, Kelly-Mooney Photography; 182, Alan Sirulnikoff / SPL; 183, T Harcourt Education Ltd; B Shout / Alamy; 185, Etit Claude / Corbis Sygma; 186, Pledge; 187, T Getty Images / PhotoDisc; B Corbis; 188, T Dacorum Gold / Alamy; B Jean-Francois Cardella / Construction Photography; 189, Honda; 190, Russell Sach; 191, T Harcourt Education Ltd; M Harcourt Education Ltd, B Cn Boon / Alamy; 192, Andrew Lambert Photography / SPL; 193, T Sheila Terry / SPL; B imagebroker / Alamy; 194, Harcourt Education Ltd; 195, T Getty Images / PhotoDisc; B Renee Morris / Alamy; 198, Getty Images / PhotoDisc; 199, SPL; 200, Getty Images / PhotoDisc; 201, T Sipa Press / Rex Features; B John Greim / SPL; 202, Getty; 203, Getty Images / PhotoDisc; 204, Gabe Palmer / Corbis; 206, Illustrated London News; 207, Bob Krist / Corbis; 208, T Ian M Butterfield / Alamy; B Chris Priest / SPL; 209, Getty Images / PhotoDisc; 210, Corbis Sygma; 211, T Bettmann / Corbis; B Digital Stock; 213, Roger Ressmeyer / Corbis; 214, Getty Images / PhotoDisc.

The authors and publisher would like to thank the following individuals and organisations for permission to reproduce copyright materials: 21, TL Relative rates graph for the human body, - Advanced Biology Principles and Applications by Clegg and Mackean, published by John Murray/ BR Growth curves for boys head size and weight - Child Growth Foundation; 112 pH universal indicator - Letts GCSE Classbook Science by D Baylis, published by Letts Educational Ltd; 140 Water Purification diagram - IGCSE Chemistry by Earl and Wilford, published by Hodder Education; 142 Reservoir capacity in England and Wales 2004/2005 - www.environment-agency.gov.uk.

Every effort has been made to contact copyright holders of material reproduced in this book. Any omissions will be rectified in subsequent printings if notice is given to the publishers.
Tel: 01865 888058   www.heinemann.co.uk

Introduction

This student book covers the Foundation tier of the new OCR Gateway Science specification. The first examinations are in January 2007. It has been written to support you as you study for the OCR Gateway Science GCSE.

This book has been written by examiners who are also teachers and who have been involved in the development of the new specification. It is supported by other material produced by Heinemann, including online teacher resource sheets and interactive learning software with exciting video clips, games and activities.

As part of GCSE Additional Science you have to do a skills assessment. This involves a research task, a data task and an assessment of your practical skills made by your teacher. You will find out more about these on pages 218–223.

If you are following this Additional Science course, you will either have completed or are progressing towards the Science Core GCSE award. The emphasis in the Core is on how science affects our everyday lives. For Additional Science the emphasis changes. It is more about the work of scientists, both in the past and also today. You will cover topics such as atomic structure, genetics and some quantitative physics. As a result of studying Additional Science, you may be encouraged to follow a science-based course or to seek employment in a science-related area.

The next two pages explain the special features we have included in this book to help you to learn and understand the science, and to be able to use it in context. At the back of the book you will also find some useful tables, as well as a glossary and index.

About this book

This student book has been designed to make learning science fun. The book follows the layout of the OCR Gateway specification. It is divided into six sections that match the six modules in the specification with two for Biology, two for Chemistry and two for Physics: B3, B4, C3, C4, P3, P4.

The module introduction page at the start of a module (e.g. below right) introduces what you are going to learn. It has some short introductory paragraphs, plus 'talking heads' with speech bubbles that raise questions about what is going to be covered. There is also a 'What you need to know' box highlighting what you need to remember from key stage 3.

Each module is then broken down into eight separate items (a–h), for example, B3a, B3b, B3c, B3d, B3e, B3f, B3g, B3h.

Each 'item' is covered in four book pages. These four pages are split into three pages covering the science content relevant to the item plus a 'Context' page which places the science content just covered into context, either by news-related articles or data tasks, or by examples of scientists at work, science in everyday life or science in the news.

Throughout these four pages there are clear explanations with diagrams and photos to illustrate the science being discussed. At the end of each module there are three pages of questions to test your knowledge and understanding of the module.

There are three pages of exam-style end of module questions for each module.

The numbers in square brackets give the marks for the question or part of the question.

The talking heads on the module introduction page raise questions about what you are going to learn.

The bulleted text introduces the module

This box highlights what you need to know before you start the module.

Context pages link the science learnt in the item with real life.

This box highlights what you will be learning about in this item.

General approach to the topic

Question box at the end.

Some amazing facts have been included – science isn't just boring facts!

When a new word appears for the first time in the text, it will appear in **bold** type. All words in bold are listed with their meanings in the glossary at the back of the book. There is also a Keywords box at the end of the three pages covering the content which lists all the keywords used in the item.

Questions in the text make sure you have understood what you have just read.

Clear diagrams to explain the science.

The Keywords box lists all keywords in the item.

B3a Molecules of life

DNA fingerprints

Dr Pete MacDonald works in a laboratory dealing with DNA fingerprinting. In genetic fingerprints, only about one in four 'fingerprint' bands match between people who are not related. Genetic fingerprinting is often used to decide relationships between different people.

Today Pete is working on the case of two babies who were found abandoned outside a hospital. Ten days after the babies were found a woman and a man have come forward claiming that the babies are theirs.

The authorities want Pete to check whether the two babies are related and whether the woman and the man are the parents. He takes DNA samples from the woman and the man, and then tests them against DNA from the babies. His results are shown in the diagram.

Questions
1. Which of the children could be the offspring of the woman and the man?
2. Do you think that child 1 and child 2 are related?
3. If the two babies were identical twins, what would their genetic fingerprints look like?
4. Suggest how genetic fingerprinting could be useful at a crime scene.

6

B3b Diffusion

Spreading far and wide

In this item you will find out
- how diffusion happens
- the importance of diffusion in animals
- how diffusion occurs in plant leaves

Have you ever played a trick on someone with a stink-bomb from a joke shop?

If you break the bottle, a terrible smell soon spreads out across the room. After a while, the smell disappears. This is because of **diffusion**. The molecules of the gas are spreading out throughout the room, eventually reaching the noses of the people in the room.

▲ Stink-bombs work by diffusion

◄ A plug-in air-freshener

▶ Why do you think the smell disappears after a while?

Diffusion is responsible for our ability to smell all the different scents that we come across. They need to diffuse into our noses to be detected.

Rather than making stink-bombs, other companies make air-fresheners. They have to design the air-freshener so that the scent diffuses out at just the correct rate

▶ What would happen if the scent diffused out too quickly or too slowly?

Some air-fresheners plug into electric sockets. This allows the scent to be heated up or cooled down.

Many of our household devices rely on diffusion, but so do many processes in our bodies and in the tissues of plants.

Amazing fact
The US Army is developing a device for dispersing crowds, using the strongest smelling artificial chemical (2 parts chemical to 1 million parts air).

7

P4b Uses of electrostatics

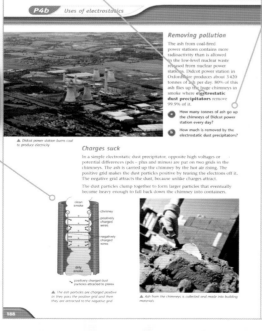
▲ Didcot power station burns coal to produce electricity

Removing pollution

The ash from coal-fired power stations contains more radioactivity than is allowed in the low-level nuclear waste released from nuclear power stations. Didcot power station in Oxfordshire produces about 1420 tonnes of ash per day. 80% of this ash flies up the huge chimneys in smoke where **electrostatic dust precipitators** remove 99.9% of it.

▶ How many tonnes of ash go up the chimneys of Didcot power station every day?

▶ How much is removed by the electrostatic dust precipitators?

Charges suck

In a simple electrostatic dust precipitator, opposite high voltages or potential differences (pds – plus and minus) are put on two grids in the chimneys. The ash is carried up the chimney by the hot air rising. The positive grid makes the dust particles positive by tearing the electrons off it. The negative grid attracts the dust, because unlike charges attract.

The dust particles clump together to form larger particles that eventually become heavy enough to fall back down the chimney into containers.

▲ The ash particles are charged positive as they pass the positive grid and then they are attracted to the negative grid.

▲ Ash from the chimneys is collected and made into building material.

Charging paint

Paint spraying a car is much faster than painting by hand. But a lot of paint is wasted as it sticks to everything, and not just to the car. One way to save paint (and money) is to charge up the spray gun so that the paint droplets pick up electrostatic charge. This means all the particles have the same type of charge and so they repel each other. This makes the droplets of paint spread out and become a fine spray.

The car is charged opposite to the spray and so the spray is attracted to the car and gives an even coating. This is because unlike charges attract. The whole process is much less wasteful and more effective and the spray will find its way into cracks and crevices that the operator could not see.

◄ Charging the spray means that the car attracts the paint

▶ Explain why charging paint gives a fine, spread out spray?

▶ Why does the paint stick well to the car?

Copying... copying... copying

Photocopiers use static electricity to make copies. There is a huge round drum in the copier made of a material that can be charged up. Inside the copier a bright light reflects off the paper you want to copy onto the drum. The white bits on the page reflect lots of light onto the drum and the drum loses its electrostatic charge.

The black bits do not reflect the light so those parts of the drum stay charged. The ink (toner) sticks to the parts of the drum that are charged. As the drum goes round it sticks the toner onto the paper and a heater warms up the paper to make it stick permanently.

A laser printer is similar. In a laser printer the laser writes the page and discharges the drum, leaving the background with a positive charge and the written areas with a negative charge. The toner is positive so sticks to the letters and not to the background.

▲ Electrostatic charge sticks the ink to the drum in a photocopier

Keywords
defibrillator • electrostatic dust precipitator • photocopier

188

189

Contents

B3 Living and growing

We are twins. We must be as strong as each other because we have the same genes.

- You may have noticed how some of your friends look similar to their parents or even their grandparents. Everybody knows that it is something to do with their genes. But what are genes and how are they passed on from one generation to another? This module looks at how genes control living organisms.

- You have probably heard about cloning, genetic engineering or genetic fingerprinting. After studying this module you should know more about these processes and understand more about what is possible and what should be allowed.

- Being an organism made of millions of cells gives many advantages but it means that systems are needed to move substances around. You will be looking at how some of these transport systems work.

Does that mean we are clones? I thought clones were made in a lab?

What you need to know

- Simple details about the human reproductive and breathing systems.

- Plants need sunlight, water and carbon dioxide to make their own food by photosynthesis.

- The structure of plant and animal cells and the importance of proteins in the body.

Building blocks for organisms

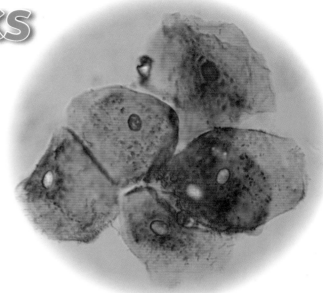

▲ Cheek cells

In this item you will find out

- how cells produce proteins

- what DNA fingerprints are used for

- the functions of enzymes

You, as well as all other living organisms, are made up of cells. But what do these cells look like? Using the naked eye we can see detail down to about the size of 0.1 mm. Cells are smaller than this, so we need to use microscopes to study them.

You have probably used a light microscope to look at cells and seen images like the one in the photograph.

All cells have a **cell membrane**, **cytoplasm** and a **nucleus**. These structures do different jobs.

Structure	Job
cell membrane	controls the movement of chemicals in and out of the cell
cytoplasm	the site of many chemical reactions
nucleus	carries the genetic information

The different structures found in cells are made up from different chemicals – one of the most important of these is **protein**. Proteins are needed for the growth and repair of cells and tissues. Some proteins are **enzymes** and control chemical reactions in cells. There are many different proteins and they can be used in different ways. What makes one cell different to another is the type of protein it makes.

a Why do you think teenagers need large amounts of protein?

b If the cell membrane of the cell is damaged, the cell might die. Suggest why this might happen.

▲ Rhinoceros horn and hair are both made from protein

3

Mitochondria

It is now possible to look more closely at the cytoplasm in cells. Using an electron microscope, very small structures such as **mitochondria** can be seen. Each mitochondrion is only about 0.002 mm long.

Mitochondria contain enzymes that carry out the final stages of respiration and this provides all the energy for life processes.

 c Arrange the following in order of increasing size: cell, mitochondrion, nucleus.

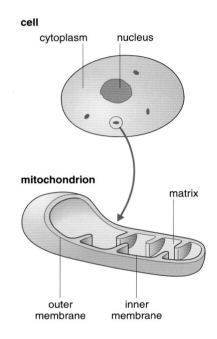

▶ *Inside mitochondria*

Coding for proteins

It has been known for a long time that the nucleus of the cell is the control centre. It manages the activities of the cell by controlling which proteins the cell makes.

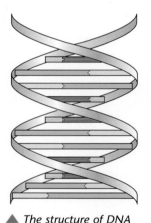

▲ *The structure of DNA*

 d What are some of the jobs of these proteins?

Each different protein is made up of a chain of amino acids. The amino acids are in a specific order. This order controls the shape of the protein and how it works. The nucleus must therefore have a code for the order of the amino acids. For many years people wondered what this code was.

Then in 1953 two scientists – Watson and Crick – worked out the structure of a chemical called **DNA**. The nucleus always contains DNA. They found that DNA was made of two strands of organic bases twisted up to make a spiral or **double helix**. There are four different bases. Pairs of bases hold the two strands together with cross-links. This makes a DNA molecule look a little like a twisted ladder.

Watson and Crick realised that this structure allowed DNA to code for proteins and so control the production of the different proteins (protein synthesis). The whole base sequence that codes for one protein is now called a **gene**. Each gene codes for a particular protein. Genes make up the chromosomes in the cell nucleus.

A cell needs lots of amino acids to make proteins. These are obtained from our food.

Before a cell divides the DNA copies itself (DNA replication). This means that each cell has exactly the same DNA. Watson and Crick's model for DNA has helped us to understand how DNA can do this.

Watson and Crick's work has led to many further discoveries about the workings and uses of DNA. One of these is the development of DNA **fingerprinting**.

Although much of our DNA codes for proteins, some does not. Scientists have found that this non-coding DNA is different in each person, so it can be used to identify you as a unique individual.

Enzymes

One of the most important types of protein produced by all cells is enzymes. Enzymes are biological catalysts. This means that they will speed up the rate of chemical reactions in organisms but will not get used up themselves. The reactions they speed up include respiration, photosynthesis, protein production and digestion.

All enzymes also share the following characteristics:

• they work best at a particular temperature
• they work best at a particular pH (the optimum)
• each enzyme will only work on one substrate in a particular reaction (they are specific).

The graphs show how the rate of reaction changes with temperature and pH.

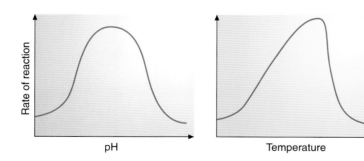

At very low or very high temperatures or pH levels, enzymes will work very slowly. The best temperature for most of our enzymes to work is about 37°C.

 Why do you think our enzymes work best at about 37°C?

 Biological washing powders contain enzymes. Why are they not used in very hot washes?

child 1   mother   child 2   possible father

DNA fingerprints

Dr Pete MacDonald works in a laboratory dealing with DNA fingerprinting. In genetic fingerprints, only about one in four 'fingerprint' bands match between people who are not related. Genetic fingerprinting is often used to decide relationships between different people.

Today Pete is working on the case of two babies who were found abandoned outside a hospital. Ten days after the babies were found a woman and a man have come forward claiming that the babies are theirs.

The authorities want Pete to check whether the two babies are related and whether the woman and the man are the parents. He takes DNA samples from the woman and the man, and then tests them against DNA from the babies. His results are shown in the diagram.

Questions

1 Which of the children could be the offspring of the woman and the man?

2 Do you think that child 1 and child 2 are related?

3 If the two babies were identical twins, what would their genetic fingerprints look like?

4 Suggest how genetic fingerprinting could be useful at a crime scene.

Spreading far and wide

In this item you will find out

- how diffusion happens

- the importance of diffusion in animals

- how diffusion occurs in plant leaves

Have you ever played a trick on someone with a stink-bomb from a joke shop?

If you break the bottle, a terrible smell soon spreads out across the room. After a while, the smell disappears. This is because of **diffusion**. The molecules of the gas are spreading out throughout the room, eventually reaching the noses of the people in the room.

▲ Stink-bombs work by diffusion

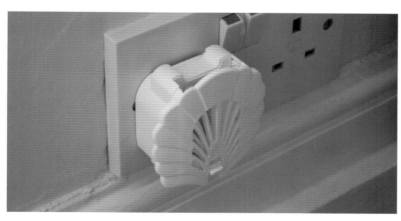

◄ A plug-in air-freshener

a Why do you think the smell disappears after a while?

Diffusion is responsible for our ability to smell all the different scents that we come across. They need to diffuse into our noses to be detected.

Rather than making stink-bombs, other companies make air-fresheners. They have to design the air-freshener so that the scent diffuses out at just the correct rate.

b What would happen if the scent diffused out too quickly or too slowly?

Some air-fresheners plug into electric sockets. This allows the scent to be heated up or cooled down.

Many of our household devices rely on diffusion, but so do many processes in our bodies and in the tissues of plants.

Amazing fact

The US Army is developing a device for dispersing crowds, using the strongest smelling artificial chemical (2 parts chemical to 1 million parts air).

What is diffusion?

Diffusion is the movement of a substance from an area of high concentration to an area of low concentration. It works because particles are constantly moving about at random and so tend to spread out.

A cell loses waste products and gains useful substances by diffusion through the cell membrane. This is because a cell is constantly making waste products and using up certain substances. The molecules move through the cell membrane from areas of high concentration to areas of low concentration.

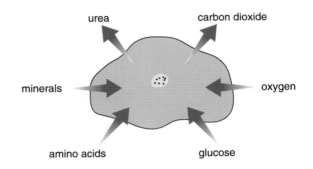

▶ *A cell needs certain substances and produces other waste substances*

Diffusion in mammals

Amazing fact

A large tree will lose over 1000 litres of water a day through its leaves.

Substances can pass in and out of cells by diffusion and this allows animals to exchange substances with their surroundings. In the small intestine, tiny digested food molecules are absorbed into the bloodstream.

The inside of the small intestine is covered with finger-like projections called villi. The digested food diffuses through the walls of the villi into the bloodstream. It is then carried to the tissues of the body where it leaves the blood. This is shown in the diagram below.

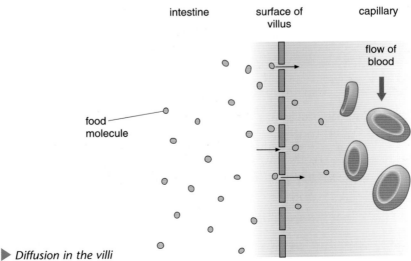

▶ *Diffusion in the villi*

In the lungs, oxygen diffuses into the bloodstream and carbon dioxide diffuses out. This happens in small air sacs called **alveoli**, which have a rich blood supply. There are millions of these alveoli in each lung.

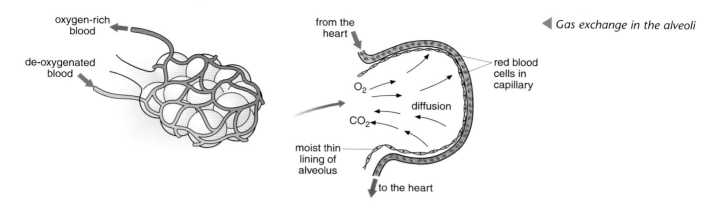

Gas exchange in the alveoli

In the body tissues, diffusion occurs in the opposite direction. Carbon dioxide diffuses into the bloodstream and oxygen diffuses out into the tissues.

A **fetus** also needs food and oxygen while it is growing, but it gets these from its mother. Early in pregnancy the fetus grows a structure called a **placenta**. This is a disc of tissue that is attached to the wall of the uterus. Food and oxygen diffuse through the placenta to the fetus, and carbon dioxide and waste diffuse in the other direction to the mother.

c Why does a fetus need a large supply of food?

d Where does the carbon dioxide go after it diffuses across the placenta into the mother's blood?

Diffusion in plants

In plants, oxygen and carbon dioxide diffuse in and out through the leaves. During the day, carbon dioxide will diffuse in because it is being used by the leaf. Oxygen is being produced and so will diffuse out.

e What process uses carbon dioxide in the plant?

f Why do you think carbon dioxide does not diffuse in during the night?

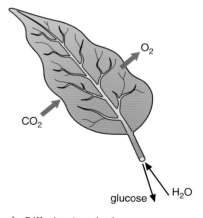

▲ *Diffusion in a leaf*

As gases diffuse in and out of the leaf, water molecules also diffuse out. Plants lose large amounts of water by diffusion from their leaves. This process is known as evaporation. They have to take up water from the soil in order to replace the water that is lost.

Keywords

alveolus • diffusion • fetus • placenta

Fat-free chips

Scientists have produced a new type of fat molecule called olestra. It tastes like normal fat, but the molecules are bigger. This means that they do not get digested by the normal fat-digesting enzymes in the body and the molecules cannot diffuse into the bloodstream.

This new fat can be used for everything that normal fats and oils can be used for, such as baking or frying.

Fat in food contains twice as much energy per gram as protein or sugar. This means that if you eat lots of fatty foods – like crisps, chips or pizza – and you do not exercise, you will put on weight.

The trouble is that fat in food often makes the food taste nice. Fat-free foods never taste quite the same as full-fat foods. Olestra means that you could eat lots of fatty foods and, because the fat passes straight through your body, you would not put on weight.

But there are a couple of problems with olestra. Some vitamins that are fat-soluble, such as vitamins A and E, get dissolved in the fat and pass straight out of the body without being absorbed. Olestra may also cause some people to have problems with stomach cramps and loose bowel movements.

In the USA crisps containing olestra are on sale, but olestra has not yet been passed for use in the UK.

Questions

1   If 1 g of sugar contains 17 kJ of energy, how much does 1 g of normal fat contain?

2   How does olestra stop fat being absorbed by the body?

3   What are the problems with olestra?

4   Why do you think manufacturers in the USA are particularly keen to use olestra?

Blood is thicker than water

In this item you will find out

- about the jobs of different parts of the blood

- about the role of the blood vessels

- how the heart works and how heart problems can be overcome

For thousands of years, humans have known about the importance of blood to life. For much of this time people did not understand what blood was made of. They tried to explain its importance by giving it magical powers.

We now know what blood is made of and the jobs of its different parts. This means that we can understand how changes to our blood can affect us.

When people started to climb the highest mountains, they found that above 3000–4000 m their muscles became tired much more quickly. They found it hard to get enough oxygen to their muscles. If they spent some time at these heights they started to find it easier to move. When their blood was tested, it was found to contain higher than normal numbers of **red blood cells**.

▲ A mountaineer

There are about 5 million red blood cells in every cubic millimetre of blood and their function is to carry oxygen around the body. A red blood cell is shaped like a small disc with a dent in each side – this shape is called a biconcave disc.

Red blood cells are small cells so they can fit through the narrowest blood vessels. They contain a red protein called **haemoglobin**, which carries oxygen around the body. The shape of red blood cells gives them a large surface area, so that they can lose or gain oxygen more quickly. They do not have a nucleus so that more haemoglobin can fit in.

 What is the job of the red blood cells?

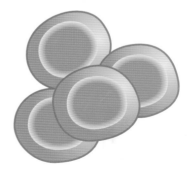

▲ The structure of a red blood cell is adapted to its function

Cells for all jobs

Blood contains three types of cells and they all carry out different jobs. As well as red blood cells there are **white blood cells** and **platelets**.

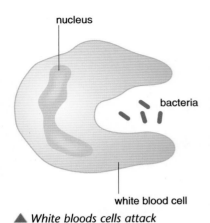

White blood cells are twice as large as red blood cells and there is one white cell to every 500 red cells. The function of white blood cells is to engulf and destroy disease organisms. To allow them to do this, they can change shape so that they can squeeze out of the blood vessels and surround the invader.

b **Explain how white blood cells destroy bacteria.**

Platelets are pieces of cells that are smaller than red or white blood cells. Their job is to gather at wounds and make the blood clot.

c **Suggest why it is important that the blood clots.**

▲ White bloods cells attack bacteria

All the cells are carried around the body by the liquid part of the blood called **plasma**. Most of the plasma is water, but it also contains hormones, dissolved food, antibodies and waste products.

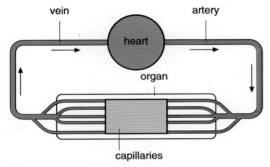

▲ Arteries, veins and capillaries

Moving blood

The blood is carried around the body in blood vessels. There are three types of blood vessels: **arteries**, **capillaries** and **veins**. Arteries carry blood away from the heart and veins carry blood back to the heart. Capillaries join arteries to veins and it is here that substances can pass in and out of the tissues.

How the heart works

The job of the heart is to pump the blood around the body. It is really two pumps in one. The right side pumps the blood to the lungs. The left side pumps the blood to the rest of the body. This is shown in the diagram.

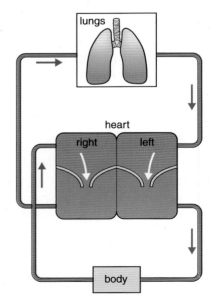

▶ How the heart pumps blood around the body

Examiner's tip

Remember the right side of the heart is on the left as you look at it.

The heart is made up of four chambers. The top two chambers are called **atria** and they receive blood from veins. The bottom two chambers are called **ventricles**. They pump the blood out into arteries.

The top two chambers, the atria, fill up with blood returning in the **vena cava** and **pulmonary veins**. The two atria then contract together and pump the blood down into the ventricles. The two ventricles then contract, pumping blood out into the **aorta** and **pulmonary arteries**.

Blood in the arteries is under higher pressure than in the veins, because there is little pressure remaining to force it along when it leaves the capillaries to return to the heart.

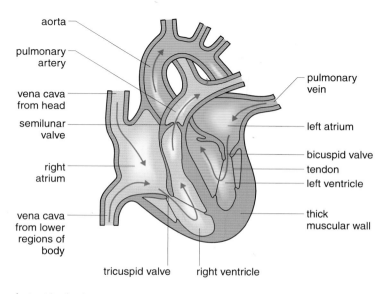

▲ *Inside the heart*

The muscle wall of the left ventricle is always thicker than the muscle wall of the right ventricle. This is because it has to pump blood all round the body, compared with the short distance to the lungs.

In the heart there are two sets of valves. The job of the valves is to prevent blood flowing backwards. In between the atria and the ventricles are the **bicuspid** and **tricuspid** valves.

These valves stop blood flowing back into the atria when the ventricles contract. The pressure of blood closes the flaps of the valves and the tendons stop the flaps turning inside out. There are also **semilunar** valves between the ventricles and the arteries.

d Why does blood flow faster in arteries than veins?

e Which chambers of the heart contain oxygenated blood?

f Why do the tendons in the heart have to be very strong?

Keywords

aorta • artery • atrium • bicuspid • capillary • haemoglobin • plasma • platelet • pulmonary artery • pulmonary vein • red blood cell • semilunar • tricuspid • vein • vena cava • ventricle • white blood cell

Replacing hearts

Most people now realise that too much fat is bad for their heart. It is not all types of fat that are bad, but two main types: saturated fats and cholesterol.

Large amounts of these fats in the diet can cause cholesterol to build up in arteries. This may restrict or block blood flow, or damage the heart. If the damage is bad, parts of the heart such as a valve – or even the whole heart – may need to be replaced.

If a whole heart is needed then it is possible to have a heart transplant. The heart could come from a human donor or could possibly be a whole mechanical heart.

Although mechanical hearts have been built, they have several problems:

- it is difficult to make the heart small enough
- they need an energy source to power them
- it is hard for a mechanical heart to change its rate like a real heart does during exercise.

Most people who need a new heart receive a human heart. However, there is a shortage of heart donors, and even when a donor heart is found it is not always the right size, age or tissue match.

Also, when a heart transplant takes place, the person who receives the heart has to take drugs for a long time to stop the heart being rejected.

Questions

1 How can certain types of fats affect the heart?

2 What are the problems with mechanical hearts?

3 Suggest how a mechanical heart could be powered.

4 What are the problems with finding suitable donor hearts?

Cell multiplication

In this item you will find out

- how organisms produce new cells for growth

- the advantages to an organism of being multicellular

- how organisms produce sex cells for reproduction

We all know that every organism is made up of cells – in the case of humans, it is a very large number of cells. One major question that scientists have asked for hundreds of years is where do all these cells come from?

For an organism to increase in size or grow, its cells can get bigger. But there seems to be a limit to the size of cell that one nucleus can control.

So most growth involves an organism's cells splitting into two or dividing. This means that the cells increase in number. The type of cell division that is used for growth is called **mitosis**.

Mitosis is also used to make new cells as replacements for worn-out cells or for repairing damaged tissues.

In the body cells of humans and all mammals, the nuclei contain chromosomes that occur in pairs. They are said to be **diploid**. In humans there are 23 pairs in each body cell, making 46 chromosomes. These chromosomes are copied in mitosis.

a Why do cells divide by mitosis?

b Why is it important that chromosomes are copied exactly in mitosis?

▲ *We are all made up of lots of cells*

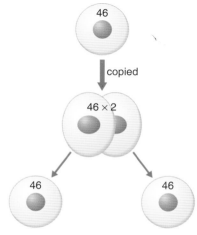

46

copied

46×2

46

46

▶ *How cells divide by mitosis*

Multicellular v unicellular

Mitosis allows an organism to increase from being one cell (unicellular) to being composed of many cells (**multicellular**).

It may seem obvious that it is an advantage to be multicellular, but why? There are a number of possible reasons. It allows an organism to have different cells specialised to do different jobs. This is called **differentiation** and makes the cells more efficient. An organism can also become larger and more complex. This means that it can protect itself more easily.

> **Amazing fact**
>
> The human body is made of up to 100 000 000 000 cells, but almost half of these are bacteria living in our guts.

c Many factories have differentiation in the jobs that their workers are trained to do. In a car factory, each worker may make a particular part of the car. What can happen to the factory if a particular worker is not able to work?

d What is a possible disadvantage of differentiation in the body?

Cell division for reproduction

Some organisms can reproduce by splitting into two, but this produces identical offspring. This is because their cells are all made by mitosis.

Another type of reproduction is sexual reproduction. This involves **sex cells (gametes)** combining at **fertilisation** to form a **zygote**.

▶ A sperm joining with an egg

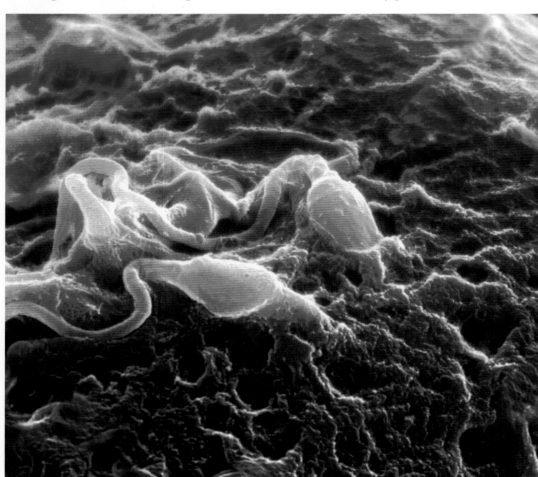

The sex cells – the sperm and eggs – have half the number of chromosomes of a normal body cell. In humans, the sperm and eggs each have 23 chromosomes instead of the usual 46. They are said to be **haploid**.

This means that when the sperm and the egg join, the number of chromosomes becomes 46 again and the zygote has the diploid number of chromosomes. This is shown in the diagram on the right.

The type of cell division that makes gametes is called **meiosis**. Each gamete has a different combination of genes. During fertilisation, any sperm can fertilise any egg. This means that the zygote can have any one of a number of possible combinations of genes. This explains why all organisms look different and how meiosis introduces variation into a species.

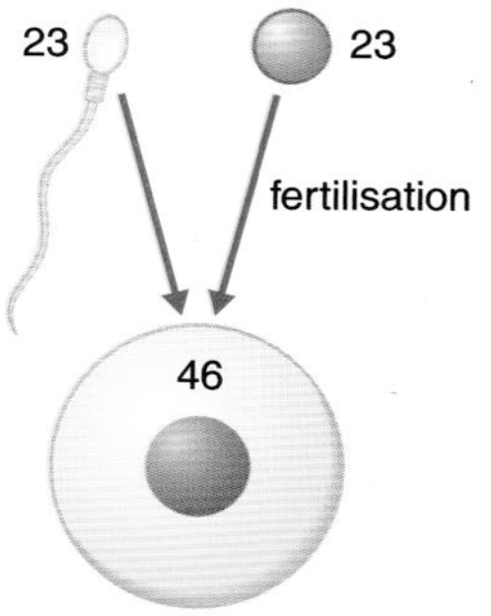

▲ *Sperm and egg join to form a baby's first cell*

Eggs and sperm

The eggs and sperm are very well adapted for their jobs in reproduction.

Sperm:

- are small and have a tail to swim to the egg
- have lots of mitochondria to provide energy to power the tail
- have a large nucleus, which contains the genes for the zygote
- are produced in large numbers to increase the chance of one finding an egg
- have a special bag of enzymes called the **acrosome** so that they can digest the egg membrane and get into the egg.

Eggs also have a nucleus to carry genes, but they are larger because they have a store of food for the zygote to use after fertilisation.

Examiner's tip

Because the words 'mitosis' and 'meiosis' are so similar make sure you spell them properly.

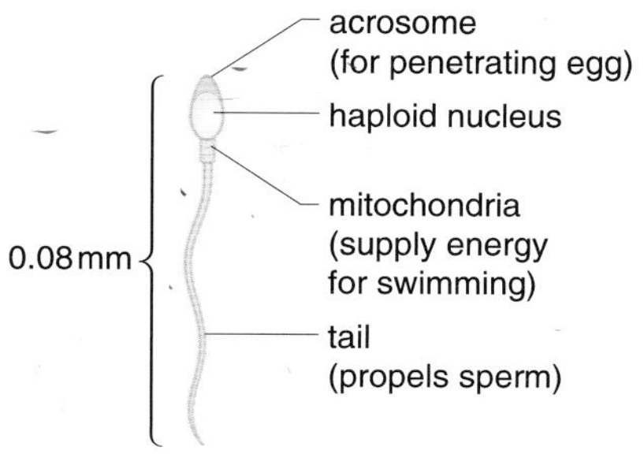

▲ *A sperm cell*

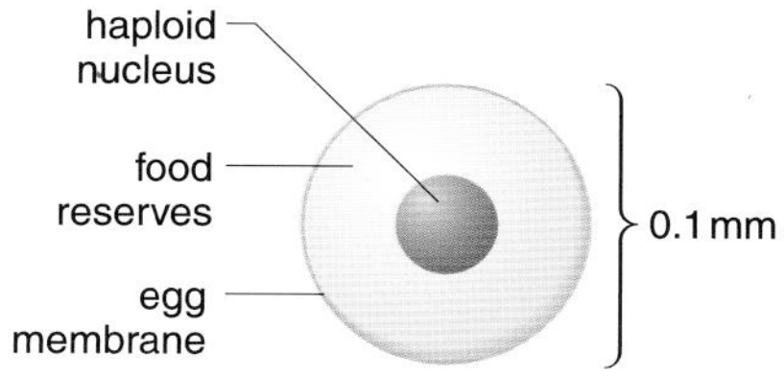

▲ *An egg cell*

Keywords

acrosome • differentiation • diploid • fertilisation • gamete • haploid • meiosis • mitosis • multicellular • sex cell • zygote

e **Why does the sperm need so much energy?**

f **Why does the zygote need food after fertilisation?**

The bare necessities

Once scientists worked out the details of how a sperm and egg joined during sexual reproduction, they could use this information in many different ways.

Giant Pandas are very rare animals. There are only about 1000 left living in the bamboo forests of China and Nepal. To stop them becoming extinct, zoos are trying to breed them.

However, this is proving very difficult for several reasons:

- the female pandas only produce about one egg every year
- the male pandas do not seem very interested in the female pandas and so they do not try to mate
- many of the male pandas in zoos are quite old. This means that they produce lower numbers of sperm. Also, the sperm do not swim so well.

Scientists are now trying to make female pandas pregnant by injecting sperm into them that has been taken from a male panda. This is called artificial insemination. If a Giant Panda does become pregnant, the embryo grows into a very small baby. When it is born it is about 0.1% of its mother's weight, but it soon grows.

Questions

1 Suggest why there are so few Giant Pandas left in the wild.

2 A female panda produces about one egg a year. What is the name of the type of cell division that makes this egg?

3 The sperm of male pandas in zoos do not swim very well. Why do you think this means that the female panda is less likely to get pregnant?

4 Why is it important for male animals to produce many sperm?

5 A Giant Panda baby weighs 0.1% of its mother's weight. In humans a 60 kg woman may have a 3 kg baby. What percentage of the mother's weight is this?

6 The panda baby soon grows by making more cells. What is the name of the type of cell division used?

Growth spurts

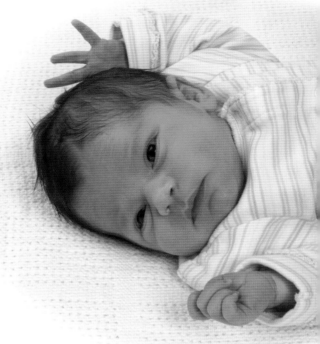

▲ *A baby is made up of millions of cells*

In this item you will find out

- about the differences between plant and animal cells

- how plants and animals grow

- about the main stages of human growth

You probably know that it takes about 9 months for a fertilised egg to grow into a human baby. During that time the number of cells has increased from one to many million.

To produce a baby from a fertilised egg involves cell division followed by the cells becoming specialised for different jobs.

We have seen that both plants and animals increase in size or grow during their lives. They do this by a combination of making new cells and by the new cells enlarging.

Most animals, including babies, tend to stop growing when they reach a certain size, but plants can often carry on growing for the whole of their lives. Some plants become very large indeed.

The largest living organism in the world is a tree called General Sherman. It is over 80 m tall, is thought to be over 2200 years old and is still growing!

a What is the difference between animal growth and plant growth?

Humans, like most animals, stop growing because their cells stop dividing. The growth of babies is regularly measured to make sure that their growth does not slow down too early. As cell division slows down it becomes harder to replace any cells that are damaged. This is all part of getting older and it means that injuries heal a lot slower. It also means that we cannot live forever, even if we do not catch diseases.

Plants tend to increase in size throughout their lives and can grow to enormous sizes.

b What problems would an animal face if it grew as large as General Sherman?

▲ *General Sherman is still growing!*

Plant and animal cells

Plant and animal cells both contain certain important structures such as the cell membrane, cytoplasm and nucleus.

There are, however, important differences. Only plant cells have:
- **chloroplasts** that absorb light energy for photosynthesis
- a **cell wall** to help support the plant
- a large **vacuole** that stores cell sap and also provides support.

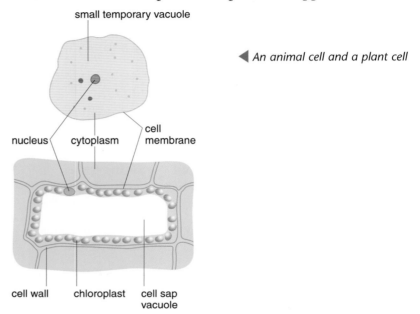

◀ *An animal cell and a plant cell*

Looking at cells

You can look at cells yourself if you have a microscope. Just use an onion and peel off a very thin strip of tissue from one of the many layers. This strip will be one cell thick.

You can then put this strip on a microscope slide. Add a few drops of a liquid such as iodine solution onto the strip – this will stain the cells. Place a cover slip on top and with the use of a microscope you should be able to see onion cells.

Differentiation and stem cells

Once new cells have been made by mitosis they take on different jobs. This is called differentiation. In animals the cells become muscle cells, nerve cells, blood cells and all the other types of cells that make up the different tissues. In plants they also become different types of cells. The difference is that plants keep a large number of cells in reserve that can still form different types of cells. You can easily show this, because a small piece cut from a plant can grow into a whole new plant.

Modern research has shown that animals, including humans, do keep some cells that still have the ability to differentiate. They are called **stem cells**. These stem cells are easy to find in an embryo but much harder to find in the adult body.

Animal growth

The length of time between fertilisation and birth is called the **gestation period**. During this time the zygote divides to form a ball of cells called an embryo. Once the embryo has formed all the organs and tissues of a baby, it is called a fetus.

c What is the difference between a zygote, an embryo and a fetus?

d What effect does the size of the baby have on the gestation period?

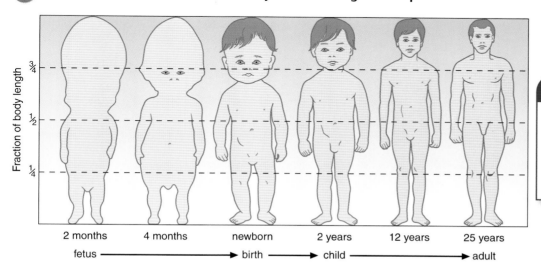

◀ *Different parts of the body grow at different rates*

Amazing fact

It takes about 90 weeks for a baby elephant to grow but only about 3 weeks for a baby mouse!

Different animals have different lengths of gestation period. The most important factor controlling this is the size of the animal.

So the babies of various animals grow at different rates, but there are also differences in the growth of different parts of the same baby. The diagram above shows that the head and brain of an early fetus grow very quickly compared with the rest of the body. Later, the body and legs start to grow faster and brain and head growth slows down.

Growing up

Humans grow quickly or slowly at different times in their lives. The graph on the right shows how human growth changes over a person's lifetime. During infancy a child grows very quickly. Growth slows down slightly during childhood, but there is a growth spurt during adolescence (puberty). Once a person reaches adulthood they stop growing.

e Look at the graph. What are the differences between male and female growth patterns?

f What happens to growth in old age?

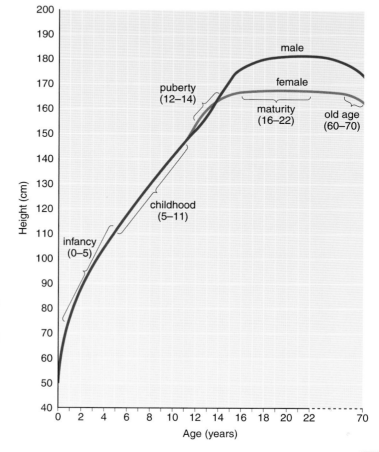

Keeping an eye on Adam

Adam is taken to a clinic by his parents to have his mass and head size measured. The diagram shows these measurements just after he was born and now that he is 1 year old.

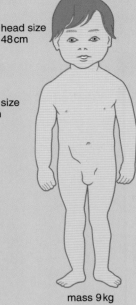

head size 48 cm

head size 35 cm

mass 3 kg   mass 9 kg

All babies grow at different rates. After the nurse measures Adam's head size and his mass, she checks the results against a graph that shows the range of results that are considered normal.

Head size (cm) vs Age (weeks): values 24–52, ages 34, 38, 2, 10, 20, 30, 40, 50. Labelled *average*, *normal range*.

Mass (kg) vs Age (weeks): values 0–13, ages 34, 38 | 2, 10, 20, 30, 40, 50. Labelled *average*, *normal range*. birth. Age (weeks)

Questions

1 Use the charts to check Adam's mass and head size just after he was born. What can you say about his measurements from the chart then?

2 Check Adam's measurements now against the chart. Is he growing normally?

3 The nurse uses different growth charts for boys and girls. Suggest why she does this.

4 The human growth graph on page 21 shows the five main phases of human growth. What phase is Adam in now? How old will he be when he enters the next phase?

Growing around corners

In this item you will find out

- that plant growth is controlled by chemicals called hormones

- about some different plant responses that are controlled by hormones

- how these hormones can be used to change plant growth

 Rotting apples

Have you heard of the old saying 'one bad apple spoils the rest'? Many people pack apples into boxes for storage in a cellar. The cool temperature of the cellar helps to keep the apples from ripening until you want to eat them during the winter. You have to be careful not to include an overripe apple in with the rest. If you do, then all the apples will tend to go soft and mushy.

We now know that fruits produce a chemical that makes them ripen. This chemical is a gas and so it can spread from apple to apple.

You can show this quite easily by taking some unripe bananas and putting some in a plastic bag with a brown banana, and some in a bag on their own. After a week the bananas in the bag with the brown banana will have ripened more.

a **Why do the bananas with the brown banana ripen more quickly?**

Scientists have found a number of different chemicals that control not just ripening but many other aspects of plant growth too. We can now control plant growth ourselves.

For example, poinsettias have attractive red leaves and are in great demand at Christmas. The production of these leaves is controlled by chemicals in the plants, and growers can make sure that the poinsettias are ready in time for Christmas.

▲ Poinsettia

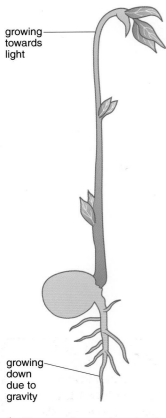

growing towards light

growing down due to gravity

▲ *Phototropism and geotropism*

Responding to light and gravity

Like any other living organisms, plants must be able to respond to changes in their environment. This is called sensitivity. Animals often respond to stimuli by moving about, but plants cannot do this. They respond by growing in a particular direction. These plant growth movements in response to stimuli from a particular direction are called tropisms and the growth is called a tropic response.

Two of the most important stimuli that plants respond to are light and gravity. A response to light is called **phototropism** and a response to gravity is called **geotropism**.

Different parts of the plant will respond differently to these stimuli. Shoots grow towards light so they are positively phototropic. Roots grow downwards in response to gravity so they are positively geotropic. This is shown in the diagram on the left.

b It is very important for the plant's shoots to grow towards light. Why is this?

c Why is it also important that the roots grow in response to gravity?

When a seed starts to grow in soil the shoot grows upwards. This happens even though it is in the dark. So as well as being able to grow towards light, shoots must also grow against gravity.

Stimulus	Growth response	
	Shoots	Roots
Gravity	away = negatively geotropic	towards = positively geotropic
Light	towards = positively phototropic	away = negatively phototropic

Experiments have shown that these growth movements are controlled by chemicals that can move through the plant in solution. These chemicals are **plant hormones (auxins)**.

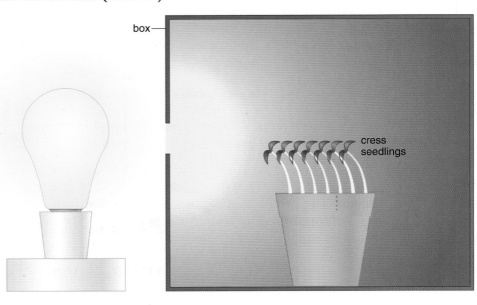

box

cress seedlings

▶ *Shoots grow towards light*

It is easy to show that shoots grow towards light. Cress plants are ideal for this experiment because they grow quickly. Two pots of cress seedlings are grown. One is then placed in a box with a hole in one end so that it only receives light from one direction. The other is left in the open receiving light from all directions. Before long the shoots in the box will be growing towards the light.

Uses of plant hormones

Plant hormones control three main aspects of plant growth:

- growth of shoots and roots
- flowering
- ripening of fruits.

Plant hormones can be used in agriculture to alter plant growth. When they are sprayed on plants at high concentrations, they cause the plants to grow very quickly and then die. Narrow-leaved plants such as grass do not take up these chemicals, so they can be sprayed onto lawns. They will only kill the weeds and so are called **selective weedkillers**.

Other plant hormones encourage shoots to grow roots from their cut end. Gardeners use these hormones in **rooting powder** so that they can produce more plants by taking cuttings.

As plant hormones can control how fast fruits ripen, they can be used to control fruit ripening by slowing it down or speeding it up. This means that fruit, such as bananas, can be transported long distances and then ripen at just the right time in the shops.

Seeds, flowers and buds all start growing at the best time of the year to give the plant the best chance to survive. If conditions are tough they will not develop and this is called **dormancy**. Plant hormones can be used to control this dormancy so that plants and flowers can be available all year round.

Amazing fact

Bananas have now been produced that taste of apple, vanilla or strawberries when they are ripe.

◀ Bananas picked before they are ripe

d **Why is it useful to be able to transport fruit such as bananas before they are ripe?**

e **Why is it important for many flowers to open in the summer rather than in the winter?**

Keywords

auxin • dormancy • geotropism • phototropism • plant hormone • rooting powder • selective weedkiller

Working with plants

Jenny is spending some time doing work experience in a large garden. She is helping the gardener with different jobs.

On Monday he is working on the lawns. He sprays the lawns with water containing lawn weedkiller. He tells Jenny that it will kill the weeds but not the grass.

On Tuesday he is working in the greenhouses taking cuttings. Before he plants the cuttings he dips them in hormone rooting powder. He tells Jenny that this will help them to grow into new plants.

Later in the week, Jenny is invited into the house. The owner shows her around and Jenny asks her about a large plant she sees growing in a dark corner.

'Ah,' says the owner, 'that is an aspidistra! In Victorian times it was about the only plant that people could grow indoors. It was the only plant that would grow in the very dim rooms. It could also survive a chemical in the gas that was used to light the rooms.'

▲ *Aspidistra*

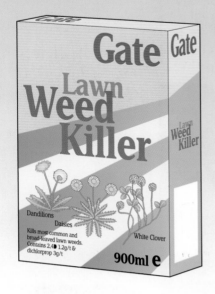

Questions

1. The lawn weedkiller contains a chemical called 2,4D. This is a chemical made to copy the effects of a plant hormone. Which of these chemicals is a plant hormone?

   adrenaline   auxin   chlorophyll   sugar

2. The gardener says that the weedkiller will not kill the grass. Why is this?

3. How does the hormone rooting powder help the cutting to grow into a plant?

4. Aspidistras have very dark green leaves. What causes this dark green colour?

5. Because they are very dark green, aspidistras could survive in dim Victorian rooms. Why is this?

6. The gas used to light Victorian rooms contained a plant hormone. How would this get into the house-plants? Choose from this list:

   diffusion   evaporation   osmosis   transpiration

Controlling the changes

In this item you will find out

- what mutations are
- how selective breeding is used
- that genes can be moved from one organism to another

Most people have heard of the word **mutation** and may describe organisms that are unusual as mutants. But what is a mutation and what causes it to happen?

In many science-fiction films, strange organisms are produced by mutation. This is often caused by leaks of radiation or unusual chemicals. The mutant seems to take on a new form and always seems to be dangerous. Is this really what mutation is all about?

There is some truth in these stories. Mutations are in fact changes in the genes of organisms and they can occur spontaneously. These changes can alter how an organism looks or behaves.

Most mutations are harmful and many will kill the organism. However, occasionally a useful mutation occurs. This can allow types of organisms to change and become more advanced. We are all mutants – without mutations we would not be here!

A mutation usually happens when the genes are copied before a cell divides. Under normal conditions, mutations usually happen at a very slow rate. But the rate can be speeded up by:

- radiation, such as X-rays or ultraviolet light
- certain chemicals, such as the tar in cigarette smoke.

Scientists can use radiation to try to change the genes of organisms, but the mutations are too random.

a Why do people who take X-rays stay behind protective shields when they are working?

▲ Albino rabbits result from mutations that occur naturally

Amazing fact

Every time a human gene is copied there is less than a one in a million chance that a mistake is made.

Selective breeding

If you look at all the different types of dogs that live today, it is difficult to believe that they are all members of the same species. All the different types have been produced as a result of **selective breeding**.

Some have been bred to be fast runners, others as guard-dogs and some as gentle pets. Selective breeding always works like this:

- two animals are chosen that have the characteristics that are wanted, such as speed
- these animals are allowed to mate – if they come from different breeds this is known as **cross-breeding**
- when the offspring are produced, the ones with the most desirable characteristics are chosen again and mated
- this happens for many generations until the animal with all the right characteristics is produced.

In this way humans have produced different breeds of dogs and champion racehorses.

Selective breeding can be carried out in the same way with plants. We can breed crop plants that are stronger, more resistant to disease or that are ready for harvesting quicker. This leads to improved agricultural yields.

b Why does selective breeding take so long?

c What features do you think a farmer might selectively breed for in his cows?

Moving genes

One of the problems with selective breeding is that it takes a long time to produce the organism that is needed. Scientists can now choose what characteristics an organism has by changing its genes. **Genetic engineering** or **genetic modification** involves transferring genes from one living organism to another. This will produce an organism that has different characteristics.

▲ Members of the same species

Genetic engineering is useful because it produces new organisms quickly with the characteristics that we want. However, the new genes inserted into an organism may have harmful effects that the scientists are not expecting.

Some people are worried about this. They are concerned about eating food containing genetically modified crops and about the effects these crops will have on the environment.

Genetic engineering at work

In many parts of the world people eat a lot of rice and not many vegetables or dairy products. This means they can become deficient in vitamin A, which can lead to problems with their eyes. Vitamin A can be found in the beta-carotene in carrots. Scientists have been able to take the genes from carrots that control beta-carotene production and insert them into rice. When people eat this genetically modified rice, they can convert the beta-carotene in the rice into vitamin A.

▲ *Genetically modified rice*

Bacteria can be genetically modified to produce human insulin, and this can be used by diabetics to control their blood-sugar levels. It is also possible to genetically modify crop plants, such as maize or wheat, so that they become resistant to frost damage, disease or herbicides.

d Why might a farmer want a crop that is resistant to herbicides?

e Bacteria reproduce very quickly. Why do you think they are useful for making human insulin?

◀ *This protestor is demonstrating against genetically modified crops*

Keywords

cross-breeding • genetic engineering • genetic modification • mutation • selective breeding

▲ A quagga

▲ Zebras

Bring back the quagga

The quagga was a type of zebra that lived in South Africa until the 1800s. It looked different to most other types of zebra because it only had stripes on its head and neck.

Due to overhunting by humans, the quagga became extinct in South Africa and the last one died in a zoo in Holland in 1883.

Scientists have argued for many years about whether the quagga was a special type of zebra or a totally different species. By studying tissue from old skins, they now know that it was a special type of zebra.

With this news, scientists in South Africa have set up the Quagga Project. They want to choose particular zebras and breed them. Over many years of breeding they hope to produce animals that look just like the extinct quagga.

Questions

1 How is a quagga different to a zebra?

2 Was the quagga a different species or a special type of zebra? How do scientists know this?

3 The differences between the quagga and the zebra were probably made by a natural change in the gene of a zebra. Such a change in a gene is called (choose from the list):

   mating   mutation   radiation   reproduction

4 The scientists want to bring back the quagga by choosing zebras to mate and repeating the process many times. Which zebras would the scientists choose to mate with each other?

5 What is this type of process called?

Cloning around

In this item you will find out

- how plants and animals can be cloned

- the advantages and disadvantages of using cloned plants

- some of the possible uses of animal cloning

A **clone** is a genetically identical copy of an organism. Most people think that clones are made by scientists in laboratories, but this is not always the case. You may know people who are identical twins. Identical twins like those in the photo are formed from an embryo splitting into two at an early stage. They are therefore genetically identical and so are clones.

▲ *Identical twins have the same genes*

For a long time people have been very interested in making clones. In the film *Jurassic Park*, dinosaurs were cloned using blood that was found in ancient mosquitoes. The mosquitoes had been sucking the blood of dinosaurs.

When the film was made, cloning of animals or humans was thought to be science-fiction. But gradually scientists have made breakthroughs. First they managed to clone simple animals and then more complicated animals with backbones, like frogs. Finally they managed to clone a mammal using cells from another adult mammal. This happened in 1996, when they produced a cloned sheep called Dolly.

Cloning in plants happens naturally and has been carried out artificially by humans for a long time. It is the cloning of animals – and maybe even humans – that has caught people's interest and not everybody thinks that it should be allowed.

a Why were people more worried about cloning animals like Dolly than they were about cloning frogs?

Amazing fact

People can pay companies to make a clone of their favourite pet so that its genes will be preserved forever. Farm animals that have the characteristics that the farmer wants can be cloned to make large identical herds.

▲ *Dolly the sheep*

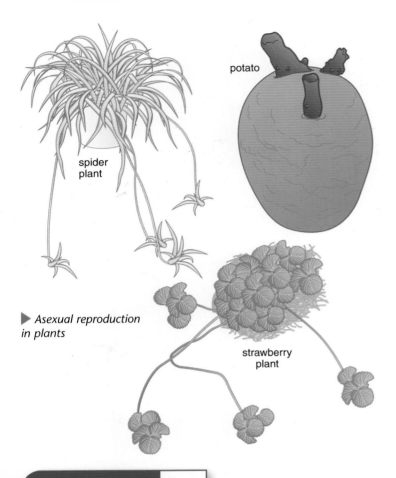

▶ *Asexual reproduction in plants*

Cloning plants

Cloning is not new for gardeners. Many plants clone themselves naturally. This is an example of **asexual reproduction** and cell division makes new plants. Plants do this in many different ways. Three different methods are used by spider plants, potatoes and strawberry plants. This is shown in the diagram on the left.

A spider plant grows miniature plants on the ends of long shoots.

A strawberry plant produces runners that touch the soil and grow roots. The runner rots away leaving new plants.

A potato tuber can grow into a potato plant which may have dozens of tubers attached. Each one of these tubers can grow into a separate plant during the next summer.

Many gardeners encourage cloning by cutting lengths of stem from a plant. These are called **cuttings**. With the help of hormone rooting powder they will grow into new plants.

b Suggest why the cuttings find it difficult to take up water.

c Why do you think the cut end of the stem is dipped in hormone rooting powder?

Examiner's tip

Remember that most plants, such as strawberry plants, can also reproduce sexually by producing flowers.

▶ *How to take a cutting*

1 Cut shoot from a plant

2 Dip cut end into hormone rooting powder

3 Plant in pot of soil as soon as possible after cutting

Amazing fact

The plant that produces the largest flower is called the Titan Arum. The flower is nearly 3 m tall. It flowers only once in 1000 days, so new plants are usually produced by cloning.

Producing plants commercially by various cloning methods has some advantages and some disadvantages.

Advantages	Disadvantages
• you know what you are going to get because all the plants will be genetically identical to each other and the parent • it can be used to reproduce plants that do not flower very often or are difficult to grow from seeds • it is possible to produce large numbers of plants	• the population of plants will be genetically identical – there will be little variety • because they are all very similar, a disease or change in the environment could wipe them all out

Cloning animals

One way to clone an animal is to copy what happens in nature when identical twins are produced. An embryo is produced by a sperm fertilising an egg and then the embryo is split into two at an early stage. This is how cows can be cloned.

The scientists collect sperm from the bulls they have chosen. They then **artificially inseminate** selected cows with this sperm. When the embryos are large enough they are collected and split into two, forming clones.

These embryo clones are implanted into cows who will act as **surrogate** mothers and the calves are born normally. This process is shown in the diagram.

The problem with using this process to produce cattle is that you are never quite sure what you will get. Although the parent animals may be champion cattle, sexual reproduction is still involved. That means variation.

What should be allowed?

Since Dolly was born in 1996, other animals such as pigs, cats, cows and horses have been cloned.

But why should scientists want to do this? Animals could be genetically engineered so that they contain some human genes – cloning these animals could produce a supply of organs for human transplants.

 Why would a supply of animal organs for transplants be very useful?

If animals, such as sheep, can be cloned then it should be possible to clone a human. Some people are very worried about the possibility of this happening and do not believe that it is ethically acceptable.

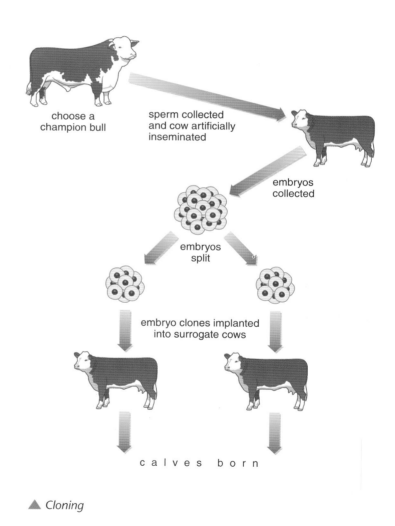

▲ Cloning

choose a champion bull

sperm collected and cow artificially inseminated

embryos collected

embryos split

embryo clones implanted into surrogate cows

c a l v e s   b o r n

Keywords

artificially inseminate •
asexual reproduction • clone
• cutting • surrogate

▲ *Gaur*

▲ *Bucardo*

Jurassic Park *in action?*

Can we really clone endangered or even extinct animals like in *Jurassic Park*?

So far, the most successful attempt to do so has been the cloning of a gaur, a rare ox that lives in Asia. Scientists produced an embryo by cloning and placed it into a cow to allow it to grow. But 2 days after the cow gave birth, the baby died from a common infection.

Scientists are now trying to clone the bucardo.

This is a type of mountain goat that lived in Spain. The last bucardo died on 6 January 2000 – it was crushed by a tree. Before it died, scientists took some cells from its ear. If the cloning succeeds, it will only produce female clones. To solve this problem, scientists hope that they may be able to remove one female chromosome and add a male chromosome from a different type of goat.

Cloning extinct animals such as the woolly mammoth or the dodo is much more difficult. This is because genetic material does not survive very well after death.

Questions

1. Why do you think the scientists put the gaur embryo into a cow to let it grow?
2. Why would the bucardo only produce female clones?
3. Why do the scientists want to replace one female chromosome with a male chromosome?
4. Why is cloning extinct animals difficult?

B3a

1 The diagram shows an animal cell.

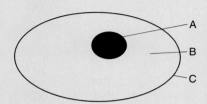

Copy the diagram and label it using the words from the list:

nucleus   cell membrane   cytoplasm [3]

2 Where in an animal cell do the following descriptions refer to? Finish the sentences by using the letters A, B or C from the above diagram.

The part of the cell that contains DNA is ___(1)___ .
The part of the cell that controls the movement of substances in and out is ___(2)___ .
The part of the cell where most of the chemical reactions take place is ___(3)___ . [3]

3 Finish the sentences by using words from the list.

**chromosomes   DNA   genes   nucleus
protein**

The genetic information in the cell is carried on long strands called ___(1)___ . They are made of a chemical called ___(2)___ and can be divided into sections called ___(3)___ . [3]

4 Where in a cell are mitochondria found and what is their function? [2]

5 Read the following statements about DNA. Which are true?

A DNA controls the production of proteins
B DNA consists of three chains wound together
C The DNA molecule contains long chains of bases
D DNA controls the production of amino acids [2]

B3b

1 In the body carbon dioxide and oxygen pass in and out of the blood. Copy the diagram and write on each arrow either CO_2 or O_2 to show which way these gases move. [4]

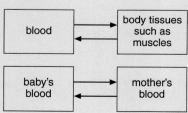

2 Finish the sentences by using words from the list.

**cell membranes   cell walls   food   lungs
small intestine   waste**

To allow it to grow, a fetus needs to get ___(1)___ from its mother. This enters all the cells of the foetus through the ___(2)___ . The mother will absorb these nutrients into her blood through her ___(3)___ after she eats. [3]

3 The diagram shows part of an alveolus and a blood vessel.

a Where in the body are alveoli found? [1]
b Where on this diagram is the concentration of oxygen highest? [1]
c Explain why and how oxygen passes from the air in the alveolus into the blood. [3]
d Which way does carbon dioxide move? Explain why. [2]

B3c

1 Match the correct function with each type of blood cell. Choose the functions from the list.

**carries oxygen   helps blood clotting
defends against disease**

a platelets   [1]   **b** red blood cells   [1]
c white blood cells [1]

2 Complete these sentences.

Blood moves around the body in arteries, veins and ___(1)___ . The highest pressure is found in the ___(2)___ . The right side of the heart pumps blood to the ___(3)___ and the left side pumps it to the ___(4)___ . In some people the arteries may become partly blocked by a type of fat called ___(5)___ . [5]

3 This table shows some differences between arteries and veins. Copy and complete the table, filling in the empty boxes.

Feature	Arteries	Veins
direction of blood flow		
type of wall		
are valves present?		

[6]

B3d

1 Complete these sentences.

Complex animals like humans are made up of millions of cells. Some of the cells are producing new cells by ___(1)___ . These new cells could be used for ___(2)___ or for ___(3)___ . [3]

2 This table shows some differences between sperm and egg cells. Copy and complete the table by putting a tick or a cross in each of the empty boxes.

Feature	Sperm	Egg
does it have a tail?		
does it have large food reserves?		
does it have a nucleus?		
is it produced in large numbers?		

[4]

3 Explain why a sperm cell needs:

a many mitochondria [2] **b** an acrosome [2]

4 This diagram shows how sperm and egg are produced and also shows one sperm joining with one egg.

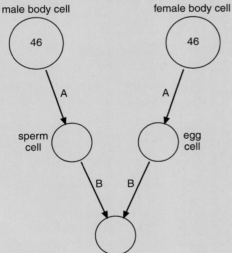

a The body cells have 46 chromosomes. What is the number of chromosomes in: (i) the sperm cell; (ii) the egg cell; (iii) cell X? [3]

b The type of cell division shown at A makes gametes. What is the name of this cell division? [1]

c Process B shows the gametes joining. What is the name of this process? [1]

d What is the name given to the type of cell labelled X? [1]

e The gametes are said to be haploid. What does this mean? [1]

f Why is it important that the gametes are haploid? [2]

B3e

1 Look at the diagram of a plant cell.

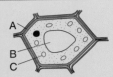

a The diagram has three structures labelled A, B and C. What are they? [3]

b Copy the table and write A, B or C in each of the empty boxes to show which parts of the cell do each job.

Job	Part of the cell
absorbs light	
contains cell sap	
made of cellulose and provides support	

[3]

2 Make a list of the structures that are found in both plant cells and animal cells. [3]

3 Look at the diagram on page 21 showing the growth of different parts of the body.

a Approximately what percentage of the body length is the head at birth? [1]

b Why do you think that the main growth of the head happens before the main growth of the arms and legs? [2]

B3f

1 Finish the sentences by using words from the list. You can use each word once, more than once or not at all.

**chemicals   flowers   gravity   light
leaves   nerves   sugar**

Plant hormones are ___(1)___ that control plant growth. When a seed is planted, plant hormones make sure that the root grows towards ___(2)___ . The shoot will grow towards ___(3)___ but away from ___(4)___ . When the plant reproduces, it produces ___(5)___ at a particular time in the year. This is also controlled by plant hormones. [5]

2 The diagram shows a simple experiment to show the action of plant hormones on a cut shoot.

a What effect does the plant hormone (auxin) have on the cut shoot? [1]

b Suggest why one shoot is placed in a beaker of water? [1]

c Explain how a gardener can use this property of plant hormones? [2]

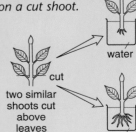

3 The table contains some statements about plant growth. Copy and complete the table by putting a tick or a cross in each empty box.

Feature	Roots	Shoots
contain plant hormones		
show positive phototropism		
show negative geotropism		

[3]

4 Read the following paragraph and then answer the questions.

Plant hormones control how plants grow and so are often used in agriculture to alter plant growth. They might be used to change the rate at which fruit ripens. This is particularly helpful with fruit such as bananas, where they have to be transported long distances. They can also be used as selective weedkillers, because certain hormones will only kill the types of plants that have broad leaves.

a Why is it helpful to change the rate at which fruit ripens? [2]

b What is a selective weedkiller? [1]

c Why can selective weedkillers be used on crops such as wheat and barley but not on tomatoes or lettuce? [2]

B3g

1 In 1791 a strange type of sheep was born that had short crooked legs. It could not jump over fences. A farmer called Seth Wright decided that he wanted a whole flock of these sheep on his farm.

a This sheep was produced as a result of a change in the normal genes of a sheep. What is this type of change called? Choose your answer from the list.

diffusion   mutation   reproduction
replication   [1]

b Why do you think that Seth Wright wanted a whole flock of these sheep on his farm? [2]

c What process could Seth Wright use to produce such a flock?
A use a selective breeding programme
B use random mating
C cross-breed the sheep with a small goat
D self-fertilise the sheep [1]

2 Complete the sentences.

A mutation is usually ___(1)___ to an organism and can be caused by being exposed to ___(2)___ or ___(3)___ . A more controlled way of changing the ___(4)___ of an organism is by genetic engineering. This is now used to make organisms such as ___(5)___ produce human insulin in large quantities. [5]

3 A type of cat has been bred that has very short front legs. These cats do not move around like normal cats but hop rather like kangaroos. This means that they cannot scratch with their paws or hunt animals.

a These cats have been produced by selective breeding. Explain the steps that would have been taken to do this. [3]

b Some people are keen to own these cats as pets. Others think that it is wrong to breed them. Describe the arguments that these two different groups of people might use. [4]

B3h

1 Finish the sentences by using words from the list.

asexual   genes   identical   sex cells
sexual   similar

A clone is an ___(1)___ genetic copy of an organism. This means that it has the same ___(2)___ as the parent. Clones are produced in ___(3)___ reproduction. [3]

2 Which pairs of organisms are clones?

A two strawberry plants grown from runners
B identical twins
C two strawberry plants grown from seeds
D a brother and sister [2]

3 Clones can be produced by splitting up embryos produced from fertilised cows' eggs.

a Write down the stages A to E in the correct order.
A cow artificially inseminated
B sperm collected from champion bull
C embryos collected from cow
D cloned embryos put into surrogate cow
E embryo split up [4]

b Why do the farmers use a champion bull to provide the sperm? [2]

c What is a surrogate cow? [1]

4 Read the paragraph about a gardener and then answer the questions.

George the gardener has a favourite geranium plant. He says that it is the same plant that was passed on to him by his father 30 years ago. Although it dies every winter, he takes cuttings in the autumn and keeps them in a greenhouse for the next summer. This way, he says, he knows they will have attractive flowers of the same colour.

a What does George do when he 'takes a cutting'? [3]

b George has a whole flower-bed full of these geraniums. Why does he have to be extra careful that they do not get a plant disease? [2]

I don't like eating vegetables or fruit. I wouldn't worry if they didn't exist. I'd be happy just to eat meat.

- A walk in the woods can be very different in June compared with November. In the summer, the leaves are so efficient in trapping light and so very little light reaches the ground. In the autumn all the leaves fall and the ground is covered in dead leaves. In this module you will find out what makes leaves so good at absorbing light and how a thick carpet of dead leaves can disappear in a few months.

- As well as sunlight, plants need water and minerals to be able to produce their food and grow. The water has to pass many metres up to the leaves from the soil. You will find out how plants manage to do this. The minerals come from the leaves that have been lost and broken down. A study of how this happens can tell us a lot about how to stop our food decaying.

But if we didn't have plants in the world then there wouldn't be any meat for us to eat!

What you need to know

- Where diffusion occurs in plants.

- The word equation for photosynthesis.

- What a food chain shows.

Leaves for life

In this item you will find out

- the main parts of a leaf
- how a leaf is adapted for photosynthesis

The next time you are out for a walk, have a look around at all the different types of leaves on plants and trees. Leaves come in all sorts of shapes, sizes and colours. The main job of leaves is to produce food for the plant by photosynthesis.

This process uses the green chemical, **chlorophyll**, to trap sunlight and it gives leaves their colour. While most leaves are green, some can vary in colour and sometimes there are even different colours on the same leaf. You can see this in the photograph of ivy leaves.

The different colours of some leaves are produced by other chemicals in the leaf that hide the colour of the chlorophyll.

In autumn, many leaves that are normally green become red and orange. This is because the chlorophyll in the leaves starts to break down. So the red and orange chemicals show themselves more clearly.

▲ Ivy leaves

a How do you think plants can tell when it is autumn?

In some plants, leaves do other jobs as well.

The Venus fly-trap plant has special leaves that trap unsuspecting flies if they touch the hairs.

The leaves of the stinging nettle help to protect the plant. They have thousands of tiny hairs that are filled with poison. They break when you touch them and inject the poison into your skin.

So leaves carry out many different jobs for plants but their main role is photosynthesis. Without this, plants would not be able to make their own food and we would starve!

Amazing fact

The largest leaf in the world is on the Raphia palm. Its leaves can grow up to 25 m in length.

▲ Leaves in autumn

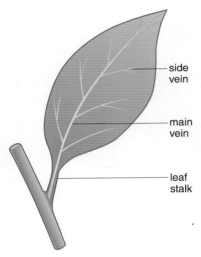

▲ *The structure of a leaf*

The structure of a leaf

Although leaves come in all shapes and sizes, they all have certain things in common. The diagram on the left shows the external features of a leaf. You can see a series of **veins** that spread throughout the leaf. These carry water that has been absorbed by the roots to the cells of the leaf. They also transport away the sugar that is made by photosynthesis.

When you look at a thin section of a leaf under a microscope, you can see details of the cells inside.

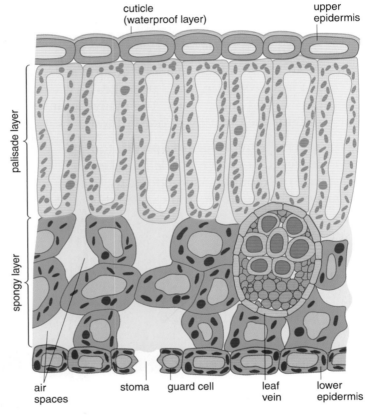

▲ *A cross-section of a leaf*

There is a waxy layer called the **cuticle** on the top of the leaf. Under the cuticle are different layers of cells. There are four main layers of cells: the **upper epidermis**, **palisade mesophyll**, **spongy mesophyll** and **lower epidermis**. All the cells have a large central vacuole containing sap, as well as a tough cellulose cell wall. Some of the cells also have chloroplasts that contain the green chemical chlorophyll and so can carry out photosynthesis. The job of the chloroplasts is to absorb light energy.

b What do you think the waxy cuticle is for?

c Not all plant cells contain chloroplasts. Why do you think that leaf cells contain chloroplasts but root cells do not?

On the bottom of the leaf are pores called **stomata**, which are opened or closed by **guard cells**. They allow gases in and out of the leaf.

Photosynthesis

The process of photosynthesis is carried out by all green plants, mainly in their leaves. It traps the energy from sunlight and uses it to produce a sugar called glucose. The plant can then convert the glucose into all the other chemicals that it needs to live and grow.

During photosynthesis, water and carbon dioxide are converted into glucose and oxygen. The carbon dioxide is absorbed by the leaf through its leaf pores (stomata), while the water is taken up by the plant's roots. The oxygen then needs to leave the plant and it gets out through the stomata.

If you look at a leaf it is usually greener on the top than on the bottom. This is because the cells that have the most chloroplasts are closer to the top of the leaf than the bottom. These are the leaf palisade cells and form the palisade mesophyll layer. This is where most photosynthesis takes place.

Adaptations of a leaf

Although some photosynthesis occurs in the stems of some plants, it is the leaves that do most of the work. Leaves have evolved over millions of years to become efficient at photosynthesis. They:

- are broad so that they have a large surface area to absorb the light
- are very thin so that the gases in photosynthesis, like carbon dioxide, do not have far to travel from the air through the leaf to get to the plant cells
- have a network of veins that support the leaf, and carry water in and sugar out
- have stomata to allow gases to diffuse in and out
- have chlorophyll to absorb sunlight.

▲ Leaves use sunlight to produce energy

d Why does carbon dioxide diffuse into the leaf during the day rather than diffusing out?

e If a leaf is dipped into boiling water, air bubbles can be seen coming out of the bottom of the leaf. Why is this?

Keywords

chlorophyll • cuticle • guard cell • lower epidermis • palisade mesophyll • spongy mesophyll • stoma • upper epidermis • vein

A shady character

Nathan was looking out of the window at a tree growing in the corner of his garden.

He was looking at the different leaves. He thought that the leaves lower down on the tree were bigger than the leaves higher up. He decided to investigate this.

Nathan measured the length and width of three leaves from the top of the tree and three leaves from further down. His results are shown in the table.

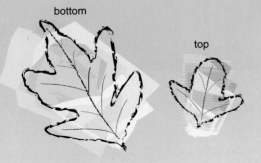

bottom

top

	Top leaves		Bottom leaves	
	Length (cm)	Width (cm)	Length (cm)	Width (cm)
sample 1	2.0	2.3	2.6	3.2
sample 2	1.9	2.2	2.8	3.5
sample 3	2.1	2.1	3.0	3.5
average	2.0	2.2		3.4

When he looked at the leaves he noticed other differences. The leaves from the bottom of the tree seemed to be darker green than the leaves near the top. They also seemed to be different shapes. He drew two of the leaves, one from the top and one from the bottom of the tree.

Questions

1. Work out the average that is missing from the table and draw a bar chart to show Nathan's average results.

2. Nathan thought that the leaves were different sizes at different heights of the tree. What do his results show?

3. Look at Nathan's drawings of the leaves. Write down any other differences that you can see.

4. Why do you think that leaves lower down the tree were greener?

Looking at osmosis

In this item you will find out

- about osmosis

- some of the roles of water in plants

- how plants try to reduce water loss

▲ *This plant has been well watered*

Have you ever looked after a house-plant? If you forget to water it, its leaves and stems will **wilt** and droop.

But why do plants wilt if they do not get enough water?

Water moves in and out of plant cells through the cell wall and cell membrane. Most of the water is stored in the vacuole. When the vacuole of a plant cell is filled with liquid, it is under pressure and presses up against the cell wall. The cell wall is inelastic and does not stretch, so it supports the plant cell.

When the vacuole does not have enough liquid in it, it cannot press up against the cell wall. The plant cells collapse inwards and the plant wilts.

This means that both the inelastic cell wall and water are needed to support plants.

a Explain how the cell wall helps to support a plant.

Gardeners also know about the importance of water in supporting plants. They know that if they want to move a plant then it is much better to take a large amount of soil with the roots. This helps prevent too much damage to the roots and stops the plant wilting when it is replanted. When the plant is replanted it must always be watered.

▲ *Someone forgot to water this plant!*

Amazing fact

The Atacama desert is the driest place in the world and in some areas it has not rained for over 400 years. Plants have to get water from mists and fog.

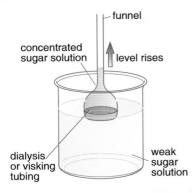

concentrated sugar solution

funnel

level rises

dialysis or visking tubing

weak sugar solution

▲ *Osmosis is a special type of diffusion*

▼ *The cell on the right has shrunk because it has lost water*

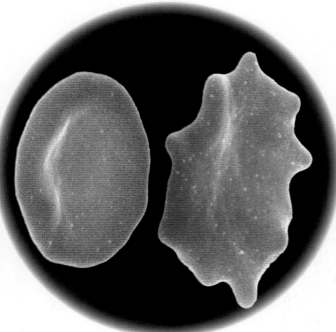

Osmosis

Water moves in and out of plant cells by a special type of diffusion called **osmosis**. Plant cells are surrounded by a cell wall and a cell membrane. The cell wall is **permeable** and so lets quite large molecules through. The cell membrane is **partially permeable**. This means that small molecules like water can diffuse through but larger molecules cannot.

Osmosis is the movement of water from an area of high water concentration (a dilute solution) to an area of low water concentration (a concentrated solution) across a partially permeable membrane. You can see how this works by looking at the diagram.

Water passes into the concentrated sugar solution from the weak solution, and the level of the concentrated sugar solution rises. This is because there is less water in the concentrated solution. The dialysis or visking tubing acts as a partially permeable membrane.

b Why can water molecules get through a partially permeable membrane but sugar molecules cannot?

If plant cells are placed in water they take up water by osmosis. Under a microscope the cells can be seen to swell up and then stop. The liquid inside the vacuole starts off as an area of low water concentration and the water moves into the plant cells. When the plant cells have taken up enough water, the cell wall stops any more water from entering.

Animal cells behave differently to plant cells when surrounded with water. They take up too much water by osmosis and burst. In a concentrated solution, they lose water and shrink.

c When plant cells swell up they do not burst but animal cells do. Why is this?

How water travels through a plant

Plant leaves are covered in thousands of small pores called stomata. They allow gases to diffuse in and out of the leaf, but they also let water molecules evaporate out by diffusion. This loss of water is called **transpiration**.

Plants have to replace this water or they will wilt. Water is taken up (absorbed) from the soil into roots by osmosis. The younger parts of the roots are covered in fine projections called root hairs.

The root hairs increase the surface area to speed up the absorption of water. The water is then transported up the stem to the leaves. Healthy plants have to balance water uptake with water loss.

More about transpiration

Although plants cannot stop losing water, the flow of water to the leaves does help the plant in several ways:

- it helps to cool the plant down, rather like sweating in animals
- it provides the leaves with water for photosynthesis
- it brings minerals up from the soil
- it makes sure that cells stay stiff to stop the plant wilting.

◀ *Water moves up from the roots to the leaves*

A balancing act

Although transpiration has its uses, plants try to lose as little water as they can. They have a waxy cuticle on the top of the leaves, which stops water leaving the leaf. They also have only a small number of stomata on the upper surface of the leaf. This cuts down on loss of water through evaporation from the stomata, when the Sun's energy hits the leaf. As most of the energy hits the top of the leaf, if there are few stomata then water evaporation is reduced.

d **Leaves on plants like grass grow straight upwards. Where would you expect their stomata to be found?**

Keywords

osmosis • partially permeable • permeable • transpiration • wilt

▲ Oak leaf

▲ Holly leaf

Counting stomata

Reshma carried out an experiment to count leaf stomata. She painted leaves with a small amount of clear nail varnish. When the varnish was dry, she peeled it off and stuck it onto a glass microscope slide. The nail varnish carried with it an imprint of the stomata. She carried out this technique with both the top and bottom surfaces of holly leaves and oak leaves.

Reshma then put the slides under a microscope and counted the stomata. The diagrams show what she saw.

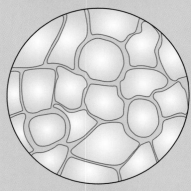

top of holly leaf

top of oak leaf

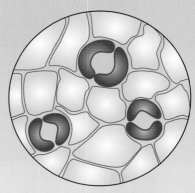

bottom of holly leaf

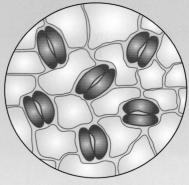

bottom of oak leaf

Reshma drew a blank table for her results.

Type of plant	Number of stomata in a field of view	
	Top leaf surface	Bottom leaf surface
holly		
oak		

She then read about holly and oak trees. The book said that holly leaves are adapted to lose water at a slower rate than oak leaves. This is why they have a thicker waxy cuticle.

Questions

1 Why did Reshma use a microscope to see the stomata?

2 Why do you think Reshma made a transparent imprint of the stomata rather than putting the whole leaf under the microscope?

3 Copy out Reshma's table and fill in her results.

4 On which surface of the leaves are most stomata found? Why do you think this is?

5 What differences between holly and oak do Reshma's results show? Suggest an explanation for the differences.

Xylem and phloem in action

In this item you will find out

- how plant structure relates to its function
- about xylem and phloem
- what affects the rate of transpiration

Do you put sugar in your tea or coffee? Most of us eat sugar in some form every day. About 70% of our sugar comes from a plant called sugar-cane and this can only grow in tropical countries. The main producers are in the West Indies and Brazil.

Sugar-cane can grow about 5 m tall and it produces the sugar in its leaves. The sugar is then transported down the stem of the sugar-cane. Farmers cut down and crush the stem. Hot water is used to dissolve out the sugar and then the water is evaporated. This leaves crystals of sugar that we can use.

Different parts of a sugar-cane plant do different jobs. This is the same for all plants. You can see this in the photograph on the right.

The stem transports substances up and down the plant and provides support. Photosynthesis – which provides the plant with energy – is carried out in the leaves, while the flowers enable the plant to reproduce. The roots take up water and minerals from the soil, and grow into the ground to anchor the plant.

a Explain what the stem of a plant does.

Amazing fact

During 1999 each person ate an average of 90 kg of sugar – that's nearly two large bags a week.

▲ Sugar-cane grows in tropical countries

flower contains the sex organs for reproduction

leaf for photosynthesis

stem for support and transport

soil level

roots for taking up water and minerals and for anchoring the plant

Xylem and phloem

In animals there is one main transport system that moves all substances around the body. In a plant there are two different transport systems, and they move different substances around the plant. The two different systems are called **xylem** and **phloem**. You can see how they are arranged in the roots, stem and leaves of a **dicotyledonous** plant (it has two seed leaves) in the diagram.

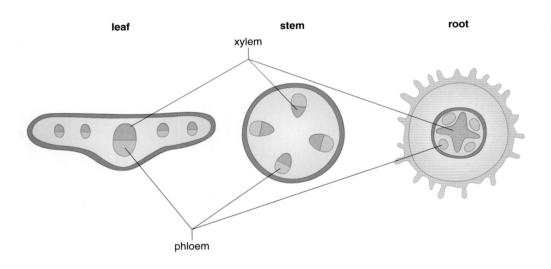

Xylem transports water and dissolved minerals. The water and dissolved minerals are taken in by the roots and move up to the leaves and shoots, where the water is lost in transpiration.

Phloem transports dissolved food substances (sugars) around the plant. Unlike the transport of water, the food may be transported up or down the stem. It may move from the leaves where it is made up to the tips of the shoots where growth is happening. It may also be sent down the stem to storage organs such as swollen roots. This movement of food substances by the phloem is called **translocation**.

The xylem vessels and phloem tubes run continuously from the roots to the stem and into the veins of the leaves. In the stem they are gathered together into collections called **vascular bundles**.

 A small amount of the water is not lost in transpiration but is used by the leaves. Which process uses water in the leaves?

     digestion   excretion   photosynthesis   respiration

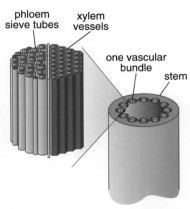

▲ *Phloem tubes and xylem vessels are arranged in bundles*

Transpiration rate

As we have already seen, transpiration is the diffusion of water out of leaves through the stomata and its evaporation. When water is lost through the stomata, this creates a suction force that helps to pull more water up from the roots to the leaves through the xylem vessels.

We can carry out various experiments using a potted plant to see what affects the rate of transpiration. The plant is placed on an accurate balance that will measure the mass of the plant, the pot and the soil. If the plant loses water, then the mass goes down.

c What prevents water from evaporating from the soil into the air during the experiment?

d Why is it important to stop this evaporation?

Plants that live in areas where it is warm and windy are in danger of losing too much water. These plants often have a number of adaptations to limit transpiration. They may have many hairs on the leaves or the leaves may curl up.

e How would these adaptations help to reduce transpiration?

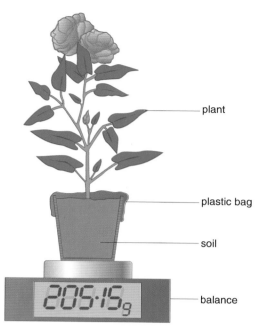

▲ The apparatus that can be used to measure transpiration

These are the results.

- *Experiment 1:* A plant was kept on a sunny windowsill. A similar plant was kept in a darkened room. The plant on the sunny windowsill lost more mass than the plant in the darkened room. This means that it lost more water.
- *Experiment 2:* A plant was kept in a cold room. A similar plant was kept in a room with the heating turned up. The plant in the cold room lost less water than the plant in the hot room.
- *Experiment 3:* A plant was kept on a windowsill. A similar plant was also kept on a windowsill but it had a fan blowing air at it. The plant with the air blowing at it lost more water than the other plant.
- *Experiment 4:* A plant was kept in a dry room. A similar plant was kept in a room that was kept humid by boiling a kettle. The plant in the drier atmosphere lost more water than the other plant.

So how are these results explained? Transpiration rate is increased by an increase in light intensity, because the stomata are open wider in bright conditions. This means that more water can escape.

Transpiration is also increased by a warmer temperature, because the warmth makes the water molecules move faster and so they escape faster. More air movement increases the rate of transpiration because it blows the water molecules away.

Transpiration is also increased by a decrease in humidity, because this means the air is less saturated with water and so more can evaporate.

Keywords

dicotyledonous • phloem • translocation • vascular bundle • xylem

Does beer grow on trees?

If you visit Malaysia you may be lucky enough to see an unusual scene. Early in the morning a local worker appears with pots, a knife and a bamboo ladder. He then climbs a tree called a toddy palm.

Once he is close to the top, he uses his knife to slice into the shoots, which cuts into the phloem tubes. He hangs pots under the cut shoots, leaving the pots there for several hours while he moves to another toddy palm tree. When he comes back, a sweet liquid has dripped out of the cut shoots into the pots. This is called toddy juice.

The man brings the pots down and the juice is left in the sun. Yeast in the juice starts to ferment it, and before long it has turned into an alcoholic drink called toddy beer. So beer really can grow on trees!

Questions

1 Which tissue in the plant does the toddy juice drip out of?

2 Write down one substance that is in the toddy juice.

3 Suggest why the yeast ferments the toddy juice faster if it is left in the sun.

4 What is the difference between toddy juice and toddy beer?

A healthy diet

In this item you will find out

- how plants take up minerals

- what plants use minerals for

- what happens to plants if they lack minerals

Most people know that to be fit and healthy it is important to have a balanced diet. Among other things, a balanced diet contains **minerals** and vitamins. The actual amounts needed are small but without them our health would suffer. Plants also need minerals to survive.

The difference is that we get our minerals from food but plants get their minerals from the soil. All plants can make their own food by photosynthesis, but they need minerals in order to grow properly and produce flowers and seeds.

The minerals that plants need are absorbed by their roots from the soil. The minerals are dissolved in water in quite low concentrations.

Minerals are so important to plants that plants go to great lengths to get them. Many plants will extend their root system out for long distances to try to take up as many minerals as they can from the soil. There are also plants that grow in soil that is very low in minerals. Some of these plants catch insects and extract the minerals they need from them. They are often called carnivorous plants.

 How do you think the pitcher-plant catches insects?

▲ *Humans and plants both need minerals*

◀ *Pitcher-plants catch insects*

Amazing fact

Frogs, mice and even rats have sometimes been found trapped in pitcher-plants.

What do plants need minerals for?

Plants can make sugars during photosynthesis using carbon dioxide and water. But in order to turn these sugars into other important substances such as protein, they need minerals.

For plants to stay healthy and reproduce, they need different minerals for different processes. The table shows how plants use certain minerals.

Mineral	Used by plants for:
magnesium	photosynthesis
nitrates	production of proteins that are needed for cell growth
phosphates	respiration and growth
potassium	photosynthesis and respiration

Fertilisers

Farmers may add **fertilisers** to the soil to help their crops grow. These fertilisers contain various combinations of minerals, such as nitrates, potassium, magnesium and phosphate compounds. This is because some plants need more of one type of mineral than another. The photograph below shows a bag of fertiliser with an **NPK** value on it. This stands for nitrogen, phosphorus and potassium, and tells the farmer the proportion of each of these minerals in the fertiliser.

▶ *A bag of fertiliser showing the NPK value*

 The photograph says that the NPK ratio is 21:8:11. There is 42 g of nitrogen in a sample of fertiliser from the bag. How much phosphorus and potassium will there be in the same sample?

Mineral deficiencies

If a plant grows without enough minerals it will not develop properly. This may be caused by a lack of one or more minerals in the soil. It is called a **deficiency**. It is possible to show the effect of the lack of a mineral by growing plants in solutions that are missing particular minerals. You can see this in the photograph below.

COMPLETE | −N | −P | −K | −Ca | −Mg | −S | −Fe

◀ *The effects of mineral deficiencies*

Different mineral deficiencies can affect plants in different ways.

Mineral	Effect of deficiency on growth
magnesium	yellow leaves
nitrate	poor growth and yellow leaves
potassium	poor flower and fruit growth and discoloured leaves
phosphate	poor root growth and discoloured leaves

c Look at the two tables. The mineral magnesium is needed for chlorophyll to be present in leaves. If a plant does not get magnesium, why would its leaves go yellow?

d Why do you think that a lack of nitrate leads to poor growth?

Keywords

deficiency • fertiliser • mineral • NPK

The most valuable bird in the world?

The Guanay Cormorant is a large sea-bird that lives on the coast of Peru in South America. In the early 1900s there were about 20 million of these birds living in the area.

The bird releases some of its faeces on the land. On many of the islands these droppings – called guano – were collected by local people. They realised that guano was an excellent fertiliser that could increase crop yields. Peruvian people sold the guano to Europe for large amounts of money. This made Peru very wealthy and the Guanay Cormorant became known as the most valuable bird in the world.

Unfortunately, in Europe people discovered how to produce fertilisers using chemicals. So they stopped buying the guano. In desperation, the Peruvian people started to catch large amounts of small fish called anchovies. They sold these as food for cattle.

In 1960 they caught about 9 000 000 tonnes of the fish. But this has caused various problems. The yield of anchovies caught each year has dropped dramatically. The cormorants feed on anchovies and there are now less than 1 million of the birds in Peru. Also, the number of larger fish such as tuna has dropped.

Questions

1 Write down the name of one mineral that might be present in guano.

2 How does this mineral help plants to grow?

3 Suggest why European farmers started using chemically produced fertilisers rather than guano.

4 Why do you think each of the following are going down in number: **(a)** the number of anchovies caught; **(b)** the number of cormorants living in Peru?

Pass it on

In this item you will find out

- about pyramids of numbers and biomass

- how energy flows through a food chain

- how we can use biomass for fuel

All living things need energy to live. Ultimately this energy comes from the Sun.

Plants can absorb the energy from sunlight and store it in the form of starch, sugars, fats or oils.

Plants can be used as food by animals, including humans. This transfers the energy from plants to animals.

As well as using plants for food, humans also use them for fuel. Wood has been burned for thousands of years, but now there are many other ways in which humans are trying to use plants for fuel.

One idea has been put forward by a group of Japanese scientists. They want to build 100 vast nets that will float in the middle of the ocean. On the nets will grow quick-growing seaweed.

The nets will then be towed back to land and the seaweed harvested. It will be dried and burned to produce electricity.

a Suggest one advantage of burning the seaweed for energy rather than burning coal.

Amazing fact

Celery has energy trapped in its cells, but it takes more energy for humans to digest the celery than is released.

▲ Plants absorb energy from sunlight

▲ We use plants as food

Examiner's tip

Don't confuse the words 'trophic' and 'tropic'. They mean different things.

Pyramids of numbers and biomass

You can see how organisms rely on each other for food if you draw a simple food chain like the one in the diagram below.

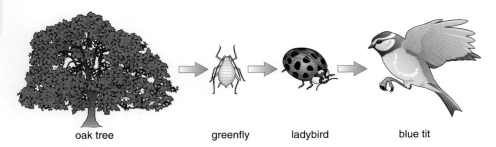

oak tree
greenfly
ladybird
blue tit

In every food chain the first organism is the **producer**. This means that it can make its own food using the energy from sunlight. All the other organisms in a food chain are **consumers**. They need to take in food because they cannot produce their own.

To give more information about the numbers of organisms in a food chain, you can construct a **pyramid of numbers**. The number of organisms at each stage in the food chain (**trophic level**) is counted. Each box in the pyramid is drawn so that the area represents the number of organisms.

The trouble with this type of pyramid is that it does not take into account the size of the organism. One oak tree takes up as much area as one greenfly!

blue tits
ladybirds
greenfly
oak tree

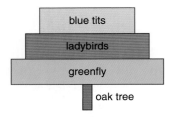

▲ *Pyramid of numbers*

An alternative is to draw a **pyramid of biomass** like the one shown on page 57. **Biomass** is the mass of living material of an organism. The mass of all the organisms at each level is measured and the boxes are drawn to show the mass at each stage in a food chain or web.

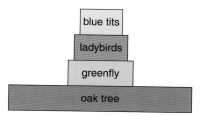

▲ *Pyramid of biomass*

b What type of organism is always at the bottom of a pyramid of numbers or biomass?

c Why is the oak tree box much larger in the pyramid of biomass?

d Why is it hard to find out the biomass of an organism such as an oak tree?

Energy flow

Some scientists study the flow of energy through food chains. The energy enters the food chain when plants absorb sunlight. The producers trap some of this energy in photosynthesis, although a large amount of the energy is reflected off the plants and is not used.

The light energy that is trapped is converted into chemical energy in compounds such as glucose. This energy then passes along the food chain as each organism feeds on other organisms and takes in the compounds. This energy flow is shown in the diagram below.

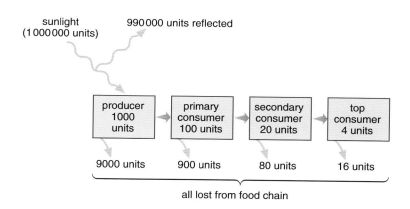

◀ *Energy flow in a food chain*

The diagram shows that energy is leaving the food chain at each stage. This is because organisms give out heat that has been made in respiration. Some energy is also lost in material that is ejected from animals (**egestion**). This is food that has passed all the way through an animal and has not been digested.

e In the diagram showing energy flow, the producer contains 10 times more energy than the primary consumer. How much more energy does the producer have compared with the top consumer?

Keywords

biomass • consumer • egestion • producer • pyramid of biomass • pyramid of numbers • trophic level

▲ *A Brazilian poster promoting gasohol*

▲ *An Indian dung digester*

Energy from biomass

Plants produce biomass when they photosynthesise. Humans can use this biomass in different ways as fuels.

In Brazil they grow lots of sugar-cane. They use yeast to ferment this to produce alcohol, which they mix with petrol. The mixture is called gasohol and can be used in cars once they have been modified.

In some places, such as India, waste material like animal dung is placed in tanks called digesters. Bacteria feed on the waste and produce the gases methane and carbon dioxide. The mixture of these gases is called biogas and this can be burnt as a fuel.

Forests of fast-growing trees have been planted in Scandinavia. These trees can be cut down at regular intervals and the wood burnt for fuel. The tree stumps that are left produce new shoots and these can be cut again in several years' time.

Questions

1. All three new types of fuel described here are examples of biomass. How do plants produce biomass?

2. The sugar-cane and the trees mentioned above are called producers. What is a producer?

3. The sugar-cane in Brazil is turned into alcohol. What type of microorganism carries out this process and what is the name of the process?

4. The biogas digesters in India are often buried in the ground. Why do you think this is?

5. Why are fast-growing trees used in energy forests?

▲ *Machines at work in an energy forest*

Food for everybody

In this item you will find out

- some of the advantages and disadvantages of intensive farming

- how plants can be grown without soil

- about organic farming

There are a lot more people alive today than ever before. The world's population has doubled nearly four times in the last 500 years. This increase in numbers has meant that more food is needed.

Up until the last 100 years, farming methods in Britain had changed little for centuries. Farmers ploughed small fields using animals to pull ploughs. Seeds were planted and crops harvested by hand. The manure from the farm animals was spread on the fields to fertilise the soil.

Recently there have been major changes in farming methods. Crops are now grown in large fields and crop yields have gone up tremendously. This is due to **intensive farming**. Intensive farming means trying to produce as much food as possible from a certain area of land and from the plants or animals that are farmed.

The graph below shows the yield of one crop, corn, in the USA in recent years. You can see how the yield compares with a crop of corn in Guatemala, where animals are used rather than machinery.

▲ *In some countries people still use animals to pull ploughs*

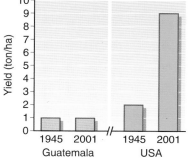
◄ *Crop yields in Guatemala and the USA*

a By using intensive practices the USA has increased the yield of corn that is grown. By how much has the yield increased in 2001 compared with 1945?

Intensive farming is not popular with everybody. Many people think that we should use **organic farming** techniques.

Pesticides and herbicides

Intensive farmers often use **pesticides**. These are chemicals that kill pests. For example, **insecticides** kill insects that may eat crops and **fungicides** kill fungi that may cause diseases. Farmers may also use **herbicides** to kill plants such as weeds in crop fields.

b Why do you think that weeds stop crops from growing so well?

Although farmers can produce more food if they practise intensive farming and use herbicides and pesticides, these practices can damage the environment and harm the health of plants, animals and humans, which raises ethical dilemmas.

Pesticides may harm useful organisms such as insects that pollinate flowers. They may also enter the bodies of organisms and their concentration may build up in consumers higher up the food chain. This can be seen in the diagram.

▶ *How pesticides travel up a food chain*

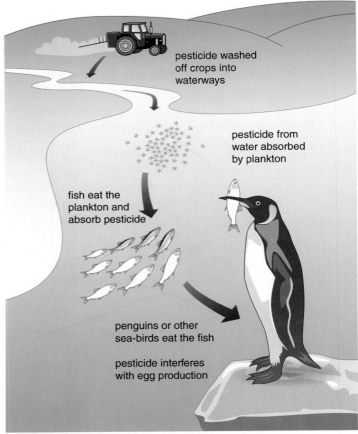

pesticide washed off crops into waterways

pesticide from water absorbed by plankton

fish eat the plankton and absorb pesticide

penguins or other sea-birds eat the fish

pesticide interferes with egg production

Fish or chicken?

Battery farming involves keeping hundreds of animals, such as chickens, in controlled conditions indoors. Chickens are fed special food to make them grow quickly, so they can be slaughtered earlier than chickens that grow naturally. Fish are often grown in the same way in special enclosures called **fish farms**. They are protected from predators and fed so that they grow quickly. Fruit and vegetables can also be grown in glasshouses in carefully controlled conditions.

c **Suggest one condition that farmers might control in a battery farm.**

Some people think that raising animals in this way is unethical. Chickens, for example, have very little room to move around in. Also, because they grow so quickly, their legs often cannot support their bodies.

Soil-free

The growing of plants without soil is becoming more popular in many areas. This is called **hydroponics**. Proper hydroponics means growing crops in water, but now farmers may use an artificial soil. This technique may be very useful in areas where the soil is poor (or barren, as it is known) or for growing plants like tomatoes in greenhouses.

Going organic

Due to the problems caused by intensive farming, lots of people think that plants should be grown without artificial fertilisers, herbicides or pesticides. This is called organic farming.

There are a number of alternative methods that organic farmers can use:

- animal manure and compost can be dug into the soil as fertiliser
- crops that can fix nitrogen in the soil, such as clover, can be grown
- crop rotation can be used so that the same plant is not grown in the same field each year and pests cannot build up in the soil
- crops can be weeded by hand
- farmers can vary seed planting times.

Instead of using pesticides and insecticides to control pests, you can use living organisms. This is called **biological control**. Often the organism used is a predator that eats the pest.

Care must be taken when biological control organisms are introduced because they may have effects on the food web. If they wipe out the pest completely then this may mean that other animals in the food web may starve and die out. Sometimes the control organism or other animals may increase in numbers and become pests themselves.

▲ Growing tomatoes by hydroponics

◀ A ladybird eats an aphid

Keywords

battery farming • biological control • fish farm • fungicide • herbicide • hydroponics • insecticide • intensive farming • organic farming • pesticide

▲ *An Indian mongoose*

The great wall of Japan

You have probably heard of the Great Wall of China but now the Japanese are planning a wall. This wall is not designed to keep out invading armies but the vicious Indian mongoose.

Seventeen mongooses were released onto the island in 1910. This was to try to control a poisonous snake that bit and killed hundreds of islanders every year. Although the mongooses can attack the snakes, they have had little effect on them. This is because the snakes tend to come out at night when the mongooses are asleep.

Instead, the mongooses are attacking the nests of rare birds. One bird called the rail is now endangered. In 1986 there were 1800, but in 2005 there were only 1000.

The rail has retreated to the north of the island and the Japanese are going to build a wall to keep the mongooses out. The wall will be covered in slippery material and will have very deep foundations.

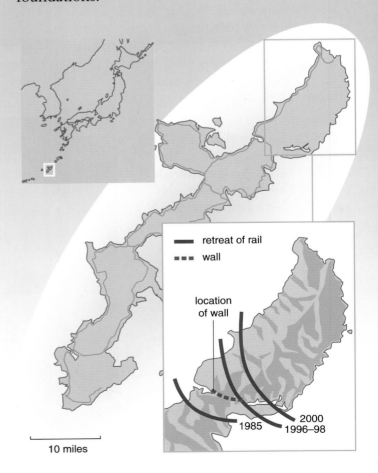

retreat of rail

wall

location of wall

1985

2000

1996–98

10 miles

Questions

1 Why were the Japanese so keen to introduce the mongooses to the island?

2 Why were the mongooses unsuccessful in controlling the snakes?

3 What was the decrease in the number of rails between 1986 and 2005?

4 Why do you think that the Japanese chose the narrowest part of the island to build the wall?

5 Suggest why the wall will be 'covered in slippery material and will have very deep foundations'.

To rot or not to rot?

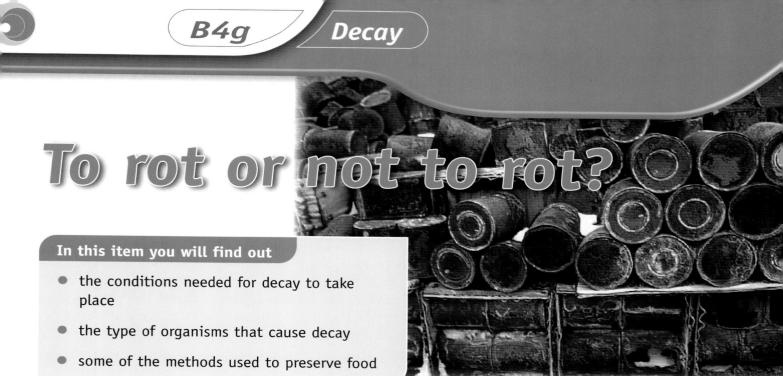

In this item you will find out

- the conditions needed for decay to take place

- the type of organisms that cause decay

- some of the methods used to preserve food

These cans of food were taken by the explorer Shackleton when he went to the Antarctic in 1914.

Nearly 90 years later, some of these cans were brought back to England. When they were opened, the food inside was found to be in good condition.

The question is, how could the food in the cans have lasted so long without going bad? The main reason is the cans themselves. But the low temperatures also had a part to play.

a What cannot get into cans after they are sealed?

In September 1991 two people walking in the mountains near the border between Austria and Italy made an amazing discovery. Half-buried in the ice was the body of a dead man. They thought that he had died recently.

▼ *Otzi the iceman*

When people looked more closely they found that he had a copper axe. They soon realised that this body was very old – in fact, it turned out to be 5300 years old! The amazing thing was that the body and all the possessions were wonderfully preserved.

These two examples show how dead materials, including food, can be prevented from breaking down. These ideas are used in preserving our food.

b Suggest how they estimated the age of Otzi.

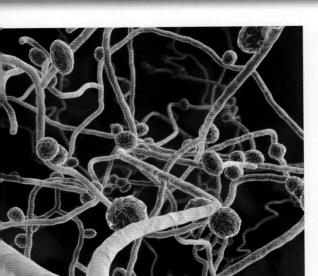

▲ *Fungus can break down dead organic material*

Causing decay

Organisms that break down dead organic material are called **decomposers**. They are very important because they allow chemical elements to be recycled. If decomposers did not do this, all the chemical elements needed for life would build up inside dead organisms. The two main groups of decomposers are bacteria and fungi. They feed on dead material and digest it.

You can show how important bacteria and fungi are as decomposers by a simple experiment. Samples of fruit and vegetables can be treated with disinfectant to kill bacteria and fungi. If the samples are kept in sterile dishes, the rotting of the food can be compared with samples that have not been treated with disinfectant.

c Why is the food put into sterile dishes after being treated with disinfectant?

d Why is it important to have two samples, one treated with disinfectant and one which has not been treated?

e Peatbogs are acidic. What effect do you think this will have on the enzymes?

There are organisms that help the decomposers to do their job. Animals such as earthworms, maggots and woodlice feed on pieces of dead and decaying material (**detritus**). They are called **detritivores**.

Detritivores increase the rate of decay by finely breaking up material so that it has a larger surface area. This means that it can be broken down faster by the decomposers.

We can use microorganisms that are decomposers to break down human waste (**sewage**). Plant waste (**compost**) can also be broken down by detritivores and microorgansims.

▶ *Earthworms are detritivores and create casts*

Conditions needed for decay

In order for organic material to decay, several things need to be present. There need to be microorganisms, oxygen and water. It also needs to be warm enough.

The rate of decay can be changed if the temperature changes. If the temperature is too hot or too cold, decomposition will not occur. Lack of oxygen or lack of water will also stop decay occurring.

We can use this knowledge about how to alter the rate of decay to preserve food and stop it rotting.

Keeping food good

We can use different techniques to reduce the rate of decay of food. This is called **food preservation**. Most food preservation techniques work by removing one of the factors that the microorganisms need. Some examples are shown in the table.

Preservation method	Details of method	How decay is prevented
canning	food is heated in a can to about 100°C and then the can is sealed	the high temperature kills the microorganisms, and water and oxygen cannot get into the can after it is sealed
cooling	food is kept in refrigerators at about 5°C	the low temperature slows down the growth and respiration of microorganisms
drying	dry air is passed over the food, sometimes in a partial vacuum	microorganisms cannot respire or reproduce
freezing	food is kept in a freezer at about –18°C	microorganisms cannot respire or reproduce
adding salt or sugar	food is soaked in a sugar solution or packed in salt	the sugar or salt draws water out of the microorganisms
adding vinegar	the food is soaked in vinegar	the vinegar is too acidic for the microorganisms

f Suggest why the can is sealed after heating and not before?

g Why do you think that food still goes bad in a refrigerator?

Amazing fact

Dried wheat seeds have been found in the tombs of ancient Egyptians. They are several thousand years old. When water was added to them, some of them started to sprout!

Keywords

compost • decomposer • detritivore • detritus • food preservation • sewage

Making compost

Alison wants to have a compost heap in her garden. It will allow her to get rid of garden waste such as grass cuttings and leaves. It will also make compost, which she can dig into the soil. She finds a photograph of a traditional compost heap in a gardening magazine.

But on the next page she sees an advert for a plastic composting drum.

Plastic composter

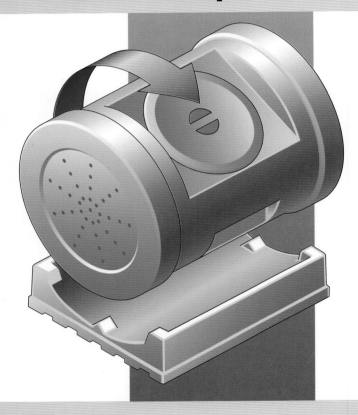

Put all your garden and kitchen waste into the drum through the hatch. (Do not add diseased plants.) Turn the drum at least three times a week. The more often you turn the drum, the faster the compost is made. Add enough water to keep the compost moist but not waterlogged. In the winter compost will not be made, but freezing will help to break up the material and will make it decompose quicker in spring.

Questions

1 The traditional compost heap is made using chicken wire with holes in it. The holes let in things that are useful in making compost. What do you think they are?

2 Why do you think that turning the composting drum helps to make the compost quicker?

3 Animals, such as worms, cannot get into the drum easily. Why is this a disadvantage when making compost?

4 Why is compost made much more slowly in winter in the drum?

Cycles for life

In this item you will find out

- about natural recycling

- how carbon and nitrogen are recycled

Recycling of materials is becoming more popular. You have probably seen one of the recycling banks that have been set up in many towns. We now recycle lots of different materials, such as glass and metals. This saves energy and raw materials.

 Suggest one reason why recycling is a good idea.

We have moved into recycling quite recently, but other organisms have been at it for millions of years. Natural recyclers such as bacteria and fungi break down dead material and make the chemical elements available again for living organisms.

During their lives, animals and plants take in these chemicals and use them to build their bodies. Without the natural recyclers, animals and plants would run out of carbon, nitrogen, oxygen and all the other elements that are needed for life.

Nitrogen often causes the largest problem for living organisms. Although we are surrounded by nitrogen, it is not in a form that is easy to use but it is desperately needed by plants.

The German scientist Fritz Haber developed a process in 1909 to combine nitrogen from the air with hydrogen. The ammonia that is produced can be turned into fertiliser for plants. Now about half of the nitrogen needed by all the plants grown in the world comes from the Haber Process.

Amazing fact

In every kilogram of soil there are about 5 g of living organisms many of which are microorganisms.

▲ *These leaves will soon be recycled*

▲ *Diamonds are pure carbon*

The carbon cycle

The element carbon is the basis for all molecules that make up living organisms. Carbohydrates, proteins and fats all contain carbon. In nature, pure carbon is found as diamonds and graphite, but animals and plants cannot use this carbon.

The main source of carbon is carbon dioxide in the air. Plants remove carbon dioxide from the air when they photosynthesise. The carbon is trapped in carbon compounds like sugar and then passed on from organism to organism along food chains or webs. It returns to the air as carbon dioxide when animals or plants respire. This cycling of carbon is shown in the diagram below.

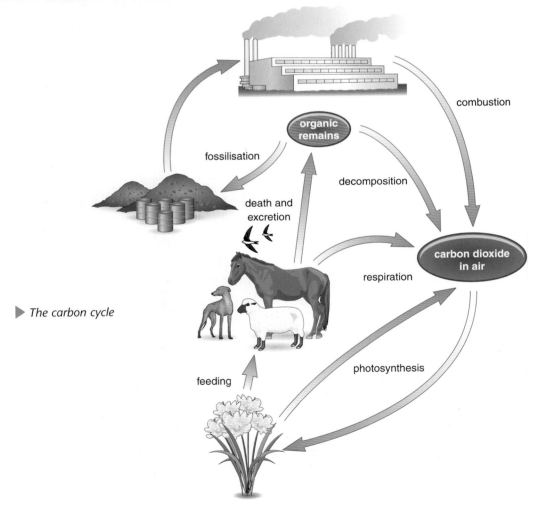

▶ *The carbon cycle*

b How does the carbon get from plants to animals?

Soil bacteria and fungi acting as decomposers also release carbon dioxide into the air when they feed on dead material.

Sometimes, dead animals and plants do not decompose. Instead, over millions of years they are changed into fossil fuels. This process of fossilisation traps carbon in coal, oil and gas. That is why these fuels are called fossil fuels. Burning (combustion) of these fossil fuels will release this carbon again as carbon dioxide.

▲ Burning coal releases carbon dioxide into the air

The nitrogen cycle

We have already seen how important nitrogen is for plants and animals. They are surrounded by air that contains 78% nitrogen, but they cannot use it directly because it is too unreactive.

Plants take in nitrogen as nitrates from the soil through their roots. They use the nitrates to make nitrogen compounds (proteins) for growth. This protein passes down the food chain as animals eat plants and other animals.

Eventually all this trapped nitrogen is released again when decomposers break down dead plants and animals into nitrates that return to the soil. You can see this in the diagram below.

◀ The nitrogen cycle

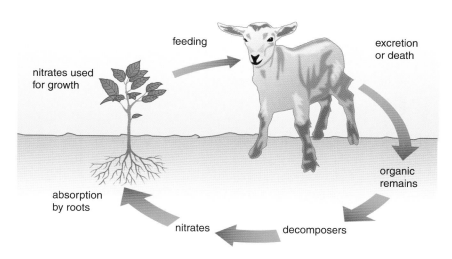

c Farmers try to encourage the nitrogen cycle by adding organic remains to their fields. Which of these substances are organic remains added by farmers?

compost   herbicides   manure   pesticides   water

d Why is it important for plants that nitrates can dissolve in water in the soil?

Keywords

recycling

Fish, ferns and food

A little fern is proving to be a very valuable plant for the Chinese. Azolla is a tiny fern that floats on the surface of lakes and rivers. The important thing about the fern is that it is very rich in amino acids.

In China, rice is grown in large flooded fields. The Chinese also farm fish in the same flooded fields. This provides them with extra food and the fish eat the rice pests, which helps the rice to grow.

The problem is that there is not much food for the fish in the fields. This problem has been solved by adding Azolla to the fields. The fish eat the fern, which is rich in amino acids, and can use the amino acids to make protein.

The fish also help the rice to grow by producing nitrogen-rich faeces. So by adding the fish and the fern, the farmers no longer need to buy expensive fertilisers and pesticides.

Questions

1 Draw a food web to include rice, fish, Azolla and rice pests.

2 The article says that the fish grow well because they feed on the fern, which is rich in amino acids. How does this help the fish to grow?

3 Explain why the farmers do not need to buy fertilisers or pesticides now.

B4a

1 A plant absorbs light to make food. What is the name of the process that makes this food?

**diffusion   osmosis   photosynthesis
respiration**   [1]

2 Finish the sentences by using words from the list.

**chlorophyll   chloroplasts   roots   stomata
vacuoles**

Light energy is trapped by a green chemical called
____(1)____ . This green chemical is found in small
structures called ____(2)____ . Water is taken into a
plant by the ____(3)____ . Carbon dioxide is made by
the plant and exits leaves through ____(4)____ .   [4]

3 The diagram shows
a section through a leaf.

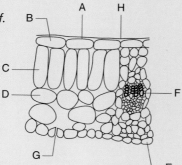

Write down the letter on the diagram that matches the
following structures:

a palisade mesophyll layer   [1]
b cuticle   [1]
c a structure that supplies the leaf with water   [1]
d a structure that allows gaseous exchange   [1]

4 Explain how each of the following features help a leaf
to photosynthesise:

a a broad shape   [2]
b being thin   [2]
c palisade cells with many chloroplasts   [2]

B4b

1 Finish the sentences by using words from the list.

**cell membrane   cell wall   chloroplasts
stem   evaporation**

Water passes up to the leaves of a plant through the
____(1)____ . To get into the cells of the leaf it must first
pass through the ____(2)____ . It then needs to pass
through the ____(3)____ . Water passes out of the leaves
by ____(4)____ .   [4]

2 Explain what happens to a plant if it loses water faster
than it takes it up.   [1]

3 The diagram shows two
solutions in a glass beaker.
They are separated by a
partially permeable membrane.

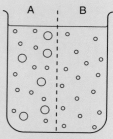

In compartment A there is a
concentrated sugar solution.
In compartment B there is water.

○ sucrose
∘ water molecule

a Which way will the water move?   [1]
b What is the name of the process that causes the
water to move?   [1]
c The sugar molecules cannot move across the
partially permeable membrane. Why is this?   [1]

4 What is the difference between

a osmosis and diffusion?   [2]
b roots and root hairs?   [1]

B4c

1 Copy and complete the table by writing the correct
function in each box. Choose the functions from the list.

**mineral uptake   photosynthesis   transport
reproduction**

Part of the plant	Function
flower	
leaf	
stem	
root	

[4]

2 A plant loses water by transpiration. Give two
conditions that may cause a plant to lose more water
than normal.   [2]

3 Complete the following sentences by adding a word or
words in each gap.

In the plant stem the xylem and phloem are arranged
in groups called ____(1)____ . In the stem the ____(2)____
is on the outside and the ____(3)____ is on the inside of
each of these groups. The xylem transports ____(4)____
up the stem and the phloem transports ____(5)____ in
____(6)____ directions. The evaporation of water out of
the leaves is called ____(7)____ .   [7]

B4d

1 Plants need minerals to grow. Plant fertilisers often have
figures printed on them called NPK. What does each of
the letters stand for?   [3]

2 Write down one other mineral that plants need to get from the soil so that they can grow properly. [1]

3 Jane buys a packet of fertiliser to use on her garden. On the packet it says:

'This fertiliser contains all the minerals needed for your plants to grow. Simply dissolve in some water in a watering can and water the soil. Only use a small amount of the powder – plants are not used to too many minerals.'

  a Why should water and a watering can be used to apply the fertiliser? [2]

  b Why are plants not used to too many minerals? [1]

  c Which mineral in the fertiliser would be needed for cell growth? [1]

4 An experiment was carried out to investigate the effect of growing plants without different minerals. The results are shown in the photograph on page 53.

  a Why is each of the solutions in this experiment made using distilled water? [2]

  b Which plant grew best and why? [2]

  c What is the difference in colour between the nitrogen-free plant (–N) and the plant grown with all the necessary minerals (complete)? [1]

  d What effects do lack of phosphate (–P) have on the plant? [2]

B4e

1 Which energy sources are examples of biomass?

  A alcohol   B nuclear fuel
  C wave power   D wood [2]

2 Finish the sentences by using words from the list.

chlorophyll   **consumers**   **food chains**
producer   **Sun**

A green plant is called a ___(1)___ because it can make food using simple molecules. To do this it uses the energy from the ___(2)___ . Once the energy has been trapped in food it can be passed along ___(3)___ . This allows organisms called ___(4)___ to take in food. [4]

3 Several animals live in a garden. The table shows what they eat.

Animal	Food
snail	grass
rabbit	grass
mice	grass seeds
fox	rabbit, mice
blackbird	snail

  a Which organism in the table is a producer? [1]

  b Draw a food web for the organisms listed in the table. [3]

  c Many tiny fleas live in the fur of the fox. Draw a pyramid of numbers for this food chain:
grass plants → rabbits → fox → fleas [2]

  d Draw a pyramid of biomass for the same food chain and explain why it looks different to the pyramid of numbers. [3]

4 The diagram shows energy being lost as it passes through a food chain.

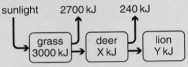

  a Calculate the amount of energy available to the deer for growth. [1]

  b Calculate the amount of energy available to the lion. [1]

  c Name two ways in which energy is lost by the deer. [1]

B4f

1 Copy and complete the following table by writing the correct word in each of the empty boxes.

Type of chemical used by farmer	Organisms that are killed
pesticide	pests
fungicide	
insecticide	
herbicide	

[3]

2 Finish the sentences by using words from the list.

chemicals   **intensive**   **organic**   **pollution**
predators   **prey**

Some farmers use chemicals on their fields to try to produce as large a crop as possible. This is called ___(1)___ farming. Some farmers do not use chemicals on their fields because the chemicals can produce ___(2)___ . Farming without using these chemicals is called ___(3)___ farming. To try to get rid of pests these farmers might use ___(4)___ to eat the pests. [4]

3 Tomato plants can be grown in glasshouses. They are often grown without soil.

  a Why are tomatoes often grown in glasshouses? [1]

  b What name is given to the method of growing tomatoes without soil? [1]

  c Explain why these two methods mean that tomatoes can be grown in areas where they could not otherwise have been grown. [2]

4 A small red spider often feeds on the leaves of tomato plants. It is possible to control the red spider by releasing another type of spider called *Phytoseiulus* into the glasshouse.

    a Suggest how *Phytoseiulus* controls the red spider. [1]

    b What is the name given to this type of control? [1]

    c Why is this type of control ideal for a greenhouse but less easy to use in a field? [1]

    d Suggest why the owner of the greenhouse must stop using pesticides when *Phytoseiulus* is used? [1]

B4g

1 The following waste materials may be found in a rubbish bin. Which would decay on a compost heap?

crisp packet   dead flowers   milk bottle   potato peelings   tin can [2]

2 Finish the sentences by using words from the list.

compost   dry   glass   nitrogen   oxygen wet   sewage

Microorganisms can be used to break down waste products such as ____(1)____ and ____(2)____ . To do this they need certain conditions such as a supply of ____(3)____ . Conditions must not be too ____(4)____ or the microorganisms will not be active. [4]

3 Match each food preservation technique with the explanation of how it works.

    1 freezing   A microorganisms are killed by heat
    2 adding vinegar B temperature is too cold
    3 adding salt   C pH is too low
    4 canning   D microorganisms are dried out [2]

4 Different organisms are responsible for decomposing dead leaves. They are:
- earthworms, which are about 5 mm in diameter
- small insects, such as maggots and woodlice, which may be 2–4 mm wide
- microorganisms smaller than 0.005 mm wide.

A scientist decided to investigate how fast leaves decompose. She put leaves into three different bags and buried them in the soil. Each bag was made of nylon with different-sized holes. Every 2 months she dug up the bags and measured how much of the leaves had disappeared. Here are her results.

Month	Percentage disappearance of the leaves		
	Bag with 7 mm holes	Bag with 4 mm holes	Bag with 0.005 mm holes
June	0	0	0
August	25	8	0
October	70	20	2
December	75	25	3

    a Which of the three types of organism can get into each of the bags? [1]

    b In which bag do the leaves decay the fastest? [1]

    c Explain why the leaves decay at different rates in the three different bags. [4]

    d How does the rate of decay change in November and December compared with June to October? [1]

    e Explain this difference in rate. [2]

B4h

1 Finish the following sentences.

In order to grow, organisms need to feed. They take in elements from their surroundings and use them to make new ____(1)____ . One of the most important of these elements is ____(2)____ . When they die or give out waste, decay occurs. This means that the elements can be used again. This is called ____(3)____ . [3]

2 The diagram shows part of the carbon cycle.

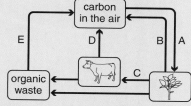

    a Write down the name of the process represented by each letter in the diagram. Choose from the list – you can use each word once, more than once or not at all.

decomposing   eating   fossilising photosynthesising   respiring [5]

    b Most of the carbon in the air is in which form? Choose from the list.

calcium carbonate   carbon dioxide carbon monoxide   limestone [1]

3 Read the paragraph about nitrogen and then answer the questions.

'Nitrogen is an important element for all organisms, from grass to giraffes and pansies to pigs. All these organisms use nitrogen for growth. But they all have a problem. Although they are surrounded by plenty of nitrogen in the air, they cannot use it very easily. Animals rely on the plants to get nitrogen from the soil. They absorb this nitrogen combined in minerals. The animals can then eat the plants.'

    a What do animals and plants make from nitrogen that is so important for growth? [1]

    b The paragraph says that there is plenty of nitrogen in the air. What is the percentage? [1]

    c Why is it so difficult for animals and plants to use this nitrogen? [1]

    d What is the main mineral taken up by plants that contains nitrogen? [1]

C3 The Periodic Table

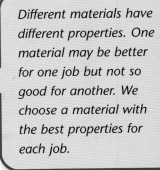

Why do we make things from different materials? My CDs are made from plastic and my bike is made from metal. Why can't I have a metal CD and a plastic bike?

Different materials have different properties. One material may be better for one job but not so good for another. We choose a material with the best properties for each job.

- Over 4 milllion substances exist on the Earth, yet these substances are made from only about 100 chemical elements. The elements are enormously varied: from mercury, a metal that is liquid, to caesium, a metal that melts if you hold it in your hand. There are gases like chlorine and oxygen, and solids like carbon, which makes both pencil leads and diamonds.

- To make sense of these quite different elements they need to be put into some sort of order. This is the Periodic Table.

- Chemists have used an understanding of how elements behave to make the materials that we use in the twenty-first century, such as polymers that stop food sticking to saucepans, dyes that colour our clothes and metals that remember their shape.

And the reason different materials have different properties is all to do with their structures: how atoms are arranged in the material and how sub-atomic particles are arranged in the atoms. This is what chemistry is all about.

What you need to know

- All substances are made from elements.

- Elements are made up of atoms.

- Elements can be divided into metals and non-metals.

Atoms and elements

In this item you will find out

- what is inside an atom
- how elements are arranged in the Periodic Table

The first atomic bomb exploded on 16 July 1945 in a desert in New Mexico, USA.

To make this bomb, scientists used their knowledge of atomic structure to find out how to split **atoms**. As atoms split, a huge amount of energy is released.

The first atomic bomb generated the same explosive power as 20 000 tons of TNT. This is the same as about 20 of the largest conventional bombs used in World War II. Modern atomic bombs can generate the same explosive power as millions of tons of TNT.

 a How do we know that splitting atoms releases a huge amount of energy?

We can now use this energy in a more peaceful way. The splitting of atoms can be controlled, so that the energy is released more slowly. This energy can be used to generate electricity.

All substances are made of atoms. Scientists worked for many years to discover what atoms are made of. Atoms contain much smaller particles called **protons**, **electrons** and **neutrons**.

 b Once atoms had been discovered, it took another 100 years for the first sub-atomic particle to be discovered. Why was it so difficult to discover these sub-atomic particles?

▲ *An atomic explosion generates a huge amount of energy*

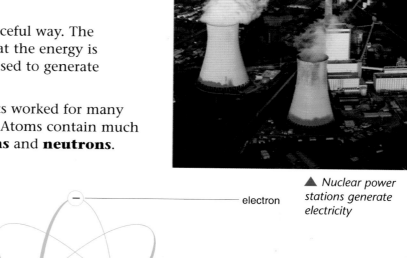

▲ *Nuclear power stations generate electricity*

electron

neutron

proton

▶ *Inside a lithium atom*

If we could look inside an atom, what would we see? In the centre of an atom is the positively charged **nucleus**. This is where the protons are. Negatively charged electrons are outside the nucleus, arranged in shells. The whole atom is neutral. Most atoms also contain neutrons in the nucleus.

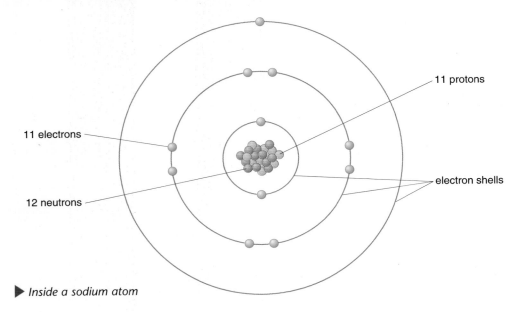

11 protons

11 electrons

12 neutrons

electron shells

▶ *Inside a sodium atom*

These three sub-atomic particles have different properties.

Sub-atomic particle	Where found	Relative mass	Relative charge
proton	in the nucleus	1	+1
neutron	in the nucleus	1	0
electron	outside the nucleus	0.0005	−1

Protons and neutrons have the same mass, but it takes about 2000 electrons to make the same mass as one proton.

c   **Which part of an atom contains most of its mass?**

The chemical elements

All of the substances that exist are made from a 'tool-kit' of just over 100 **elements**. From these elements, millions of **compounds** can be made. Each compound has two or more elements chemically joined together. A compound can be broken down chemically into the elements it contains. An element cannot be broken down chemically into smaller particles. Each element contains just one type of atom.

d   **Which of these substances are elements and which are compounds?**

     oxygen   sodium chloride   carbon   copper   sulfur dioxide   water

e   **Use a Periodic Table to identify the elements in these compounds:**

     CuO KCl ZnF_2 $FeBr_3$ H_2O Na_2SO_4 NH_4NO_3

Amazing fact

Would you like an element named after you? Glenn Seaborg had one: seaborgium. He also got a Nobel prize for discovering 10 new elements, with atomic numbers 94–102 and 106.

Atomic number and mass number

Each atom in an element contains the same number of protons. This number is called the **atomic number** of the element. It can also be called the **proton number**.

In the Periodic Table, elements are arranged in order of their atomic number.

These are the elements in the second row (called the second Period) of the Periodic Table.

Element	Lithium	Beryllium	Boron	Carbon	Nitrogen	Oxygen	Fluorine	Neon
symbol	Li	Be	B	C	N	O	F	Ne
protons	3	4	5	6	7	8	9	10
electrons	3	4	5	6	7	8	9	10

f How does the number of protons change across the second Period?

g What can you say about the number of protons and electrons in each element?

h Use a Periodic Table to: (i) find the atomic number of the elements Be, N, Ne, Ca and Br; (ii) find the names of the elements with the atomic numbers 3, 9, 13, 19 and 47.

The nucleus of an atom of beryllium contains 4 protons and 5 neutrons. Added together this comes to 9. This is the **mass number** of beryllium. It can also be called the **nucleon number.** The mass number of an element is found by adding the number of protons and the number of neutrons.

i An atom of fluorine has 9 protons and 10 neutrons. What is the mass number of fluorine?

Isotopes

In each element every atom has the same number of protons. But in most elements all of the atoms do not have the same number of neutrons. Atoms of the same element that have different numbers of neutrons are called **isotopes**.

Here is some information about the isotopes of carbon.

Isotope	Carbon-12	Carbon-13	Carbon-14
atomic number	6	6	6
mass number	12	13	14
percentage of isotope	98.9	1.1	trace

j How many neutrons are in each atom of carbon-13?

Some isotopes, such as carbon-14, are radioactive. Over a period of time they decay to form other elements, becoming less radioactive.

How old is that skeleton?

A skeleton has been found in a shallow grave.

Could this be the victim of a recent murder or did this person die hundreds of years ago? A forensic scientist is called in to find the age of the skeleton.

The forensic scientist measures the amount of the radioactive isotope lead-210 in samples from the skeleton. Tiny amounts of this isotope occur in almost all human food and get into human bones. When people die, they stop eating and drinking and so they no longer take in the lead isotope. As time goes by the lead isotope decays, and gives out less radiation.

The concentration of lead-210 in the bones of living people can also be measured. By comparing the two, it is possible to work out how long it is since a person has died.

Lead-210 has a half-life of 22 years. That means that every 22 years, the levels of lead-210 in human bones fall by half. So by just using lead levels as a measure, the forensic scientist can date bones up to 75 years old – the period of interest to the police – to an accuracy of a year.

More traditional techniques in murder investigations have so far depended on the condition of the body and even the stage of development of insects on the corpse. But these are affected by temperature: the greater the range of temperatures experienced by the body, the more uncertain the traditional dating techniques become. Using lead-210 gives a much more accurate dating of recent skeletons.

Questions

1 Why does lead-210 no longer enter a person's bones once they are dead?

2 Why does the amount of lead-210 in a person's bones fall after they die?

3 Why do you think the police are not interested in skeletons more than 75 years old?

4 Why are conventional methods for dating a skeleton less accurate than using lead-210?

5 Lead-210 is a radioactive isotope. Suggest how the lead-210 remaining in a skeleton is measured.

6 Carbon-14 is an isotope with a half-life of 5700 years. Why would this not be a good isotope for dating a skeleton less than 75 years old?

Interesting ions

For centuries people have made jewellery using the crystals in gemstones.

Gemstones are minerals dug out of the ground. They are made of crystals. This means that they reflect the light. Jewellery containing crystals has a very attractive appearance.

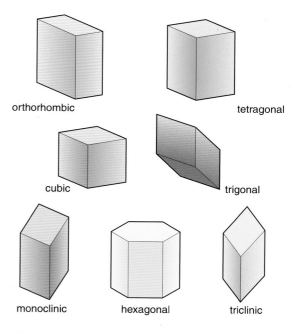

▲ *The sapphires in this jewellery are crystals*

a Why does being able to reflect light make crystals in jewellery more attractive?

Crystals have regular shapes because the particles they contain are arranged in a very orderly way. Look at the shape of a crystal of copper(II) sulfate in the photograph below.

All copper(II) sulfate crystals grow with the same shape, because the particles in copper(II) sulfate crystals are always arranged in the same pattern. There are seven basic shapes of crystal.

orthorhombic   tetragonal

cubic   trigonal

b Which of these shapes is shown in a crystal of copper sulfate?

The particles in a copper(II) sulfate crystal are called **ions**. An ion is an atom or a group of atoms with a positive or a negative charge.

Many gemstone crystals are also made from ions. Sapphire is a blue gemstone made from aluminium oxide, which contains positive aluminium ions and negative oxygen ions.

monoclinic   hexagonal   triclinic

▲ *The seven basic shapes of crystal*

▶ *A crystal of copper sulfate*

Amazing fact

The largest gem-quality diamond ever found was discovered on 26 January 1905 in South Africa. It weighed more than half a kilogram.

Are you positive?

The table shows you the names and formulae of some ions.

Name of ion	Charge	Formula
sodium	positive	Na^+
magnesium	positive	Mg^{2+}
aluminium	positive	Al^{3+}
chloride	negative	Cl^-
oxide	negative	O^{2-}
nitrate	negative	NO_3^-
carbonate	negative	CO_3^{2-}

c What sort of charge do metal ions have?

d Divide these formulae into three groups: atoms, molecules and ions.

Be^+ Ca Cl^- CO_2 CO_3^{2-} Br^- Br_2 Fe^{2+} I_2 Na^+
S SO_2 SO_4^{2-}

Ions are formed by atoms losing or gaining electrons. When a metal and a non-metal react, the metal atoms lose electrons and the non-metal atoms gain electrons. The metal atoms become positive ions and the non-metal atoms become negative ions. These ions are then attracted to one another. The number of positive protons in each atom does not change, only the number of electrons.

When sodium chloride is formed, each sodium atom loses one electron and each chlorine atom gains one electron.

e Why do sodium ions have a positive charge?

There is a very strong attraction between the positive and negative ions. This holds the ions firmly in place in a crystal of sodium chloride. This is an **ionic bond**.

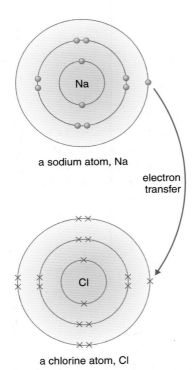

a sodium atom, Na

electron transfer

a chlorine atom, Cl

▲ *Transfer of electrons in the formation of sodium chloride: this makes positive sodium ions (Na⁺) and negative chloride ions (Cl⁻)*

◀ *A crystal of sodium chloride*

Sodium chloride

The strong forces between the sodium and chloride ions mean that a lot of energy is needed to break the ions apart. So you need to use a high temperature to melt sodium chloride.

When a material conducts electricity, electrons move through it. All of the electrons in sodium chloride are held tightly in the ions, so they cannot move. The ions are held firmly in the crystal, so they cannot move to carry electrons through the material. This means that solid sodium chloride will not conduct electricity.

When sodium chloride is melted the ions move apart. They can carry an electric current through the liquid, so molten sodium chloride conducts electricity.

Sodium chloride can be dissolved in water. In this solution the ions are free to move and carry an electric current. Sodium chloride solution conducts electricity.

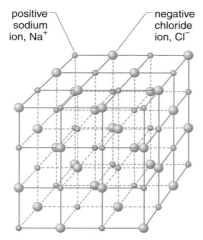

positive sodium ion, Na^+ negative chloride ion, Cl^-

▲ *A sodium chloride crystal lattice*

 Why does solid sodium chloride not conduct electricity?

Magnesium oxide

When magnesium oxide is made, each magnesium atom loses two electrons and forms a magnesium ion with two positive charges, Mg^{2+}.

Each oxygen atom gains the two electrons lost by a magnesium atom, forming an oxide ion with two negative charges, O^{2-}.

The attraction between these doubly charged ions is even stronger than that in sodium chloride. So magnesium oxide has a very high melting point and does not conduct electricity when solid.

 Why are the ions in magnesium oxide held together more strongly than the ions in sodium chloride?

When magnesium oxide is melted, the ions are free to move and carry an electric current, so molten magnesium oxide conducts electricity.

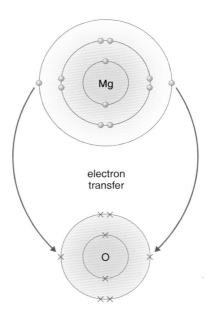

electron transfer

▲ *How electrons are transferred during the formation of magnesium oxide*

▲ *Stirring a solution*

Investigating solubility

Louise and Jamie are doing a school project on ionic compounds. They know that most compounds that contain ionic bonds are soluble in water, but the solubilities vary. Also, the solubility of an ionic compound depends on the temperature of the water it is dissolved in.

They carry out a series of experiments to test the solubility of three ionic compounds at different temperatures.

The table shows their results.

Temperature (°C)	Solubility (g per 100 g of water)		
	Sodium chloride	Copper(II) sulfate	Potassium nitrate
10	38.0	18	20
20	38.0	20	30
30	38.0	24	44
40	38.5	28	60
50	38.5	34	80
60	39	42	104
70	39	50	152

They take 100 g of water at 10 °C and add sodium chloride a little at a time, stirring between each addition. When no more has dissolved they note the mass of sodium chloride that has been added.

They repeat this at six other temperatures for sodium chloride. They then repeat the whole experiment using copper(II) sulfate and potassium nitrate.

Questions

1 How does the solubility of the three compounds change with the increase in temperature?

2 Describe the difference in the effect of temperature on the solubility of sodium chloride and potassium nitrate.

3 Which is the most soluble compound at 20 °C?

4 Which is the most soluble compound at 60 °C?

5 Use a piece of graph paper to plot solubility against temperature for sodium chloride and potassium nitrate on the same axes. At what temperature do these two compounds have the same solubility?

Bonding and beyond

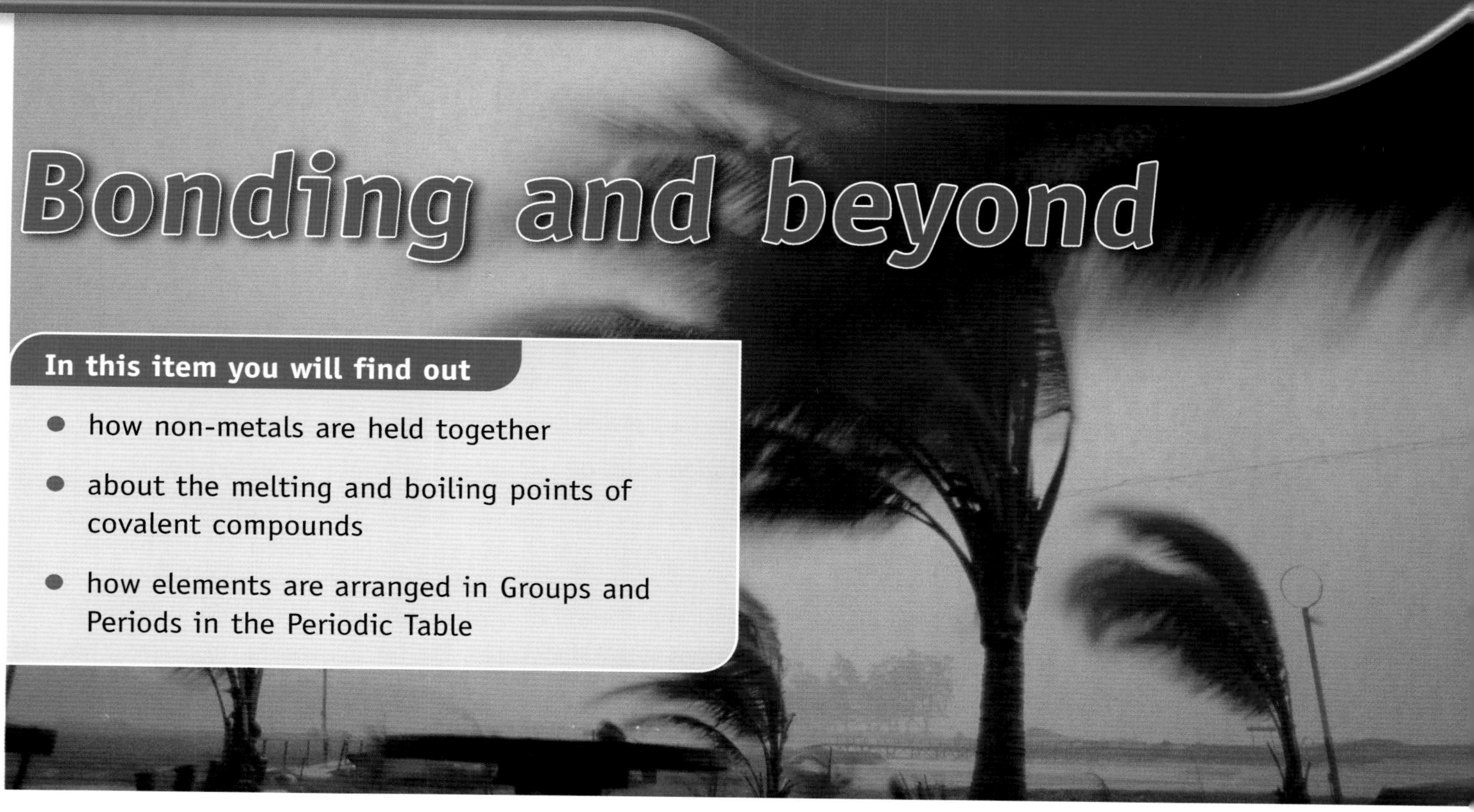

In this item you will find out

- how non-metals are held together

- about the melting and boiling points of covalent compounds

- how elements are arranged in Groups and Periods in the Periodic Table

▲ *Gases can move trees*

We move around in an atmosphere made of gases. Winds move this mixture of gases around.

The air contains elements such as nitrogen and oxygen, and compounds such as carbon dioxide and water vapour.

 Suggest how you can tell that the air contains water vapour.

Carbon dioxide and water vapour are made up of **molecules**. In each molecule two or more atoms are joined by **covalent bonds**. Covalent compounds have low melting points and boiling points.

At room temperature, most covalent compounds are gases like carbon dioxide. Some, like water, are liquids, although a lot of water is present in the air as a gas – water vapour.

The diagram shows the displayed formulae of carbon dioxide and water. The covalent bonds are shown as lines.

$$O=C=O \qquad H\diagdown O \diagup H$$

The displayed formula shows that carbon dioxide has two atoms of oxygen and one atom of carbon. The molecular formula for carbon dioxide, CO_2, also shows this.

 Use the molecular formulae of these compounds to work out how many atoms are in one molecule of each: hydrogen chloride HCl, nitrogen dioxide NO_2, ammonia NH_3, propane C_3H_8 and ethanol C_2H_5OH.

Amazing fact

Many small covalent molecules are gases with very low boiling points. Hydrogen has a boiling point of −253 °C. This is just 20 degrees above absolute zero, the coldest possible temperature.

Share and share alike

As we have seen, when an atom of a metal joins with an atom of a non-metal the atoms lose or gain electrons to form an **ionic bond**. But when two non-metal atoms combine together, they share electrons to form a covalent bond. This is how a molecule is made.

The atoms forming molecules may be from the same element, for example hydrogen forms hydrogen molecules. Or they may come from different elements, for example carbon and oxygen form carbon dioxide molecules.

c **Which of these substances has covalent bonds?**

bromine   hydrogen chloride   sodium chloride   sulfur dioxide
zinc sulfate

A molecule may contain two or more atoms. There are two atoms in an oxygen molecule, but hundreds in a poly(ethene) molecule. Some compounds are made of thousands of atoms joined together by covalent bonds. These are giant covalent structures. Examples are diamond and silicon dioxide (sand).

d **Suggest how the physical properties of giant covalent structures are different from the physical properties of small covalent molecules.**

Covalent molecules, such as water and carbon dioxide, are not charged particles so they do not conduct electricity.

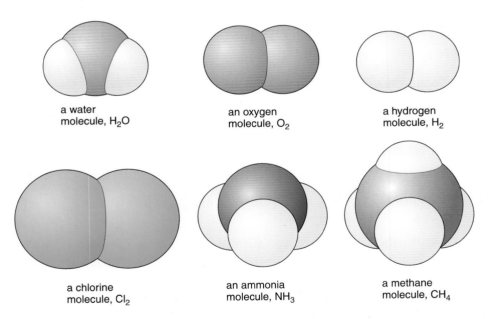

a water
molecule, H_2O

an oxygen
molecule, O_2

a hydrogen
molecule, H_2

a chlorine
molecule, Cl_2

an ammonia
molecule, NH_3

a methane
molecule, CH_4

▲ *Different molecules have different shapes*

Grouped together

The diagram shows a shortened version of the Periodic Table.

The numbers across the top row of the Periodic Table show the vertical **Groups** of elements. Lithium is in Group 1 and fluorine is in Group 7. Each Group is like a family of elements that have similar chemical properties.

1	2	3	4	5	6	7	8
1 **H** Hydrogen 1							4 **He** Helium 2
7 **Li** Lithium 3	9 **Be** Beryllium 4	11 **B** Boron 5	12 **C** Carbon 6	14 **N** Nitrogen 7	16 **O** Oxygen 8	19 **F** Fluorine 9	20 **Ne** Neon 10
23 **Na** Sodium 11	24 **Mg** Magnesium 12	27 **Al** Aluminium 13	28 **Si** Silicon 14	31 **P** Phosphorus 15	32 **S** Sulfur 16	35.5 **Cl** Chlorine 17	40 **Ar** Argon 18
39 **K** Potassium 19	40 **Ca** Calcium 20	70 **Ga** Galium 31	73 **Ge** Germanium 32	75 **As** Arsenic 33	79 **Se** Selenium 34	80 **Br** Bromine 35	84 **Kr** Krypton 36
85 **Rb** Rubidium 37	88 **Sr** Strontium 38	115 **In** Indium 49	119 **Sn** Tin 50	122 **Sb** Antimony 51	128 **Te** Tellurium 52	127 **I** Iodine 53	131 **Xe** Xenon 54
133 **Cs** Caesium 55	137 **Ba** Barium 56	204 **Tl** Thalium 81	207 **Pb** Lead 82	209 **Bi** Bismuth 83	209 **Po** Polonium 84	210 **At** Astatine 85	222 **Rn** Radon 86
223 **Fr** Francium 87	226 **Ra** Radium 88						

e Name an element in Group 5.

The number of the Group that an element belongs to tells you how many electrons there are in the outer shell of an atom of that element. All the elements in Group 1 have one electron in their outer shell. All the elements in Group 7 have seven electrons in their outer shell. All the elements in Group 8 have eight electrons in their outer shell, except for helium which has two.

f How many electrons are in the outer shell of the atoms of elements in Group 3?

Periods

From left to right across the Periodic Table the elements are arranged in horizontal rows called **Periods**. The first Period contains only hydrogen and helium. The second Period contains eight elements, from lithium to neon.

g Which of these elements are in the same Period?

argon   beryllium   oxygen   potassium   silicon   sodium

The number of shells of electrons in the atom of an element is the same as the number of the Period the element is in. Magnesium is in Period 2, so an atom of magnesium has two shells of electrons.

h How many electron shells are there in the atoms of elements in Period 3?

Lighter than air

In the 1930s aircraft were thought to be far too dangerous for passengers. Most people thought that long-distance travel was much safer by airship. Airships were filled with hydrogen gas. Because hydrogen is much lighter than air, it enabled an airship to carry passengers and cargo high above the surface of the Earth. Hydrogen is also very flammable. The photo shows the most famous airship of all, the *Hindenburg*.

On 6 May 1937, the *Hindenburg* was on a flight from Berlin to New York. As it prepared to tie up at the mooring tower, there was an explosion at the rear that quickly spread to the entire airship, bringing it crashing to the ground in flames. Of the 97 people aboard, 36 died, including 13 passengers.

Modern airships are often used for advertising. They are filled with helium instead of hydrogen. Helium is only a little heavier than hydrogen. Helium is a noble gas, in Group 8 of the Periodic Table. Helium, like other elements in this Group, is chemically inert. It does not react with other substances and therefore is not flammable. If the Hindenburg had been filled with helium, the disaster would not have happened.

Questions

1. Suggest why people in the 1930s thought that airships were safer to travel in than aeroplanes.

2. Why was the gas hydrogen chosen for filling airships?

3. Why was hydrogen not a good choice?

4. Why is helium used for modern airships?

5. Why are airships still used?

The alkali metals

In this item you will find out

- some of the properties of Group 1 elements

- how to identify Group 1 elements using flame tests

When you watch a firework display do you ever wonder how all the different colours are made?

A metal powder or metal salt is mixed with the other ingredients in each firework. Different powders or salts produce different colours. When the fireworks are burned, the metal ions in the compounds are heated to high temperatures and the coloured flames are produced.

We can see the same colours in the laboratory when metal compounds are heated in a Bunsen burner flame. This is called the **flame test**.

This test is carried out by dipping a moistened Nichrome wire into a solid sample of the compound containing the metal ion and then putting the wire into a very hot Bunsen flame.

Light given out by the metal gives the flame a colour. For example, the metals lithium, sodium and potassium give the flame colours shown in the table.

Amazing fact

A Chinese cook discovered fireworks by chance over 2000 years ago.

Group 1 element	Symbol	Flame colour
lithium	Li	carmine red
sodium	Na	golden yellow
potassium	K	lilac

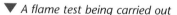
▼ *A flame test being carried out*

Scientists can use this test to identify the metal ion present in a compound.

 A scientist finds that an unknown compound turns a Bunsen burner flame lilac. Which metal ion is present in the compound?

Really reactive

Lithium, sodium and potassium are all in Group 1 of the Periodic Table and are called the **alkali metals**. They are a family of elements with similar properties. This is because each of the metals in Group 1 has atoms with one electron in the outer shell. When these atoms react, each loses this one electron to form an ion. Because the alkali metals all have the same number of electrons in their outer shell, they react in a similar way.

The photograph on the left shows samples of lithium, sodium and potassium.

The shiny metal surface of each metal quickly goes dull when exposed to air. The metal is reacting with oxygen in the air to form a coating of the metal oxide. The metals also react with water vapour in the air. Each metal is stored under oil to stop these reactions.

▶ Group 1 metals are so reactive that they have to be stored under oil

Increasing reactivity

The reactivity of these metals increases as we move down the Group: so potassium is more reactive than sodium, and sodium is more reactive than lithium.

The metals in this group behave in a similar way when they are added to water.

If a small cube of each metal is added to water in a trough, you will see that they all behave in a similar way.

▼ Lithium, sodium and potassium reacting with water

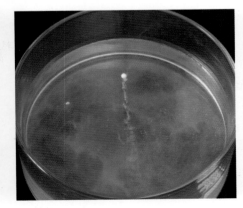
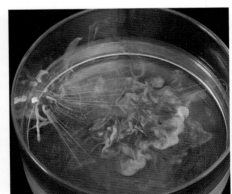

Group 1 metal	Observations when the metal is added to water	Colour of Universal Indicator added to the water
lithium	• floats on the water • remains as a cube shape • fizzes slowly • disappears slowly	purple
sodium	• floats on the water • melts to form a ball of metal • fizzes quickly • whizzes around on the surface • disappears quickly	purple
potassium	• floats on the water • melts to form a ball of metal • fizzes furiously • whizzes around on the surface • burns with a lilac flame • disappears very quickly	purple

b How does the table show that these three metals have similar properties?

c How does the table show that the reactivity of these metals increases as you move down Group 1?

d Going down Group 1, the next metal is rubidium. What do you think will happen if a cube of rubidium is added to water?

Making alkalis

In each of the three experiments, Universal Indicator turns purple when it is added to the water in the trough. This shows that an alkali is formed during the reaction.

The fizzing in these reactions shows that a gas is given off. If you collect some of this gas in a test tube and put in a lighted splint, the gas explodes with a squeaky pop sound. This shows that the gas is hydrogen.

We can write a word equation to show what is happening in this reaction:

metal + water → metal hydroxide + hydrogen

Here is the word equation for lithium:

lithium + water → lithium hydroxide + hydrogen

The alkali is lithium hydroxide. This dissolves in the water as the lithium reacts.

This is the word equation for sodium:

sodium + water → sodium hydroxide + hydrogen

e What is the alkali produced in the reaction between sodium and water?

f Write a word equation for the reaction of potassium with water.

Keywords

alkali metal • flame test

Sodium–sulfur batteries

Our increasing use of vehicles powered by petrol-burning engines is causing concern to many people. Supplies of crude oil are finite and will therefore run out in the future.

Most scientists believe that carbon dioxide emissions are causing global warming and everyone worries about the high cost of petrol.

One possible solution is the use of electric cars. A major drawback is the need to store energy to power the vehicle.

The usual lead-acid batteries used in cars are heavy and store little energy for their weight. They cannot power an electric car far enough or quickly enough for it to compete with petrol-powered cars.

The answer may lie in a revolutionary design of battery that uses the metal sodium. This is a high-temperature battery, with the molten sulfur electrolyte operating at 300°C. At this temperature the sodium contained in the battery is also liquid.

This type of battery has a very high energy output for its weight, but would be dangerous if the contents escaped. Molten sodium would explode on contact with water. Molten sulfur would burn, releasing poisonous sulfur dioxide.

In the future sodium–sulfur batteries may also be used in hybrid electric vehicles, which can be powered by both an electric motor and a petrol engine.

Questions

1. Why are battery-powered cars a good idea?

2. Why are lead-acid batteries not a good choice for these cars?

3. Why would a battery made using sodium and sulfur be a better choice?

4. What are the major disadvantages of using sodium–sulfur batteries in a family car?

The halogens

In this item you will find out

- some of the uses of Group 7 elements and their compounds

- how these elements react with alkali metals

- how the reactivity of these elements changes down the Group

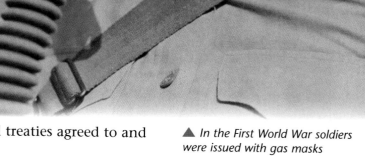

In the First World War poisonous gases were used as weapons. One of these gases was the Group 7 element chlorine.

Chlorine is a green gas. It is denser than air. When shells containing chlorine exploded, dense clouds of the gas drifted across the trenches where soldiers sheltered. Soldiers who did not have gas masks or did not put them on quickly enough breathed in the gas and died.

The use of poisonous gases such as chlorine as weapons of war is now banned by the Geneva Conventions. These are international treaties agreed to and signed by leaders of the major nations of the world.

▲ In the First World War soldiers were issued with gas masks

 Why did the chlorine gas not blow away quickly?

Chlorine is an element in Group 7 of the Periodic Table. Elements in this Group are known as **halogens**. Fluorine, bromine and iodine are also halogens. These elements have a variety of uses.

Today we use chlorine to sterilise the water used in swimming pools and the water supplied to the taps in our homes. It is also used in the manufacture of pesticides and plastics.

Iodine was also used in the First World War, not as a weapon but as a treatment for wounds. Iodine solution kills bacteria that are on the skin and in the wound. If they are not killed, these bacteria can cause an infection in the wound. If the infection was not stopped, wounded soldiers developed gangrene and had to have limbs amputated. Iodine solution is still used to sterilise wounds today.

 Why do you think chlorine is not used to sterilise wounds?

Amazing fact

You need iodine in your diet to stay healthy. If you don't get enough iodine, your thyroid gland swells to form a goitre.

The same but different

The halogens react in a similar way because they each have atoms with seven electrons in the outer shell. When these atoms react, each gains one electron to form a negative ion. Because the halogens all have the same number of electrons in the outer shell, they react in a similar way. They have similar properties.

They look very different at room temperature:

- chlorine is a green gas
- bromine is an orange-red liquid
- iodine is a grey solid.

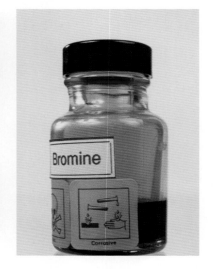

▼ Chlorine, bromine and iodine have different colours

You can see that, as we go down the Group, the state of the element changes from gas to liquid to solid. The colour of the element also gets darker.

 What does the state of each of these elements tell you about their melting and boiling points?

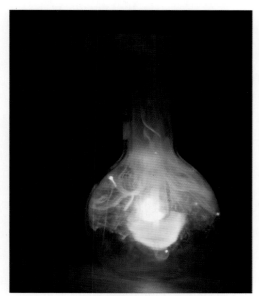

Halogens and alkali metals

All of the halogens react vigorously with the alkali metals, for example sodium. This is shown in the photo on the left.

In each reaction the product is an alkali metal **halide**. Warm sodium reacts with chlorine to make sodium chloride, with bromine to make sodium bromide, and with iodine to make sodium iodide.

▶ Chlorine reacting with sodium

This is the word equation for the reaction between sodium and chlorine:

sodium + chlorine → sodium chloride

 Write word equations for the reactions between sodium and bromine, and between sodium and iodine.

Sodium chloride, commonly called salt, has many uses. It is used as a preservative, preventing the growth of bacteria that would spoil food. Salt is also used to add flavour to food, although too much may not be good for your health. Sodium chloride is also used in the manufacture of chlorine.

The halogens react with the other alkali metals in a similar way.

 What compound is made when potassium reacts with bromine?

Sodium is a very reactive metal and chlorine is a poisonous gas, but sodium chloride is safe to add to our food. The properties of a compound are quite different from those of the elements it is made from. Eating small quantities of sodium chloride is quite harmless. Eating the elements that sodium chloride is made from would be fatal.

Displacing halogens

The reactivity of the halogens decreases down the Group. This trend can be seen in the **displacement** reaction between a halogen and a metal halide. Chlorine gas is bubbled through a solution of potassium bromide. A red colour appears in the solution. This is the element bromine that has been displaced by the more reactive chlorine:

chlorine + potassium bromide → bromine + potassium chloride

A series of experiments is carried out to give the results in the table.

Halogen	Halide solution	Result	Halogen displaced
chlorine	potassium bromide	red solution	bromine
chlorine	potassium iodide	brown solution	iodine
bromine	potassium chloride	none	none
bromine	potassium iodide	brown solution	iodine
iodine	potassium chloride	none	none
iodine	potassium bromide	none	none

These results show that chlorine displaces both other halogens, bromine displaces only iodine, and iodine does not displace either of the other two halogens. This shows that the order of reactivity, from most reactive to least reactive, is chlorine–bromine–iodine.

 Write a word equation for the reaction between bromine and potassium iodide.

Swimming in chlorine

Leroy is a maintenance engineer working for a company that builds and looks after swimming pools. He visits each pool every few months to make sure that it is clean and safe to use.

He removes leaves and other debris from outside pools. Then he cleans the filters and checks the acidity of the water. He also checks that the pump and heater are working correctly.

His most important job is to make sure that the correct amount of chlorine is being added to the water.

Chlorine is a poisonous gas, so how can we swim in it? Only a very small amount of chlorine is added to the water. This is enough to kill any algae and bacteria that are in the water. It is not enough to harm people, although it may cause sore eyes and runny noses for those who are very sensitive.

Chlorine is also added to our drinking water. An even smaller concentration is used than in swimming pools. This chlorine kills any bacteria in the water that would otherwise harm us.

In the days before water was treated in this way, many people got diseases such as cholera and dysentery from drinking water contaminated with sewage.

Questions

1 Why is chlorine added to the water in swimming pools?

2 Why does this chlorine not kill people swimming in the pools?

3 Why is chlorine added to drinking water?

4 Why are different amounts of chlorine added to the water in swimming pools and to drinking water?

Getting the metal

In this item you will find out

- what happens when electricity is passed through a molten salt or salt solution

- about the products that can be made by electrolysis of sulfuric acid

- how aluminium metal is extracted from its ore

Is your bicycle made of steel or aluminium? You can tell by trying to lift it with one hand. If it is light and easy to lift, it probably has a frame made of aluminium. If it is heavy it is probably made of steel.

Although very cheap bicycles are made of steel, those with aluminium alloy frames are not much more expensive. The main advantage of using aluminium is its low density. This makes the bicycle very light.

Another advantage of aluminium is that it has a coating of oxide that is very resistant to corrosion. If the paint on a steel bicycle is scratched, the steel underneath rusts. If the paint on an aluminium bicycle is scratched, the aluminium underneath does not corrode.

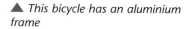 ▲ *This bicycle has an aluminium frame*

 Why is it an advantage for a bicycle to be light?

Aluminium is a good material to use because it can be made cheaply by **electrolysis**. Electricity is passed through the aluminium ore to produce the metal.

This manufacturing process uses a lot of electrical energy. It is carried out mostly in mountainous areas such as Canada and Scandinavia, where hydroelectric power is available.

 Why are mountainous areas good places to carry out the extraction of aluminium by electrolysis?

In 1886 the process used to make aluminium cheaply by electrolysis was invented. Before this, aluminium was so difficult to extract from its ore that it was very expensive.

Amazing fact

In the 1860s Napoleon III honoured guests at his court in France by using cutlery made from aluminium instead of gold.

What is electrolysis?

When an electric current is passed through an ionic compound dissolved in water, the compound is split up. This is the process of electrolysis. The solution that conducts the electricity is called an **electrolyte**.

To pass the electricity through, a positive **electrode** (**anode**) and a negative electrode (**cathode**) are placed in the electrolyte and connected to a supply of electricity.

Negative ions are attracted towards the anode and positive ions are attracted towards the cathode. Because of the electrodes they are attracted to, negative ions are called **anions** and positive ions are called **cations**.

c Which of these ions are cations and which are anions?

Na^+ Cl^- Cu^{2+} Al^{3+} O^{2-} SO_4^{2-} Ag^+

Electrolysis of dilute sulfuric acid

In the laboratory, electricity can be passed through an electrolyte that is a dilute solution of sulfuric acid, using a set of apparatus called a Hofmann voltameter.

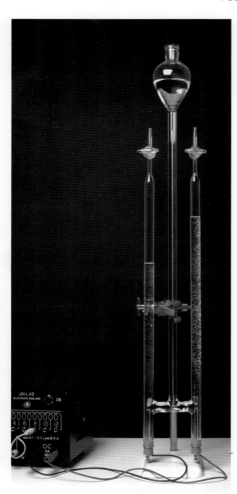

▲ A Hofmann voltameter

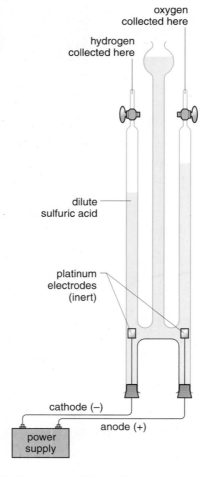

oxygen collected here

hydrogen collected here

dilute sulfuric acid

platinum electrodes (inert)

cathode (−)

anode (+)

power supply

▲ Electrolysing dilute sulfuric acid

Sulfuric acid solution contains three ions. Hydrogen ions, H^+, are positive, so they move to the cathode and are discharged as hydrogen gas. Hydroxide ions, OH^-, are negative, so they move to the anode and are discharged there, forming oxygen gas and water. The hydrogen and oxygen gases are released and collected separately in the apparatus.

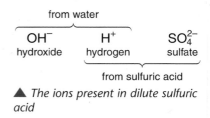

from water

OH^- hydroxide H^+ hydrogen SO_4^{2-} sulfate

from sulfuric acid

▲ The ions present in dilute sulfuric acid

You can find out which gas is which by collecting them in test tubes and carrying out these tests:

• if the gas burns with a squeaky pop when a lighted splint is brought to the mouth of the test tube, then the gas is hydrogen
• if a glowing splint relights when it is lowered into the test tube, then the gas is oxygen

Electricity is passed through the solution using platinum electrodes.

d Platinum is an expensive and very unreactive metal. So why is platinum a good metal to use for these electrodes?

Extraction of aluminium

Aluminium is found in the mineral bauxite. This contains mostly aluminium oxide, Al_2O_3. The bauxite is purified and the pure aluminium oxide is melted. The aluminium is then extracted from the molten aluminium oxide by electrolysis.

The anode and the cathode are both made of **graphite**, a fairly inexpensive form of carbon.

e Why do you think graphite is used for these electrodes instead of platinum?

Positive aluminium ions are attracted to the cathode, which is the graphite lining of the electrolytic cell. Molten aluminium is formed and collects at the bottom of the cell.

f Why does the molten aluminium collect at the bottom of the cell?

This is tapped off into moulds and allowed to cool to form solid ingots.

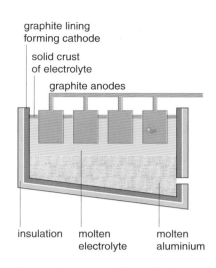

▲ *An electrolytic cell used in the manufacture of aluminium*

◄ *Solid ingots of aluminium*

Negative oxide ions are attracted to the anodes, where oxygen is given off.

This oxygen reacts with the graphite and gradually wears the anodes away.

g The graphite anodes are replaced frequently, but the graphite cathode does not need to be replaced very often. Explain this difference.

The overall reaction involved in the extraction is

aluminium oxide → aluminium + oxygen

The aluminium produced has many uses, such as for cooking foil.

Keywords

anion • anode • cathode • cation • electrode • electrolysis • electrolyte • graphite

Who got there first?

Two young scientists, Paul Héroult and Charles Hall, simultaneously invented a new electrolytic process, which is the basis for all aluminium production today. They worked separately thousands of miles apart, and were unaware of each other's work. Both inventors discovered that if they dissolved aluminium oxide (alumina) in a bath of molten cryolite and passed a powerful electric current through it, then molten aluminium would be deposited at the bottom of the bath.

Charles Hall lived in the USA. On 23 February 1886, in his family's woodshed, he produced globules of aluminium metal by the electrolysis of aluminium oxide dissolved in a cryolite–aluminium fluoride mixture.

Paul Héroult lived in France. While he was a student in Paris, he began working on the electrolysis of aluminium compounds. Paul used his father's tannery buildings for his experiments. His mother gave him her last 50 000 francs to buy a dynamo to generate the electric current he used in 1886 to produce aluminium.

The Héroult process is essentially identical to the one discovered by Hall in the same year.

For many years the two inventors battled in the courts to decide who had made the discovery first. Eventually an agreement was reached between them.

▲ Paul Héroult

▶ Charles Hall

Questions

1 Hall and Héroult were unaware of each other's discovery. Why was this not surprising in the year 1886?

2 Both Hall and Héroult were amateur inventors, working with simple apparatus in makeshift laboratories. Most modern scientific advances are made in large university or industrial laboratories. Suggest why.

3 Why do you think the two inventors spent years arguing over who made the invention first?

Metals in the middle

- which of the elements are transition metals

- some of the properties of transition metals

- some of the properties of transition metal compounds

What money have you got in your pocket or purse? You will probably have a selection of coins. But what are coins made from?

To do the job well, the material used to make a coin must be hard, durable and not corrode.

Modern coins are made from alloys containing several metals. These usually include nickel and copper. Both of these metals are **transition elements**. They have the right properties of hardness, and resistance to wear and corrosion, to last for many years of use.

Iron is also a transition element, but it is not used for coins because it rusts. A coin made of iron would corrode too quickly.

The transition elements are found together in a block in the middle of the Periodic Table.

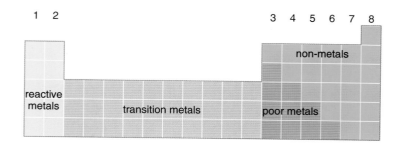

a Which of these metals are transition metals?

   aluminium   cobalt   platinum   potassium   silver   tin   zinc

b State the name and symbol of three more transition elements.

Amazing fact

Metal coins were not the first things to be used as money. The currency in China in the eighth century BC consisted of miniature farming tools.

Metal properties

Transition elements are all metals with typical metal properties, such as:

- shiny appearance
- conduction of electricity
- conduction of heat
- high melting point
- high density
- very hard.

Transition metal compounds

The compounds of transition elements can be coloured. The table shows the colours of some of them.

Transition metal ion	Colour of compounds	Example
copper(II)	blue	copper(II) sulfate
iron(II)	light green	iron(II) nitrate
iron(III)	orange/brown	iron(III) chloride

▶ Copper(II), iron(II) and iron(III) compounds all have different colours

c What colour would you expect the compound copper(II) chloride to be?

Many of the transition elements and their compounds are used as catalysts. A catalyst will speed up a chemical reaction without itself being changed at the end of the reaction. This is useful in many industrial processes. Iron is used as a catalyst in the Haber Process for the production of ammonia. Nickel is used as a catalyst in the manufacture of margarine.

d Why is it useful to speed up a reaction in an industrial process?

Breaking down compounds

Thermal decomposition is a reaction in which a substance is broken down into at least two other substances by heat. Transition metal carbonates decompose when heated. In this reaction, carbon dioxide gas is given off and a metal oxide is formed:

copper(II) carbonate → copper(II) oxide + carbon dioxide

manganese carbonate → manganese oxide + carbon dioxide

If you bubble the carbon dioxide gas given off through limewater, the limewater will turn milky. This is the test for carbon dioxide.

Similar reactions take place when iron(II) carbonate and zinc carbonate are heated. In each of these decomposition reactions there is a colour change as the reaction takes place.

e Write word equations for the thermal decomposition of iron(II) carbonate and zinc carbonate.

f How would you see that these reactions have taken place?

Identifying ions

Precipitation is a reaction that produces an insoluble solid when two solutions are mixed. When sodium hydroxide solution is added to a solution of a transition metal compound, a **precipitate** of the metal hydroxide is formed.

You can use the colour of this hydroxide precipitate to identify the transition metal.

Transition metal ion	Formula of transition metal ion	Colour of metal hydroxide precipitate
copper(II)	Cu^{2+}	blue
iron(II)	Fe^{2+}	grey/green
iron(III)	Fe^{3+}	orange

g When sodium hydroxide is added to the solution of a transition metal sulfate, a blue precipitate is formed. What is the name of this transition metal compound?

  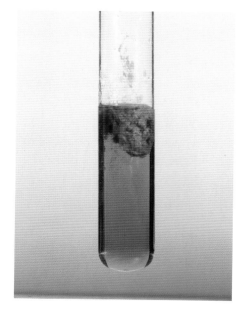

▲ These hydroxide precipitates have different colours

Metals that remember

In recent years some alloys of transition metals have been found to show a strange property, which is best described as 'remembering their shape'. A mixture of nickel and titanium, called Nitinol, is an example. After it has been bent, this metal will spring back into the shape it was before.

A popular use for these 'memory metals' is for the metal frames of glasses. An advantage is that glasses made with memory metal frames are much harder to break. You can sit on your glasses and when you get up the frames will spring back into shape.

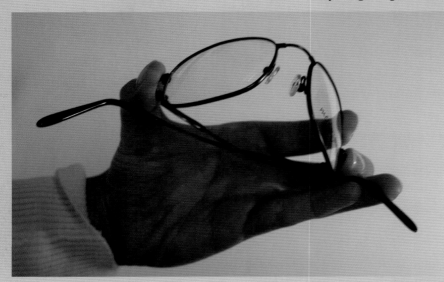

Now scientists may have found another use for memory metals: in the treatment of badly broken bones. When doctors reconstruct shattered legs and arms, they normally use stainless steel wire to hold the bones together. But the stainless steel does not always hold its shape, which means that the bones may move out of place and heal badly.

Researchers have found that Nitinol stays in position far better than stainless steel. They also think that Nitinol can help broken bones to heal faster. The trick is to cool the Nitinol, and then stretch it before wrapping it around the damaged bones. When the Nitinol heats up again it tries to return to its original shape, and while doing so it exerts a constant pressure, pushing the pieces of broken bone together.

Questions

1 Which transition metals are used to make the memory metal Nitinol?

2 Why is Nitinol a good metal to use for the frames of glasses?

3 At present doctors use stainless steel to hold broken bones together. Suggest why they do not use iron.

4 Why may Nitinol be better for this use than stainless steel?

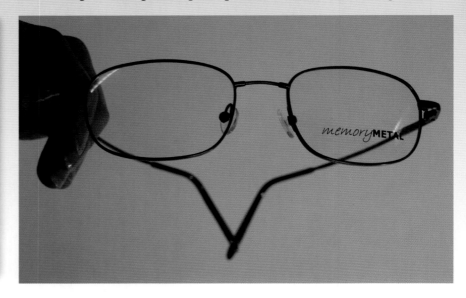

Hard and shiny

In this item you will find out

- about the properties of metals

- which metals are used for which job and why

- about superconductors

The bridge in the photograph on the right carries thousands of cars every day. It needs to be very strong and it is made of steel. Steel is made of iron mixed with a little carbon. Most modern road and rail bridges are made of steel, like the one in the photo.

Car bodies are also made of steel. Steel is easy to make into the shapes needed, and gives the car body the strength it needs.

One disadvantage of using steel is that it rusts when exposed to damp air.

 How are car bodies and steel bridges protected from rusting?

Copper is a very good conductor of electricity. It is also fairly inexpensive and resistant to corrosion. It is used to make the electrical cables and wires we use in our homes.

It is also used to make brass, which is an alloy of copper and zinc. Brass has an attractive 'gold-coloured' appearance and is resistant to corrosion. It is also hard, so it does not dent or wear away easily. Brass is used to make ornamental tools and other articles for use in our homes.

▲ Car parts being pressed into shape

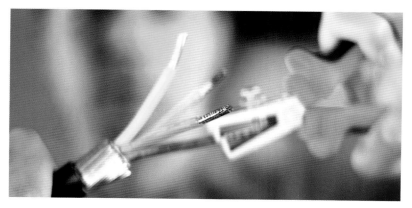

◀ This electrical cable contains copper wires

Useful metals

Most metals have a number of characteristic properties. They have:

- a shiny (**lustrous**) appearance
- a hard surface
- high density
- high **tensile strength** (they can be stretched without breaking)
- high melting and boiling points
- good heat and electrical conductivity.

Metals have many uses. For each use, a metal with the correct properties is chosen. The cables in a suspension bridge are made of steel. This has a very high tensile strength, so the cables do not stretch as cars cross the bridge.

Copper is a good metal for saucepans because it is a very good conductor of heat. Steel is stronger than copper, so many saucepans are made with a stainless steel body and a copper bottom.

b Why is it better to make a saucepan with a stainless steel body and a copper bottom, rather than a saucepan entirely from stainless steel?

Metal or non-metal	Melting point (°C)	Boiling point (°C)
aluminium	661	2467
iodine	114	185
phosphorus	44	280
iron	1535	2750
sulfur	113	445
tungsten	3407	5927

Metallic bonds

Metal particles are held together by very strong **metallic bonding**. Because the particles are hard to pull away from each other, most metals are hard and strong. This is also why most metals have a high tensile strength, which means they do not break easily when pulled.

Because the particles are held together so strongly by metallic bonding, most metals have a high melting point and boiling point.

Compare the melting points of metals and non-metals in this table.

The very high melting point of the metal tungsten means that it can be used for the filaments of electric light-bulbs. It glows white hot without melting.

Crystal structure

Metals are made of crystals. These can sometimes be seen on the surfaces of metal articles.

Metallic bonding in the metal holds the particles close together in a regular arrangement. This gives the crystals their shape.

Electrons are able to move easily through the arrangement of metal particles in the crystals, so metals are good conductors of electricity and heat.

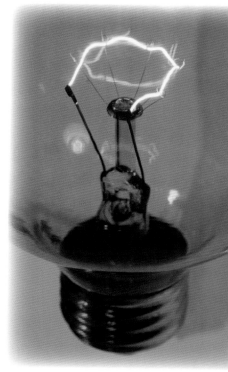

▲ The tungsten in the filament has a very high melting point

◀ If you were close enough, you would be able to see crystals on the surface of this galvanised post

Amazing fact

Some metals do not have high melting points. Caesium melts if a glass tube containing the metal is held in the hand. Mercury is a liquid at room temperature.

Superconductors

Because it is such a good conductor of electricity, copper is used for wiring. But even copper has some electrical resistance, and energy is lost in heating up the wire.

At very low temperatures some metals – including mercury, lead and tin – can be **superconductors**. These conduct electricity with little or no resistance. Superconducting metals allow electricity to move along them with no loss of energy. They can also be used to make super-fast electronic circuits and very powerful electromagnets.

d Why is it not likely that house wiring will be made of superconductors?

Keywords

lustrous • metallic bonding • superconductor • tensile strength

Choosing the right metal

It is important that the correct metal is chosen for a particular use. To make the correct choice we need to know two things:

- which properties are needed for this use of a metal
- which metal has these properties.

The table shows some properties of several commonly used metals.

◀ *Gold is a commonly used metal*

Metal	Melting point (°C)	Electrical conductivity	Density (g/cm³)	Hardness	Tensile strength	Cost
aluminium	661	good	2.70	medium	medium	low
copper	1083	very good	8.92	medium	medium	medium
gold	1065	very good	19.29	soft	low	very high
lead	328	good	11.34	soft	low	low
iron (steel)	1535	good	7.87	hard	very high	low
tungsten	3407	good	19.40	hard	high	high

Questions

1 In an electric light-bulb a metal is heated until it glows white hot. The metal is at a temperature of over 2000 °C. Explain why tungsten is chosen for this use.

2 Copper is a better conductor of electricity than aluminium, but aluminium is used for the overhead power cables that go from one electricity pylon to another. Suggest why aluminium is used.

3 A deep-sea diver carries weights to keep him on the seabed. Gold and tungsten have a very high density, but divers use weights made from lead. Why do you think lead is chosen?

4 To make electronic circuits, a metal is melted where a connection is needed. When the metal cools, it solidifies to form a joint that will conduct electricity. Which metal could be used for this job? Give reasons for your choice.

C3a

1 Copy and finish this table about the sub-atomic particles in atoms.

Sub-atomic particle	Position in atom	Charge on particle
electron	outside the nucleus	
neutron		none
	inside the nucleus	positive

[3]

2 Use a Periodic Table to answer the following questions.

a The atomic numbers of some elements are shown in the list. What is the name of each element?

11   20   9   55   6   18   16   [7]

b The names of some elements are shown in the list. What is the atomic number of each element?

chlorine   iodine   lithium
magnesium   nitrogen   sodium   tin   [7]

3 What are the names of the elements in the compounds with these formulae?

a FeS [1]   **c** NH_4NO_3 [1]
b H_2SO_4 [1]   **d** Na_2CO_3 [1]

4 Explain what is meant by the following terms:

a atomic (proton) number   [1]
b mass (nucleon) number   [1]
c isotope   [1]

5 How are elements arranged in the Periodic Table?   [2]

C3b

1 What is an ion?   [2]

2 Copy and complete this table to show which of the formulae are atoms, which are molecules and which are ions. The first one has been done for you.

Formula	Atom	Molecule	Ion
C	✓		
CO_2			
Ar			
Na^+			
NH_3			
O^{2-}			

[5]

3 Which statements show the properties of sodium chloride?

A made of crystals
B not made of crystals
C has a high melting point
D has a low melting point
E dissolves in water
F does not dissolve in water   [3]

4 Which statements are true about how sodium chloride conducts electricity?

A conducts electricity when solid
B does not conduct electricity when solid
C conducts electricity when molten
D does not conduct electricity when molten
E conducts electricity when in solution in water
F does not conduct electricity when in solution in water   [3]

5 Explain how metal and non-metal atoms combine. Use ideas about electrons, ions and attraction in your answer.   [3]

C3c

1 How many atoms are in each of the following formulae?

a SO_2 [1]   **b** HNO_3 [1]
c Na_2SO_4 [1]   **d** NH_4Cl [1]

2 How many different elements are in each of the following compounds?

a NH_3 [1]   **b** H_2SO_4 [1]
c K_2CO_3 [1]   **d** $(NH_4)_2SO_4$ [1]

3 Here are the symbols of some elements:

Ar   Be   Br   Ca   C   Cl   F   I   Li
Na   Ne

Choose from this list:

a four elements that are in the same Group of the Periodic Table   [4]
b four elements that are in the same Period of the Periodic Table   [4]

4 Non-metals combine together by sharing electrons. What is the name given to this type of bonding?   [1]

5 Copy and complete this table about Groups and Periods in the Periodic Table.

Symbol of element	Group number	Period number	Number of electrons in outer shell
Li		2	1
Cl	7	3	
Na	1		1
Ne		2	8
F	7		7
Ar	8	3	

[6]

C3d

1 What is the name given to the elements in Group 1 of the Periodic Table? [1]

2 Which of the elements in this list are in Group 1 of the Periodic Table?

Al Br C Ca K Li Mg
N Na O Rb [4]

3 Place the three metals lithium, potassium and sodium in order of reactivity, beginning with the least reactive. [2]

4 a Describe two things that you see when a small piece of potassium is dropped into a trough of water. [2]
b Write a word equation for this reaction. [2]
c Other elements in Group 1 react with water in a similar way. Use ideas about the electronic arrangement of these elements to explain why. [2]

5 A student carries out a flame test on a white powder. The flame has a lilac colour.

a Describe how this flame test is carried out. [3]
b Which Group 1 metal is present in the white powder? [1]

C3e

1 a What is the name given to the elements in Group 7 of the Periodic Table? [1]
b Which of the elements in this list are in Group 7?

Ar Br Ca Cl F He I O S [3]

2 Describe three uses for the element chlorine. [3]

3 Place the four elements bromine, chlorine, fluorine and iodine in order of reactivity, beginning with the least reactive. [3]

4 Potassium reacts violently when in contact with fluorine.

a Name the compound formed in this reaction. [1]
b Write a word equation for this reaction. [2]

5 The table shows the results of some experiments where a halogen was added to the solution of a halide. Copy and complete the table by filling in the empty boxes.

Halogen	Halide solution	Result	Halogen displaced
chlorine	potassium bromide	red solution	bromine
chlorine	potassium iodide	brown solution	iodine
bromine	potassium chloride	none	none
bromine	potassium iodide		
iodine	potassium chloride		
iodine	potassium bromide		

[6]

6 Read this paragraph about salt, sodium chloride.

Nutritionists and doctors recommend that daily salt intake should not exceed 6 g. This is about a teaspoonful. Three-quarters of the salt we eat is already in everyday foods – the main sources are bread, breakfast cereals, biscuits, ready meals, and meat products such as bacon, sausages and ham. In many foods it is used as a preservative, to prevent bacteria from rotting the food, which could cause food poisoning. It can be easy to eat too much salt without adding any yourself. And not all high-salt foods taste salty, because some also have a lot of sugar. Eating too much salt can cause high blood pressure, leading to heart disease and strokes.

a Why is it an advantage for salt to be added to some foods? [2]
b What problems can be caused by eating too much salt? [2]
c Why is it easy to eat more than 6 g of salt a day without realising it? [2]
d Most people do not worry about the amount of salt in their diet. Suggest why. [1]

7 The element bromine is a liquid that easily turns into a gas if exposed to the air. It is very poisonous and corrosive. Bromine is extracted from sea water. A major factory producing bromine is situated on the coast of the island of Anglesey.

a Suggest two reasons why it is a good idea to make bromine in a factory near to the coast. [2]
b What precautions should be taken to ensure the safety of workers in the factory and people living nearby? [2]

C3f

1 Two carbon rods are placed in dilute sulfuric acid. One rod is connected to the positive terminal of a 12 V battery. The other carbon rod is connected to the negative terminal.

a What is the electrolyte in this experiment? [1]
b The carbon rods are called electrodes. The negative electrode is called the cathode. What name is given to the positive electrode? [1]
c Which ions in the solution are attracted to the cathode? [2]

2 During the electrolysis of dilute sulfuric acid, hydrogen and oxygen are given off.

a How can you test a gas to prove that it is hydrogen? [2]
b How can you test a gas to prove that it is oxygen? [2]

3 Aluminium metal is extracted from a mineral ore.

  a What is the name of this mineral? [1]

  b Aluminium is extracted from this mineral by electrolysis. What is meant by the term electrolysis? [2]

4 During the electrolysis of dilute sulfuric acid a gas is given off at each electrode.

  a Which gas is given off at the cathode? [1]

  b Which gas is given off at the anode? [1]

5 Aluminium is extracted by the electrolysis of aluminium oxide.

  a What gas is formed at the anodes? [1]

  b The anodes are made of carbon (graphite). Why do they need frequent replacement? [2]

  c Write a word equation for the decomposition of aluminium oxide that takes place in this electrolysis. [2]

C3g

1 **a** Which of these are transition elements?

    Ag Cl Ca Cu Fe Li Mg Zn [4]

  b Which properties are typical of a transition element?
   A they conduct electricity when solid
   B they are liquids or gases at room temperature
   C they have high density and high melting point
   D they are soft and have a dull appearance
   E they are very hard and have a shiny appearance
   F they have coloured compounds [4]

2 When calcium carbonate is heated it breaks down to give calcium oxide and carbon dioxide.

  a Write a word equation for this reaction. [1]

  b What name is given to the type of reaction where a compound breaks down when heated? Choose your answer from this list:

   destruction   decomposition
   electrolysis   synthesis [1]

  c How can you prove that carbon dioxide is given off during this reaction? [2]

3 When sodium hydroxide solution is added to copper sulfate solution, solid copper hydroxide appears.

  a What name is given to the type of reaction where a solid compound is formed by the mixing of two or more solutions together? Choose your answer from this list:

   decomposition   electrolysis
   precipitation   redox [1]

  b Write a word equation for this reaction. [2]

4 Transition metals are often used as catalysts. Describe how one transition metal is used in this way. [2]

5 The table shows the colours of the precipitates made when sodium hydroxide is added to some transition metal ions in solution.

Transition metal ion	Formula of transition metal ion	Colour of metal hydroxide precipitate
copper	Cu^{2+}	blue
iron(II)	Fe^{2+}	grey/green
iron(III)	Fe^{3+}	orange/brown

Sodium hydroxide solution is added to solution X containing a transition metal sulfate. A green precipitate is formed.

  a Name the transition metal compound in solution X. [1]

  b Write a word equation for the reaction between the transition metal compound and sodium hydroxide. [2]

C3h

1 Which properties are typical of metals?

  A they are brightly coloured
  B they have a shiny appearance
  C they have low tensile strength
  D they have high melting and boiling points
  E they are poor conductors of heat
  F they are good conductors of electricity [3]

2 Metals have many uses.

  a State and explain one use for iron. [2]

  b Copper is used for making electrical wiring. Why is it a good choice for this use? [1]

  c Some metals can be used as superconductors. What conditions are needed for this use? Choose from this list:

   low temperature   room temperature
   high temperature [1]

3 Metals are made of crystals. Describe how metal particles are arranged in these crystals. [2]

4 Most metals have high melting and boiling points. Use ideas about the bonding in metals to explain these facts. [2]

5 Superconductors are better conductors of electricity than other metals.

  a How does a metal conduct electricity? [1]

  b Why do superconductors conduct electricity so well? [1]

  c State two uses of superconductors. [2]

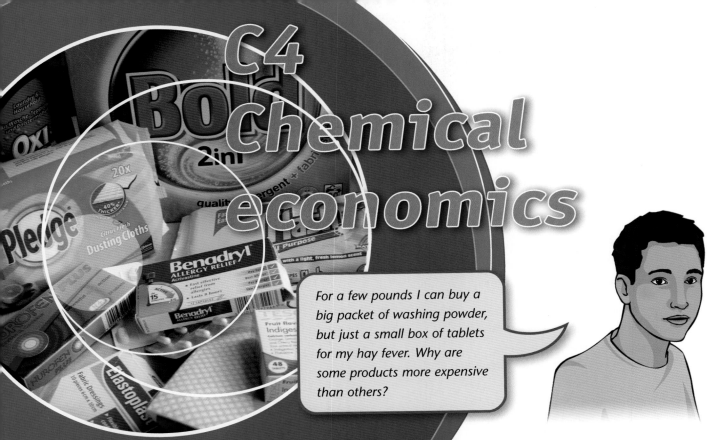

C4 Chemical economics

For a few pounds I can buy a big packet of washing powder, but just a small box of tablets for my hay fever. Why are some products more expensive than others?

- Take a look around next time you go into a supermarket. There are thousands of different products for you to buy. Have you ever thought how these products are made? Why are some things cheap to buy and others expensive?

- Most of the things we buy are made using substances produced by the chemical industry. A lot of the food we eat is grown with the help of synthetic fertilisers. Some chemicals are used in very large quantities and have to be produced cheaply, e.g. washing powder.

- New products are being invented by scientists almost every day. Some of these may have a dramatic effect on our lives in the future, making the world a better and more enjoyable place to live in.

It depends on how much it costs to make them. Different chemicals are made by different methods, so some cost more to make than others.

And it also depends on the quantity of each chemical that is made. Far fewer hay fever tablets are made than washing powder. This makes the medicine more expensive.

What you need to know

- Reactants are turned into products in a chemical reaction.

- A solute dissolves in a solvent to make a solution.

- What the terms acid, alkali and neutral mean.

Salt and acid please

In this item you will find out

- about the pH scale and Universal Indicator

- about neutralisation reactions between acids and bases

Do you like acid on your fish and chips?

If you put vinegar on your fish and chips, then you do! Vinegar is a solution of ethanoic acid, also called acetic acid. You can put a dilute solution of ethanoic acid on your food without harming yourself, because it is a weak acid.

Boric acid is so weak that it is used in eye drops. It does not harm the eyes, but does prevent infection by bacteria. Citrus fruits like oranges, lemons and limes also contain a weak acid.

a Look at the fruits that contain acid in the photograph below. How would you describe the taste of an acid?

But not all acids are weak. Sulfuric acid is a strong acid. Because sulfuric acid is very corrosive, it is used to clean metal surfaces before they are coated with other metals. This removes grease and dirt so that the metal coating will stick well. Sulfuric acid is also used in car batteries and to make fertiliser.

b Why is it safe to eat citric acid but not safe to eat sulfuric acid?

Amazing fact

When an ant bites it injects an acid, called methanoic acid, into your skin. This is why an ant bite is painful.

◀ *Citric acid is present in these fruits*

▶ *Metals can be cleaned with sulfuric acid*

The pH scale

We can measure how acidic a solution is by using Universal Indicator. When this indicator is added to a solution it changes colour to show the level of acidity. The diagram below shows the **pH scale** and the colours of Universal Indicator.

colour of Universal Indicator		red			orange	yellow	green	blue	blue-purple			purple		
pH	1	2	3	4	5	6	7	8	9	10	11	12	13	14
		strong acids			weak acids		neutral	weak alkalis			strong alkalis			

Acidity is measured on the pH scale. Below pH 7 is acidic. Above pH 7 is alkaline, which is the opposite of acidic. At pH 7 the solution is neutral – not acidic and not alkaline.

 How would you describe a solution at pH 5?

Neutralisation

A **base** is a substance that neutralises an acid. Bases are solids. Some are insoluble in water, but others dissolve to form an alkaline solution. A base that dissolves in water is called an alkali.

When an alkali or a base is added a little at a time to an acidic solution, the pH of the solution gradually changes from below 7 (acidic), to 7 (neutral) and then to above 7 (alkaline). Adding an alkali or a base increases the pH. Adding more acid decreases the pH.

The reaction between an acid and an alkali or a base is called **neutralisation**, and always makes a salt and water:

acid + base → salt + water

For example:

sulfuric acid + sodium hydroxide → sodium sulfate + water

An acid has a pH below 7. An alkali has a pH above 7. As an alkali is added a little at a time to neutralise an acid, the pH rises until it reaches 7. If an acid is added slowly to neutralise an alkali, the pH gradually falls until it reaches 7.

Making salts

The name of the salt formed during a neutralisation reaction comes from the name of the metal in the base and the name of the acid.

Name of acid	Name of salt
sulfuric acid	sulfate
hydrochloric acid	chloride
nitric acid	nitrate

Metal oxides and metal hydroxides are bases. They will neutralise acids.

 d **What is the name of the salt formed by neutralisation of nitric acid with sodium hydroxide?**

Acids can also be neutralised by carbonates. In this reaction, as well as a salt and water, carbon dioxide gas is made. For example:

hydrochloric acid + calcium carbonate → calcium chloride + carbon dioxide + water

◀ *Calcium carbonate and hydrochloric acid reacting together*

e **What is the name of the salt formed by neutralisation of sulfuric acid with sodium carbonate?**

Hydrochloric acid is made in the stomach. Sometimes too much is made, causing acid indigestion. Chewing an indigestion remedy cures the painful symptoms. Most indigestion remedies contain magnesium carbonate or calcium carbonate to neutralise the acid in the stomach.

Examiner's tip

When you are trying to work out the name of a salt formed by neutralisation, remember to take the name of the metal from what the acid is reacting with and put this with the name of the type of salt always formed by this acid.

Amazing fact

Acids in soft drinks such as cola react with carbonates in teeth. Drinking too much cola can cause serious damage to your teeth.

Keywords

base • neutralisation
• pH scale

Ted's poor plants

Ted is a farmer. He notices that in one of his fields the plants do not grow very well. He thinks that the soil in this field may not have the correct pH for the plants he is trying to grow. Many plants will not grow well if the soil is too acidic or too alkaline.

Before sowing the same type of plants in this field again, Ted takes a sample of the soil from this field.

Then Ted:

- adds distilled water to the sample and shakes to mix it
- waits for the mixture to settle, then pours the clear liquid into another test tube
- adds a few drops of Universal Indicator
- compares the colour with a pH chart for the indicator.

The colour of the indicator in the photograph on the left shows that the liquid is pH 5. To improve the soil in this field, Ted adds lime. Lime is calcium hydroxide.

A few weeks after he has spread lime onto the field, Ted tests the soil again.

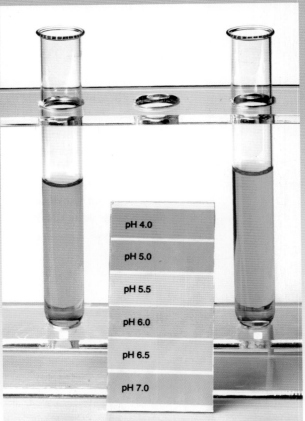

pH 4.0
pH 5.0
pH 5.5
pH 6.0
pH 6.5
pH 7.0

Questions

1 Suggest why the plants were not growing well in this field.

2 Why did Ted leave the soil and distilled water to settle, and pour off the clear liquid before testing with Universal Indicator?

3 How will spreading lime onto this field improve the growth of the plants Ted wants to grow there?

4 Why did Ted test the soil again a few weeks after spreading the lime?

Disappearing act

In this item you will find out

- how to work out relative formula mass

- how to work out reacting masses and product masses for a reaction

- how to work out percentage yield

A good magician always makes something disappear during the act. Of course, this thing does not really disappear. It is an illusion.

When chemicals react they sometimes seem to disappear, but this is also an illusion. During the reaction one or more new substances are formed.

Candle wax is a hydrocarbon – a compound containing hydrogen and carbon atoms only. As a candle burns it gets smaller. The candle wax 'disappears'.

 How can you tell that wax 'disappears' as the candle burns?

Look at the diagram on the right. A cold piece of glass is held just above the candle flame. After a few seconds water drops appear on the glass. This water is a product of the combustion of candle wax.

As the hydrocarbon burns, the hydrogen reacts with oxygen in the air to make water. In the hot flame this water is formed as a vapour. This goes into the air.

Carbon in the hydrocarbon also reacts with oxygen, forming carbon dioxide. This is a gas, and also goes into the air.

So the two products from the combustion of candle wax have both gone into the air. The candle wax seems to have disappeared, but really it hasn't.

The candle has lost the same mass that has been gained by the air. In a chemical reaction the mass of products is always the same as the mass of reactants.

▲ Candle and plate experiment

Comparing masses

Look at a Periodic Table. There are two numbers shown for each element: the atomic number (proton number) and the **relative atomic mass** (RAM).

RAMs are a way of comparing the masses of one atom of each element. An atom of magnesium has a RAM of 24, an atom of carbon has a RAM of 12 and an atom of hydrogen has a RAM of 1. This means that an atom of magnesium has the same mass as two atoms of carbon, or 24 atoms of hydrogen.

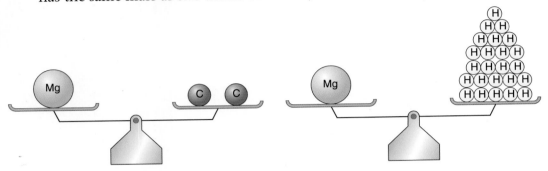

▲ Comparing the masses of atoms

b How many atoms of carbon have the same mass as one atom of titanium, Ti?

The formula of a compound tells us which atoms are joined together, and how many there are of each. For example, magnesium oxide, MgO, has one atom of magnesium and one atom of oxygen in a formula.

We can use RAMs to work out the **relative formula mass** of a compound:

Mg = 24   O = 16   MgO = 24 + 16 = 40

The relative formula mass of magnesium oxide is 40.

Sometimes a formula includes symbols in brackets. When the RAMs of the symbols in brackets have been added together, they are multiplied by the number following the brackets.

For example, for calcium hydroxide, $Ca(OH)_2$:

Ca = 40   O = 16   H = 1 $Ca(OH)_2$ = 40 + [2 × (16 + 1)] = 40 + 34 = 74

The relative formula mass of calcium hydroxide is 74.

c Work out the relative formula mass for each of the following compounds:

CaO CO_2 Na_2O $MgCl_2$ $CaSO_4$ $Mg(OH)_2$

Mass of reactants and products

During a chemical reaction, reactants are changed into products:

reactants → products

$2Mg + O_2$ → $2MgO$

> **Examiner's tip**
>
> When working out the relative formula mass of a compound that has brackets in the formula, don't forget to add the relative atomic masses of the atoms in the brackets and then multiply this by the number outside the brackets.

The total mass of the reactants at the start of a reaction is exactly the same as the total mass of the products at the end.

The greater the mass of reactants used, the greater the mass of products made. When 48 g of magnesium react with 32 g of oxygen, 80 g of magnesium oxide is made. When 24 g of magnesium react with 16 g of oxygen, 40 g of magnesium oxide is made.

 d What mass of magnesium oxide is made when 12 g of magnesium react with 8 g of oxygen?

Yield

Yield describes how much product has been collected. We can use relative formula masses to work out the maximum mass of product that can be made from the masses of the reactants used. This is called the **predicted yield**.

If we collect the product and weigh it, the mass we have is called the **actual yield**.

During the experiment some of the product is usually lost, so the actual yield is less than the predicted yield.

The product can be lost in a number of ways. This is why the yield of a product in an actual experiment is usually less than 100%. It can be lost by:

• sticking to the filter paper during filtration
• evaporation into the air
• being spilled when liquids are transferred from one container to another
• disappearing into the air during heating.

We can compare predicted yield and actual yield by working out the percentage yield:

$$\text{percentage yield} = \frac{\text{actual yield}}{\text{predicted yield}} \times 100$$

For example, when 24 g of magnesium are reacted with 16 g of oxygen, the predicted yield of magnesium oxide is 40 g. In an actual experiment using these masses of reactants, the mass of magnesium oxide made was 30 g. So:

$$\text{percentage yield} = \frac{30}{40} \times 100 = 75\%$$

 e In another experiment using the same masses of magnesium and oxygen, the mass of magnesium oxide collected was 32 g. What was the percentage yield?

The calculation of reacting masses, predicted yield and actual yield is very important in the chemical industry. When a chemical reaction is used to make a product, the correct quantities of each of the reactants must be used to make the required quantity of product. This ensures that expensive raw materials are not wasted. It is also important to make sure that the product does not contain unreacted raw materials, which could make the product dangerous to use. Finally the chemical company needs to know how much product they make from the amount of raw materials they use.

Keywords

actual yield • predicted yield
• relative atomic mass •
relative formula mass • yield

Working out yield

Magnesium sulfate, also called Epsom salts, is sometimes used as a medicine. Sandy decides to make some magnesium sulfate.

She uses this reaction:

magnesium hydroxide + sulfuric acid → magnesium sulfate + water

Sandy follows these instructions to make her Epsom salts:

- measure the correct quantities of magnesium hydroxide and dilute sulfuric acid in separate small beakers
- add the two chemicals together in a large beaker and stir
- pour the mixture into an evaporating basin and evaporate to a smaller volume
- leave the mixture to cool
- filter off the crystals
- leave the crystals to dry.

Sandy works out that the predicted yield for her Epsom salts is 85 g. She weighs the magnesium sulfate crystals she has made. They have a mass of 68 g.

Questions

1 Why did Sandy not get the 85 g of magnesium sulfate she expected?

2 Suggest how some of the magnesium sulfate was 'lost'.

3 Work out the actual yield of magnesium sulfate that Sandy made.

4 Sandy repeats the process to make more Epsom salts. How can she make more than 68 g this time?

Food for plants

In this item you will find out

- how minerals are needed by plants for their growth

- how fertilisers can be made by neutralisation reactions

In some countries food is grown by a 'slash and burn' method of agriculture. Areas of forest are cut down and the trees burned.

Plants need a number of chemical elements to grow well. These **essential elements** are contained in compounds called **minerals**.

Plants get these minerals from the soil when they take in water through their roots. Minerals are dissolved in this water.

The ash from the burned trees puts the minerals needed for plant growth into the soil.

The land is ploughed and crops planted. A good crop is grown for the first year. But each year the crop grown is poorer, because minerals needed by the plants are being removed from the soil.

After a few years the area is abandoned. Another part of the forest is cut down so that crops can be grown there. This process is repeated every few years. Huge areas of forest are devastated by this method of agriculture each year.

a   **Why can the ground be used to grow crops for only a few years?**

The problem can be solved by using **fertilisers**. A fertiliser is a chemical that contains the essential elements needed by plants.

b   **Why do you think some farmers use 'slash and burn' techniques to grow crops instead of using synthetic fertilisers?**

> **Amazing fact**
>
> If the current rate of deforestation continues, all of the world's rainforests will vanish within 100 years.

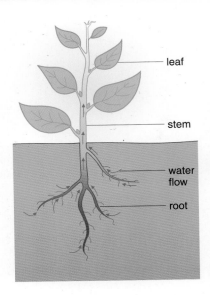

leaf

stem

water flow

root

Fertilisers at work

The three essential elements that are needed for plant growth are nitrogen, phosphorus and potassium. The minerals in fertilisers must be in compounds that are soluble in water. Plants can then take in the solution through their roots. The diagram on the left shows how plants do this. Using a fertiliser makes plants grow bigger and faster. This gives more yield from the crop.

c   **Why would an insoluble compound be useless as a fertiliser?**

One example of a fertiliser is the compound ammonium nitrate, NH_4NO_3. It is a good fertiliser because it contains nitrogen – essential for plant growth – and is very soluble in water.

The relative formula mass of ammonium nitrate can be worked out from the RAMs of the elements:

RAMs: N = 14   H = 1   O = 16

relative formula mass of NH_4NO_3 = $(2 \times 14) + (4 \times 1) + (3 \times 16) = 80$

Of this relative formula mass of 80, 28 is nitrogen. Ammonium nitrate contains a high proportion of nitrogen. A little of this fertiliser gives plants a lot of the essential element.

Making a fertiliser

A compound for use as a fertiliser can be made by a neutralisation reaction. An acid and an alkali react together to make a salt. For example:

ammonia + nitric acid → ammonium nitrate

The correct quantities of an acid and an alkali must be mixed to get a neutral solution of the salt formed. To do this, accurate measurements have to be made.

Examiner's tip

Lime (calcium hydroxide) is often spread on fields to neutralise acidity, but it is not a fertiliser. Ammonium nitrate is a fertiliser because it supplies nitrogen for plant growth.

▶ *A burette is used to make accurate measurements*

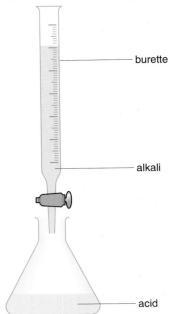

burette

alkali

acid

d Why would mixing together more acid than alkali cause a problem?

In the laboratory a burette may be used to accurately measure volumes of acid and alkali. This apparatus is shown in the photograph and the diagram on the previous page.

The acid and alkali are then mixed together. The salt solution is evaporated to a smaller volume, then left to cool.

Crystals of the salt are formed. These crystals are separated from the remaining solution by filtration. This is shown in the photograph on the right.

▶ Filtration separates crystals from the rest of the solution

Different fertilisers

By using different acids and alkalis, different fertiliser compounds can be made.

Acid	Alkali	Fertiliser
nitric acid	ammonia	ammonium nitrate, NH_4NO_3
sulfuric acid	ammonia	ammonium sulfate, $(NH_4)_2SO_4$
phosphoric acid	ammonia	ammonium phosphate, $(NH_3)_4PO_4$
nitric acid	potassium hydroxide	potassium nitrate, KNO_3

These salts can then be mixed to make a fertiliser that will provide plants with nitrogen, phosphorus and potassium.

e Which of the fertilisers shown in the table contains both nitrogen and phosphorus?

f Which of the fertilisers shown in the table contains both nitrogen and potassium?

Another fertiliser manufactured from ammonia is urea, $CO(NH_2)_2$. This compound is also present in animal and human urine.

Amazing fact

In the seventeenth century, people collected human urine in barrels. It was used as a source of ammonia. Today, human urine is still used as a fertiliser in some countries.

Keywords

essential element • fertiliser • mineral

Mandy's dad's tomatoes

Mandy and her parents are shopping at a garden centre.

Mandy's dad buys some outdoor tomato plants to grow in his garden. Mandy's mum says he should buy some fertiliser to put on the soil. She says this will grow big plants with lots of tomatoes.

They look at a display of fertiliser bags.

Questions

1 Why should Mandy's dad use a fertiliser for his tomato plants?

2 Why is 'general garden fertiliser' not good for tomato plants?

3 Why do you think the garden centre sells lots of different types of fertiliser?

4 Suggest why it is a good idea to test the pH of the soil in Mandy's garden?

Mandy's dad is confused by the many types of fertiliser for sale. He picks up a bag labelled 'general garden fertiliser'. Mandy asks one of the garden centre staff for some help. She explains that they want to buy fertiliser for tomato plants. The assistant replies that they should use a fertiliser with a high potassium content. This will give good tomatoes. He says that the 'general garden fertiliser' contains too much nitrogen. This is all right for many plants, but not for tomatoes. It will make the plants grow bigger leaves, but fewer tomatoes.

The assistant sells them a bag of fertiliser with exactly the right mix of ingredients for tomato plants. He also suggests that they buy a soil testing kit, so that they can find out the pH of the soil where they are going to grow the tomatoes.

Reversible reactions

In this item you will find out

- some of the uses of ammonia

- how ammonia is made using the Haber Process

- about the cost of producing new substances

▲ *Wheat needs a lot of fertiliser*

Ammonia is a poisonous gas with a choking smell. It is very soluble in water, forming an alkaline solution. But ammonia is very important in lots of ways. As you saw in the previous item, ammonia is used to make artificial fertilisers.

In a lot of countries, the use of artificial fertilisers means that more than enough food can be produced for all of the population. As populations increase we need to use more and more fertilisers.

Ammonia in solution is also contained in many household cleaning products. These products are very good at removing greasy stains and finger marks from kitchen work-surfaces and window glass.

 Suggest why ammonia has to be dissolved in water before it can be used to clean things.

Ammonia is used to make nitric acid, which has many uses. Most of the nitric acid made from ammonia is reacted with more ammonia to make fertilisers. Another major use of nitric acid is in the manufacture of explosives.

Amazing fact

China now uses more artificial fertiliser than any other country: over 40 million tons in 2004.

▼ *Many household cleaning products contain ammonia in solution*

The Haber Process

In the early part of the twentieth century, Fritz Haber, a German chemist, discovered a way to make ammonia on an industrial scale. This method is called the **Haber Process**.

In the Haber Process, ammonia is made from nitrogen and hydrogen. We get nitrogen gas from the air, and hydrogen from natural gas or the cracking of fractions from the distillation of crude oil.

 The air contains about 78% nitrogen and air is free. But the nitrogen obtained from this air for the Haber Process is expensive. Suggest why it costs so much to get the nitrogen.

Nitrogen and hydrogen are reacted together under carefully controlled conditions:

- a temperature of about 450°C
- a high pressure
- with an iron catalyst.

Using these conditions, about 15% of the nitrogen and hydrogen are converted into ammonia as they pass through the reaction vessel. The unreacted nitrogen and hydrogen are then recycled to make more ammonia. The diagram below shows the Haber Process.

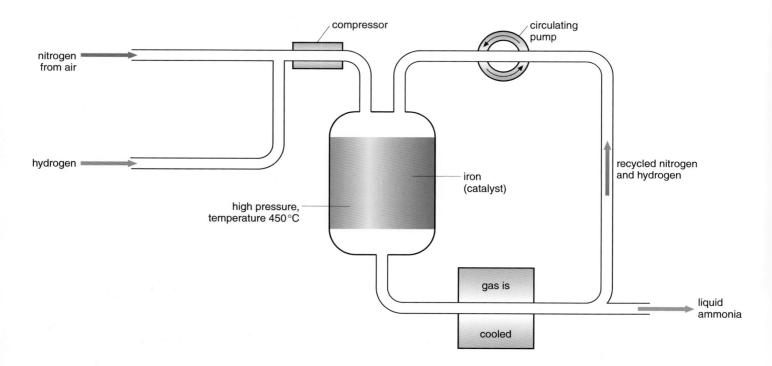

The word equation for the production of ammonia is:

nitrogen + hydrogen ⇌ ammonia

The ⇌ sign in this equation shows that this is a **reversible reaction**. It can go in either direction. For this reason, not all of the nitrogen and hydrogen form ammonia.

Counting the cost

There are a number of factors involved in the cost of making a new substance. The total cost depends on:

- the cost of equipment to make the substance
- labour costs – the wages of the workers
- the cost of the starting materials
- the cost of energy, such as gas or electricity
- the cost of any catalysts needed.

In the Haber Process, unreacted nitrogen and hydrogen are recycled into the reaction vessel. This reduces the cost of these expensive raw materials.

A high temperature is used to speed up the reaction. The higher the temperature, the higher the energy cost, and fuels such as gas and oil are expensive. But a faster reaction makes more ammonia in the same time, and so reduces the cost.

Gases in the reaction vessel are at a high pressure. This requires thick walls, making the manufacturing plant more expensive to construct. But at a high pressure more nitrogen and hydrogen react to form ammonia.

An iron catalyst is used in the process. This speeds up the reaction. Although the catalyst costs money, making more ammonia in the same time reduces the cost.

Automated control (**automation**) of the conditions used in the process – for example the flow of materials into the reaction vessel – can be carried out using computers. This reduces the number of people involved and so reduces the wages bill.

A balance must be found between the many factors that affect how much ammonia is made and how quickly it is made. These factors are controlled so that the most economic combination is used. This makes ammonia as cheaply as possible.

▲ A chemical factory

c How does recycling unreacted nitrogen and hydrogen reduce the cost of the ammonia?

d Making the reaction vessel withstand high pressures is costly. Why is it worth spending money to do this?

e Energy is very expensive. Running the process at a lower temperature would be less costly. Why is this not done?

Keywords

automation • Haber Process
• reversible reaction

▲ *A factory producing ammonia*

Controlling the process

Eddie works at a plant using the Haber Process to make ammonia. He works in the control room, where the conditions used in the process are monitored and controlled.

Eddie can change the temperature and pressure used. He studies some graphs showing how the yield of ammonia is affected by the temperature and pressure.

Eddie sets the temperature of the process to 450°C and the pressure to 200 atmospheres.

He tells his colleague Joe that this is the best compromise of conditions for the process. He says that:

- it will give a good yield of ammonia
- ammonia will be produced at a reasonably quick rate
- energy costs will not be too high
- the company will be able to sell the ammonia at a fairly cheap price.

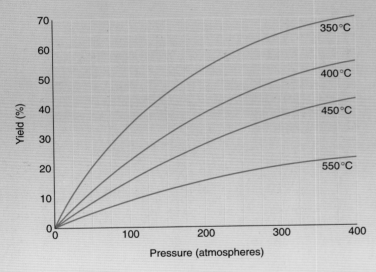

▲ *This graph shows the different yields of ammonia under different conditions*

Questions

1 What does the graph show about the effect of temperature on the yield of ammonia?

2 The higher the temperature, the faster the ammonia is formed. Suggest why Eddie does not set the temperature to 550°C.

3 What is the effect of pressure on the yield of ammonia?

4 Why does Eddie not use a pressure higher than 200 atmospheres?

5 Eddie talks about a 'best compromise of conditions'. What do you think this means?

Whiter than white

In this item you will find out

- what goes into washing powders and washing-up liquids

- how these products clean

- how dry-cleaning works

Have you ever wondered what is in a packet of washing powder? Or looked at the ingredients label and wondered what all of the things in the powder do?

Washing powders contain a number of different chemicals, each with its own job to do. The most important is the active **detergent**. This is the chemical that does the cleaning. The detergent loosens dirt from clothes. It then keeps the dirt suspended in the water so that it doesn't go back onto the clothes.

Many detergents are salts, made by the neutralisation of an acid with an alkali. Most washing powders have a synthetic detergent, made from chemicals in crude oil.

Some washing powders contain soap, made by reacting an alkali with oils or fats. Soap is less damaging to delicate fabrics than synthetic detergents.

Clothes often have labels telling you what temperature and washing powder you should use to wash them. Washing machines usually have a 'low-temperature wash' setting. This means that less energy is used to heat up the water.

Washing delicate fabrics at a low temperature is less likely to damage them. At high temperatures the dyes in some clothing may 'run' as they dissolve into the water, and the clothing may also shrink!

a Tracy buys a very expensive jumper made from wool. The label says that it should be hand-washed in soap. Suggest why.

More about washing powder

As well as detergents, washing powders contain a number of other ingredients. In many places the tap water is 'hard', because it contains dissolved calcium and magnesium salts. Hard water forms a scum with soap. Washing powders contain chemicals, called **water softeners**, which soften the water. This stops clothes being covered with scum. It also means that you can use less detergent to get the clothes clean.

Some coloured stains are difficult to remove from clothes. **Bleach** takes the colour out of these stains so that they cannot be seen.

Optical brighteners are chemicals that give white clothes a very bright 'whiter than white' appearance. Optical brighteners reflect the light from the clothes to our eyes.

Enzymes are biological catalysts. Those used in washing powder speed up the removal of food stains. They will only work in a low-temperature wash, for example at 40°C. Enzymes are destroyed at high temperatures.

 b Why should you not use detergents containing enzymes in a wash at 60°C?

Washing-up liquid

Who does the washing up in your house? We use a different product to wash dishes than we do to wash clothes – why? Washing-up liquid contains some ingredients that are similar to those in washing powders, such as detergents and water softeners. They also contain other chemicals that are designed to do different jobs.

To make the product look attractive, a colouring agent is added. Washing-up liquids are often bright, eye-catching colours. This makes people see them on a supermarket shelf. A perfume is added to give a nice smell as the dishes are washed.

Washing-up liquids also contain a chemical called a rinse agent. This helps the water run off the dishes easily, so that they dry quickly. All of these ingredients are dissolved in water. A liquid product can quickly spread in the washing-up water. Solids would take time to dissolve.

 c It is now possible to buy liquid products to use in your washing machine instead of washing powders. What advantage may these liquid products have?

◀ A rinse agent helps water run off, so dishes dry quickly

Washing symbols

Clothing manufacturers usually give details of how garments should be washed. The diagram below shows some of the washing symbols used on clothing labels.

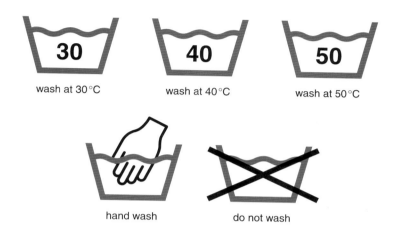

wash at 30°C   wash at 40°C   wash at 50°C

hand wash   do not wash

d Susan has a sweater with a washing symbol that has 40 on it. What washing conditions do you think the sweater needs?

Dry-cleaning

Some clothes have a label that says 'Dry-clean only'. If you wash these clothes in a washing machine they will be damaged. Often they shrink, even if washed at a low temperature.

These clothes must be taken to a dry-cleaning company. Workers at the dry-cleaning company do not wash the clothes in water. They use an organic **solvent**. A solvent is a liquid that dissolves a solid. The solid that dissolves is called a **solute**.

When a solute dissolves in a solvent, the solute seems to disappear, but it is still there. A mixture called a **solution** is formed. Different solvents will dissolve different substances.

Although dry-cleaners do not use water, it is the most widely used solvent. Dry-cleaners use organic solvents to remove stains that are **insoluble** in water, but are **soluble** in organic solvents.

e The solvents used in dry-cleaning are volatile (evaporate easily) and toxic. Suggest what precautions should be taken by the workers at a dry-cleaning company.

> **Keywords**
>
> bleach • detergent • enzyme • insoluble • optical brightener • soluble • solute • solution • solvent • water softener

▼ *A dry-cleaners*

Washing advice

Clothes in a shop window

A clothing company brings out a range of clothes made from a new material.

Scientists working for the company carry out tests to see which washing methods are best for the new material. They stain samples of the new material with household dirt and with greasy dirt.

The scientists then wash these samples with soap and with a synthetic detergent, using both hot and cool washes. They also use an organic solvent.

Their results are shown in the table.

Questions

1 Which washing method was best at removing household dirt?

2 Why may this not be the best way to wash clothes made with this material?

3 Which washing method removed 54% of the greasy dirt?

4 Which washing method was best at removing greasy dirt?

5 What advice should the manufacturers give to customers about the way that clothes made of this material should be washed?

	Percentage of dirt removed		Percentage shrinkage of material
	Household dirt	Greasy dirt	
soap at 30°C	63	36	0
soap at 60°C	86	54	14
synthetic detergent at 30°C	92	45	2
synthetic detergent at 60°C	98	78	18
organic solvent at 20°C	22	99	0

Making drugs

In this item you will find out

- about batch and continuous processes
- about the costs involved in drug research and development
- about sources of raw materials for speciality chemicals

Could eating plants make you feel better? For thousands of years plants have been used to cure illnesses.

Many years ago people with a heart condition were given herbal tea made using foxglove plants.

It was later found that foxglove plants contain a chemical called digoxin. At first this drug was extracted from foxglove plants, but now synthetic digoxin is made and used as a treatment for heart conditions.

Today many people use plants as an alternative to the treatment provided by doctors for a variety of ailments.

This table shows the medical uses of some other plants.

▲ A foxglove plant

Plant	Medical use
curare	produces a muscle relaxant used in surgery
white birch	some tests have shown it may be effective in killing melanoma (skin cancer) cells
velvet bean	used in the treatment of Parkinson's disease
willow	extracts inspired the development of aspirin
cinchona tree	quinine is extracted from the bark and used to treat malaria
wild yam	extracts are modified to produce oestrogen, which is used in birth control pills

a Which of the plants listed in the table would you use to cure a headache?

As you can see from the table, the raw materials for some **medicines** or **pharmaceutical drugs** are still extracted from plants, although many can now be made in laboratories.

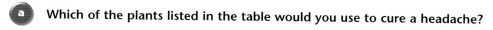

131

New drugs

Developing a new medicine or pharmaceutical drug is a long and costly process. It may take up to 15 years and cost over £300 million.

The flowchart shows the steps in the development of a new drug.

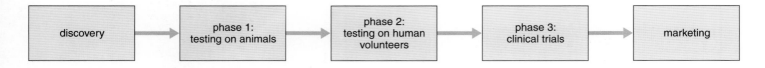

discovery → phase 1: testing on animals → phase 2: testing on human volunteers → phase 3: clinical trials → marketing

Thousands of new chemical compounds are made and tested to find one new product. The research and testing phase may take many years and is very labour-intensive.

Some of the processes involved cannot be automated and many require highly-skilled workers. Paying the wages of all these employees costs the company a lot of money.

The raw materials have to be purchased. Many of these raw materials are rare and expensive. To get some of the materials from plant sources, costly extraction processes are required.

When a promising chemical compound is found, it has to be tested. This involves testing it first on animals and then on human volunteers.

Finally, clinical trials are used to find out how effective it is at curing patients, and what unwanted side effects the drug may have.

When the drug is proved to be effective, it has to have legal approval before it is manufactured and sold.

The manufacturing process for a drug uses a lot of energy. The company has to pay for the electricity, gas or oil used in manufacture.

Finally, it can be marketed. This involves advertising and supplying the drug to hospitals and doctors. Marketing a product can be very expensive.

b Explain why the testing of a new drug is so expensive.

c It may be cheaper to make a drug by synthesising it from chemicals rather than by extracting it from a plant. Suggest why.

> **Examiner's tip**
>
> Make sure you know the meaning of, and can use, chemical terms such as batch process, bulk chemical, speciality chemical.

▲ *These road tankers are carrying a large amount of liquid ammonia*

Batch and continuous processes

The chemical industry can produce products using two types of process: a **batch process** or a **continuous process**.

The Haber Process for the manufacture of ammonia is an example of a continuous process. Nitrogen and hydrogen are passed into the reaction vessel. Here they react to make ammonia.

The ammonia gas is condensed into a liquid and collected as it is produced. This process can continue for 24 hours a day until the plant has to be closed down for maintenance.

Ammonia, like other chemicals made by continuous processes, is used in the manufacture of many other products. Because they are so widely used, very large quantities of these chemicals are made. They are called **bulk chemicals**.

Many medicines and pharmaceutical drugs are produced by a batch process. Measured amounts of raw materials are mixed and processed to produce the drug. This happens only when a new supply is required. These chemicals are not made all the time. Much smaller quantities of these chemicals are made. They are called **speciality chemicals**.

d **Bulk chemicals are much cheaper to buy than speciality chemicals. Suggest why.**

Keywords

batch process • bulk chemical • continuous process • medicine • pharmaceutical drug • speciality chemical

Extracting from plants

Husna works as a laboratory technician in the research and development department of a pharmaceutical company. One of her jobs is to extract small quantities of active ingredients from plants.

This flowchart shows how the active ingredient can be extracted from a plant.

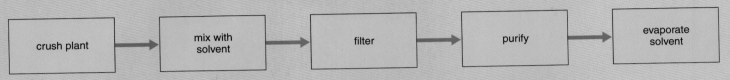

First she crushes the plant. Then she dissolves the crushed plant material in a suitable solvent. The plant contains lots of different chemicals. Different solvents can be used to separate them in order to purify the extract.

Chromatography is then used to test the purity of the extract. A spot of plant solution is placed on a piece of filter paper. The end of the filter paper is then dipped into another solvent. This solvent rises up the paper, separating out the chemicals in the plant solution. The chemicals present can then be identified.

Questions

1 Why do the plants need to be crushed before the active ingredient can be extracted?

2 Why is it necessary to use several different solvents during the purification of the extract?

3 Why is the solvent evaporated away to get the final extract?

4 Why is chromatography carried out on the final extract?

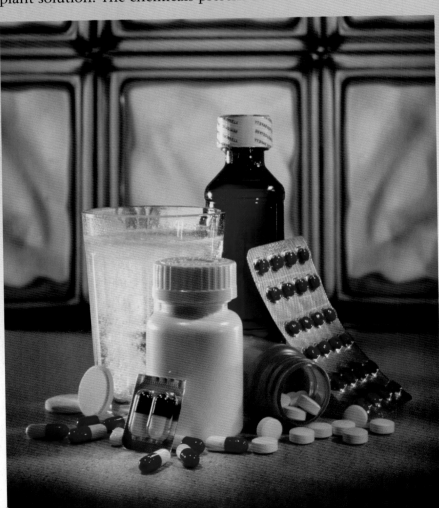

It's a small world

In this item you will find out

- about the three forms of carbon: diamond, graphite and fullerene

- about the properties and uses of these forms of carbon

- about nanochemistry

Diamond is the most valuable gemstone. It is used in the most expensive jewellery.

Why is diamond so prized and so expensive? The answer can be found in the beauty, durability and rarity of diamonds. Diamonds are lustrous, meaning that they shine.

Pure diamonds are also colourless and transparent. The fiery appearance of a diamond is caused by the separation (dispersion) of white light into the colours of the spectrum as it passes through the stone. This makes diamond the most sought-after gemstone.

 Why are diamonds considered more beautiful than other gemstones?

Diamond is the hardest naturally occurring substance. This means that the diamonds used in jewellery are impossible to scratch or damage. They truly will last forever!

In addition to jewellery, diamonds are also used to make the cutting edges of drills and saws. Diamond-tipped cutting tools are used to cut the hardest materials. Because diamond is so hard, it does not wear away quickly.

Also, diamond has a very high melting point, so it does not melt at the high temperatures caused by friction as the tools cut. Diamond itself can only be cut by another diamond.

 Why are diamonds used in industrial cutting tools?

Amazing fact

A star some 50 light-years from the Earth in the constellation Centaurus is a diamond of 10 billion trillion trillion carats. It is 4000 km across.

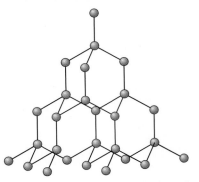

▲ *How carbon atoms are arranged in diamond*

Diamond and graphite

Diamond is one form of carbon. Another is graphite. Both of these forms of carbon are made of just carbon atoms. But the carbon atoms are arranged in a different way in each.

You can see from the diagram that in diamond each carbon atom is joined to four others. As well as being hard, transparent and shiny, diamond does not conduct electricity and it does not dissolve in water.

In graphite the carbon atoms are arranged in layers.

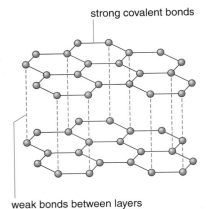

strong covalent bonds

weak bonds between layers

▲ *The layers of carbon atoms in graphite*

Graphite has different properties to diamond. It is:

- black, lustrous and opaque (does not let light through it)
- slippery
- insoluble in water
- a conductor of electricity.

Since it conducts electricity and has a high melting point, it is used for electrodes in electrolysis reactions. The graphite electrodes are used to pass an electric current through the molten material or solution to be electrolysed. One example is in the manufacture of aluminium.

The softness and black colour of graphite make it useful for pencil 'lead'. (Pencil 'lead' has no connection with lead metal.) The slipperiness of graphite means that it is a good lubricator. It is used as an additive to oils and greases.

c **Why is a high melting point a useful property for an electrode?**

Buckminsterfullerene

Until 1985 scientists believed that there were only two forms of carbon: diamond and graphite. Then a chance discovery led a small team of scientists to conclude that they had made a new form of carbon, which they called buckminsterfullerene. Within a short time other scientists were able to perform similar experiments and so confirm the discovery.

Buckminsterfullerene is made up of 60 carbon atoms joined to each other in the shape of a ball. These shapes are known as 'Bucky Balls'.

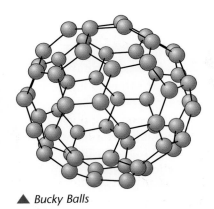

▲ *Bucky Balls*

Since this first discovery, other **fullerenes** have been made with different numbers of carbon atoms in each ball. The number of atoms ranges from 32 to 600. Buckminsterfullerene is a deep black solid, which forms a red solution in petrol.

d What is similar about the structures of all three different types of carbon?

e How is the structure of buckminsterfullerene different from that of the other two types of carbon?

Nanotubes

Fullerenes can be joined together to make tube shapes called **nanotubes**.

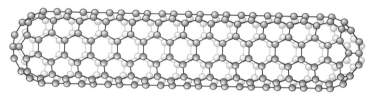

▲ How carbon atoms are arranged in a nanotube

These nanotubes are very strong and can conduct electricity. They have a number of uses, for example:

- as semiconductors in electrical circuits
- as industrial catalysts
- as a reinforcement for the graphite in tennis racquets.

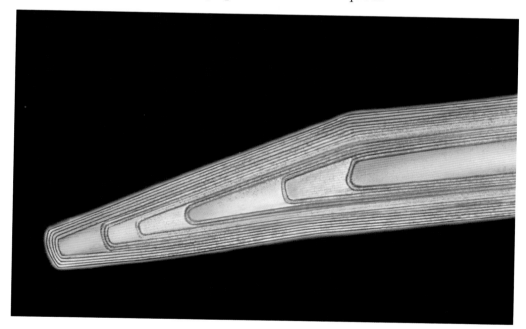

◀ Carbon nanotube fibres are used to make strong composite materials

The discovery of nanotubes has created a new area of science called **nanochemistry**. Normally chemistry works with materials on a large scale. Nanochemistry uses materials on a very small scale. It works with materials at the atomic level, with particles of incredibly small size, called **nanoparticles**. These nanoparticles have different properties to 'bulk' chemicals.

Keywords

fullerene • nanochemistry • nanoparticle • nanotube

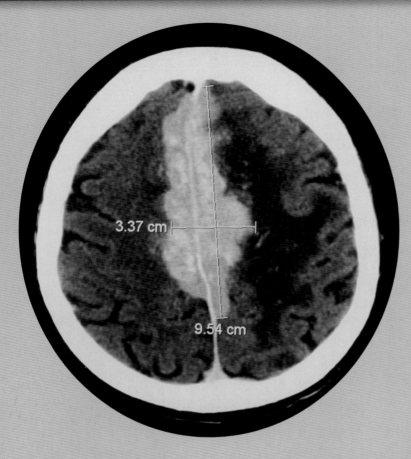

3.37 cm

9.54 cm

Nanoparticles could carry cancer drugs

Brain tumours could be tackled more efficiently by trapping the drugs used to treat them inside specially designed nanoparticles.

One problem with using chemicals to cure cancer (chemotherapy) is trying to deliver the dose needed to destroy the tumour without also destroying vital cells elsewhere in the body.

It is now possible to make tiny nanoparticles – no more than one ten-thousandth of a millimetre in diameter – from polymers. The drug is carried inside these particles.

Even at this size, the particles are so big that the only places they can leave the bloodstream are at the tumour site and at the liver. The outside of the particles is designed so that only a small number of particles can be removed by the liver.

Early attempts with polymer nanoparticles failed because they were only able to carry very small amounts of the active drug, and often they did not hold onto the drug for very long.

Scientists now believe they have improved the design. The new polymer nanoparticles should be suitable for delivering a wide range of drugs.

Questions

1 Drugs used for cancer chemotherapy attack cells. What problem does this cause?

2 How could using the new nanoparticles to carry the drugs help to solve this problem?

3 Why did early attempts to use nanoparticles in this way fail?

4 Drugs are removed from the bloodstream by the liver, making them less effective. How do the nanoparticles reduce the amount of drug removed by the liver?

Water, water everywhere

In this item you will find out

- where our water comes from and how it is purified

- about the pollutants that may be present in our water

- how to test for some substances that may be dissolved in water

When you get water from a tap, do you ever think of how it got there?

In the UK we have quite a high rainfall. The UK is well-known for the lush green plant life that can grow with such a good supply of water.

In contrast, many other countries have a very low and erratic rainfall. Droughts can destroy crops, kill animals and leave people without water to drink.

We take water from lakes, rivers and **reservoirs**. Many reservoirs have been created specially to store water by building dams.

Water is also held in rock underground. This rock is called an **aquifer**. In some places a bore hole is drilled into this rock and the water brought to the surface.

▼ A dam

a The UK has a high rainfall. Why do you think it is important for us to conserve water?

We use water every day in our homes but it is also an important resource for lots of industrial chemical processes. It is used:

- as a cheap raw material in some manufacturing processes
- as a coolant to prevent many industrial processes from overheating
- as a solvent.

Water pollution

Water pumped from a lake, reservoir or river has to be purified before it is fit for us to drink. Some of the pollutants found in water before it is purified include:

- nitrate residues – these get into the water when rain dissolves and washes fertiliser from fields into rivers and lakes
- lead compounds – these can dissolve into water from lead pipes in very old houses
- pesticide residues – if farmers spray pesticides too near to rivers or lakes, some may drift, or be washed by rain, into the water.

The water may also contain dissolved salts and minerals, microbes or insoluble materials.

How is water purified?

During water purification, those materials we do not want in the water supplied to our homes are removed. Dissolved salts and minerals are not removed, since they are harmless and even give the water a better taste.

b Which substances must be removed before water is supplied to customers?

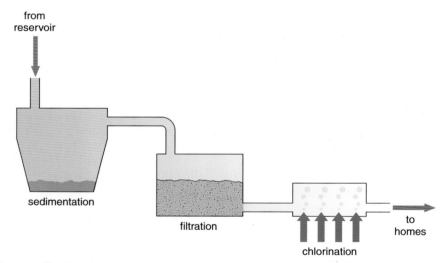

▲ *Water purification process*

Water is first passed into a **sedimentation** tank. The water contains insoluble solids. Here solid materials suspended in the water are allowed to settle to the bottom. These include sand and soil particles.

Next the water is passed through a filter made of layers of grit, coarse sand and fine sand. This traps the finer suspended materials, such as clay, that are made up of very small, light particles and do not settle out in the sedimentation tank.

c Why do not all of the suspended particles settle out in the sedimentation tank?

Finally the water undergoes **chlorination**. A very small quantity of chlorine gas is dissolved in the water. This kills microbes that might otherwise cause disease.

In many of the developing nations people get their water directly from rivers or lakes. Often this water is contaminated with sewage and contains disease-causing microbes. Aid agencies such as Oxfam are working to make clean water available to these people.

Testing water

Water can be tested to identify some of the chemicals dissolved in it. These tests involve **precipitation** reactions. This is when chemicals in two solutions that are mixed together react to form an insoluble product. The insoluble product is called a **precipitate** and makes the mixture cloudy.

To test for sulfate ions, barium chloride solution is added. For example, if sodium sulphate is present in the water:

sodium sulfate + barium chloride → barium sulfate + sodium chloride

Barium sulfate is insoluble in water and forms a white precipitate. So if the mixture turns cloudy white, it shows that there is a sulfate dissolved in the water.

In a similar way, silver nitrate solution can be used to test for chloride ions, bromide ions and iodide ions. Each of these ions forms an insoluble silver salt and turns the mixture cloudy. But each forms a precipitate with a different colour.

▲ *Clean water is very important*

Halide	Chloride	Bromide	Iodide
Name of precipitate	silver chloride	silver bromide	silver iodide
Colour of precipitate	white	cream	pale yellow

For example, with sodium halides:

sodium chloride + silver nitrate → silver chloride + sodium nitrate

sodium bromide + silver nitrate → silver bromide + sodium nitrate

sodium iodide + silver nitrate → silver iodide + sodium nitrate

d Write a word equation for the reaction between potassium bromide and silver nitrate.

e A sample of water was tested. With barium chloride it gave a clear, colourless solution, and with silver nitrate it gave a cream-coloured precipitate. What do these tests show about the water sample?

Keywords

aquifer • chlorination • precipitate • precipitation • reservoir • sedimentation

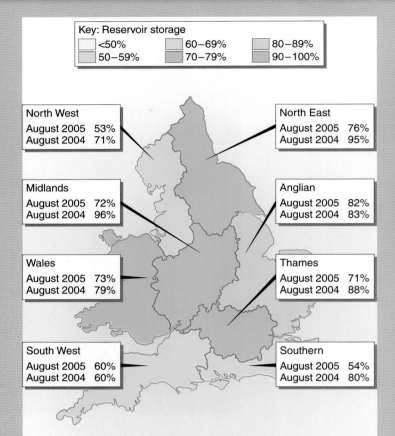

Key: Reservoir storage
- <50%
- 50–59%
- 60–69%
- 70–79%
- 80–89%
- 90–100%

North West
August 2005 53%
August 2004 71%

North East
August 2005 76%
August 2004 95%

Midlands
August 2005 72%
August 2004 96%

Anglian
August 2005 82%
August 2004 83%

Wales
August 2005 73%
August 2004 79%

Thames
August 2005 71%
August 2004 88%

South West
August 2005 60%
August 2004 60%

Southern
August 2005 54%
August 2004 80%

Water resources

Each summer in many parts of the UK water supply companies issue hosepipe bans. People are told that they are not allowed to use hosepipes to water gardens or wash cars.

They are also asked to use less water, for example by placing a brick in their toilet cistern so that it fills with less water, or by taking showers instead of baths.

The UK is usually thought of as a place that has a high rainfall. But in many parts of the country there has not been enough rain in recent years to fill the reservoirs that supply most of our water.

Southern England has been badly affected by water shortages. The area has a fast-growing population. This means that more houses are built and more water used. The map gives a comparison of how full reservoirs were in August 2004 and then one year later in August 2005. Water stored in reservoirs in each of eight regions in England and Wales is shown, as a percentage of the reservoirs' full capacity.

Questions

1 Which region has the lowest percentage of water storage capacity filled?

2 Suggest why this region has such a low amount of water stored in its reservoirs.

3 Which region has the highest percentage of water storage capacity filled?

4 Suggest why this region has such a good store of water.

5 Which region has suffered the worst fall in stored water during the year?

6 Suggest why this region has such severe water shortage problems.

C4a

1 A student tests several solutions to find the pH of each one. Her results are shown in the table.

Copy and complete the table. Put a tick in the correct box to show if each solution is an acid, an alkali or neutral.

Solution	pH	Acid	Alkali	Neutral
A	5			
B	7			
C	1			
D	9			

[4]

2 An acidic solution is added to an alkaline solution.

a What word can be used to describe the reaction that takes place? Choose from this list:

decomposition   electrolysis
neutralisation   synthesis   [1]

b Describe how the pH of the alkaline solution changes as the acid is added. [1]

3 Describe two uses of sulfuric acid. [2]

4 An acid is slowly added to a solution of a base. The word equation for the reaction that takes place is

acid + base → salt + water

a What is the term used to describe a base that is soluble in water? [2]

b Explain why the pH changes during this reaction. [2]

c Write a word equation for the reaction between an acid and a carbonate. [2]

5 Copy and complete the table by filling in the empty boxes to show the salts produced when acids are added to bases.

Acid	Base	Salt
sulfuric acid	sodium hydroxide	
hydrochloric acid	magnesium oxide	
nitric acid	lithium carbonate	

[3]

C4b

1 Use a Periodic Table to help you answer these questions.

a What is the relative atomic mass of each of the elements in this list?

aluminium   calcium   carbon   chlorine
hydrogen   magnesium   nitrogen
oxygen   sodium

[9]

b Work out the relative formula masses of compounds with these formulae:
CO_2 $MgCl_2$ NH_3 $NaOH$ $CaCO_3$
Al_2O_3 [6]

2 Four students make iron sulfide by reacting iron with sulfur. They measure the masses of the starting materials iron and sulfur used, and of the product iron sulfide made.

Student	Mass of iron in g	Mass of sulfur in g	Mass of iron sulfide in g
A	56	32	88
B	112	64	
C	23	16	
D	89	48	

a Which student makes the largest mass of iron sulfide? [1]

b What mass of iron sulfide is made by student D? [1]

3 A student heats 6 g of magnesium in oxygen until it burns to make magnesium oxide. The student uses relative atomic masses to work out that 6 g of magnesium reacts with 4 g of oxygen to make 10 g of magnesium oxide.

a If the student has a 100% yield from the experiment, what mass of magnesium oxide will he have? [1]

b If the student has a 0% yield from the experiment, what mass of magnesium oxide will he have? [1]

c If the student has a 50% yield from the experiment, what mass of magnesium oxide will he have? [1]

d Suggest why the student is not likely to get a 100% yield in this experiment. [1]

4 When calcium carbonate is heated it decomposes to form calcium oxide and carbon dioxide: 100 g of calcium decomposes to give 56 g of calcium oxide.

a What mass of calcium oxide is made when 10 g of calcium oxide decomposes? [1]

b Write a word equation for the reaction. [2]

5 A student adds 5.6 g of calcium oxide to an excess of hydrochloric acid. She evaporates some water from the solution, leaves the solution to form crystals of calcium chloride, filters off the crystals and then leaves them to dry. She then puts them into a weighing bottle.

She uses relative atomic masses to work out that the predicted yield of calcium chloride for this experiment is 11.1 g. She finds that the mass of calcium chloride she has made is 8.0 g.

  a What is the percentage yield for her experiment? [2]
  b Suggest two reasons why she did not get 100% yield? [2]

C4c

1 Farmers and gardeners put fertilisers on the soil.

  a Suggest why farmers and gardeners put fertilisers on the soil. [2]
  b Which of these are the three essential elements needed for plant growth and contained in most common fertilisers?

    carbon   nitrogen   oxygen   phosphorus potassium   sodium [3]

2 The uptake of fertilisers by plants is affected by the pH of the soil. Describe how you would test a sample of soil to find its pH. [4]

3 State the names of two nitrogen-containing fertilisers made from ammonia. [2]

4 The compounds used in fertilisers are soluble in water. Explain why this is important. [2]

5 The fertiliser potassium nitrate can be made by a neutralisation reaction between an acid and an alkali. Name the acid and alkali. [2]

C4d

1 In the Haber Process ammonia is made from nitrogen and hydrogen.

  a Where does the nitrogen for this process come from? [1]
  b Where does the hydrogen for this process come from? [1]

2 The word equation for the Haber Process is:

nitrogen + hydrogen $\rightleftharpoons$ ammonia
What does the sign $\rightleftharpoons$ show about this reaction? [2]

3 The Haber Process is used to make ammonia at a competitive price.

  a State three things that affect the cost of ammonia made by the Haber Process. [3]
  b Describe two uses for ammonia. [2]

4 State three conditions used in the Haber Process to give a good yield of ammonia in a short reaction time. [3]

5 Explain why ammonia is important in relation to world food production. [2]

C4e

1 A detergent powder contains an active detergent and a water softener. Name two other ingredients that a detergent powder contains. [2]

2 Copy and complete these sentences by using words from this list to fill in the blank spaces:

dissolve   insoluble   soluble   solute solution   solvent

Each of the ingredients in a washing powder must be ___(1)___ in water, so that it dissolves to form a ___(2)___ in which the ingredient is the ___(3)___ and water is the ___(4)___ . If any ingredient is ___(5)___ it will remain as a solid on the clothes after washing. [5]

3 Describe the function of the following ingredients:

  a active detergent in a washing powder [1]
  b water softener in a washing power [1]
  c rinse agent in a washing-up liquid [1]

4 The table shows the results of tests on two different washing powders.

Washing powder	% dirt removed at different washing temperatures		
	40 °C	60 °C	80 °C
containing synthetic detergent A	85	93	98
containing synthetic detergent B	78	89	96

  a Which detergent cleaned better at 40 °C? [1]
  b Use these results to describe the effect of increasing temperature on the cleaning power of detergents. [2]

5 Some clothes are cleaned by a dry-cleaning process.

  a How is this process different from using a washing powder? [1]

  b What are the reasons for using this process instead of a washing powder? [2]

C4f

1 Some chemicals, such as ammonia, are made by a continuous process. Other chemicals, such as many medicines, are made by a batch process.

  a What is the difference between a continuous process and a batch process? [1]

  b Describe one advantage of each process. [2]

2 State three factors that affect the cost of making and developing a new medicine. [3]

3 What is the source of many raw materials used to make medicines? Choose from this list:

  air   **plants**   **rocks**   **water** [1]

4 Making and developing a new pharmaceutical drug is usually much more expensive than a bulk chemical such as ammonia. Describe three factors that make the drug so much more expensive. [6]

5 Describe three processes used in the extraction of chemicals from plant sources. [3]

C4g

1 What are the names of the three forms of carbon? [3]

2 Copy and complete the table by ticking the boxes to show the physical properties of diamond and graphite.

Property	Diamond	Graphite
lustrous		
opaque		
slippery		
very high melting point		
conducts electricity		
soft		
insoluble in water		

[2]

3 Use the properties of diamond and graphite to explain the following facts:

  a diamond is used in cutting tools [2]

  b graphite is used to make pencil leads [2]

4 Buckminsterfullerene can be used to make nanotubes. This has led to a new branch of science called nanochemistry. How is nanochemistry different from 'ordinary' chemistry? [1]

5 Describe three uses for nanotubes. [3]

C4h

1 **a** State two types of water resources found in the UK. [2]

  b Which two of these are common pollutants in river water?

  chlorine   **copper**   **lead**   **nitrates**
  pesticides   **sulfates** [2]

2 What is the effect of the addition of chlorine to drinking water? [1]

3 Copy and complete this table about tests for ions in water.

Test	Result	Ion present
add barium sulfate solution		sulfate
add silver nitrate solution		chloride
add silver nitrate solution	cream precipitate	
add silver nitrate solution		iodide

[4]

4 Describe two ways that pollutants can get into water sources in the UK. [4]

5 Write a word equation for the reaction of potassium sulfate with barium chloride. [2]

6 The average rainfall in the United Kingdom is high, and we have lots of rivers.

  a Why do we store water in reservoirs instead of simply taking what we need from rivers? [1]

  b Suggest why using hosepipes to water gardens or wash cars is often banned in the summer, despite the large rainfall in this country. [2]

P3 Forces for transport

I'm going on holiday by aeroplane. It's quicker than taking the car on the ferry but I can't take much luggage.

- Getting from A to B is essential for all of us. We can do this by foot, bicycle, car, bus, train, boat or aeroplane. They all involve energy and forces but which methods do we choose and why? Speed, safety, convenience and environmental factors are all important.

- Which do you think is the safest way to travel? According to engineers, air travel is actually the safest way to travel. But cars still remain an extremely popular form of transport. Engineers test cars for safety features, design road calming schemes to slow us down and design speed cameras to discourage us from speeding.

Aren't aircraft more dangerous, and don't they cause lots of damage to the environment?

Actually, air travel is safer statistically – if you don't die of boredom at check-in.

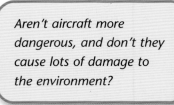

What you need to know

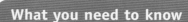

- Forces can change the movement of objects.

- Energy is measured in joules.

- Energy is needed to make things move.

146

How fast? How far?

In this item you will find out

- how to measure time and distance
- how to calculate speeds
- how to use distance–time graphs

We seem to always want to know who is the fastest:

- What is the 100 m sprint record?
- Who is the fastest bowler in cricket?
- Who has the fastest serve in tennis?

But how do we compare these very different things? Being the fastest may be interesting for some but it is hardly a matter of life or death. Road safety is crucial to all of us and an understanding of **speed** is important for safe driving. We also use the idea of speed to plan how long journeys will take.

When the Space Shuttle spacecraft goes on its long journeys accurate high speeds are needed to get it there and back home safely.

Speed is how far something moves in a certain time. To calculate speed you need to measure two things – distance and time. Speed is measured in metres per second (m/s).

If a fast object and a slow object are travelling side by side, the faster object will cover a greater distance in ten minutes than the slower object. The faster object will also cover the same distance as the slower object but in a shorter time. For example, a train is faster than a bicycle and covers more distance in ten minutes.

a The train's speed increases down a hill. How does this affect the distance it travels in ten minutes?

Amazing fact

The NASA–German *Helios* 1 and 2 solar probes reached 252 800 km/h (158 000 mph) during their orbits of the Sun.

Measuring speed

At school, if you are measuring distance outside you may use a tape measure for short distances or a trundle wheel for longer distances. You can use a stopwatch to measure time accurately.

Angela measures the distance between the speed bumps outside her school using a trundle wheel.

Sanjeev measures the time it takes for a car to pass this same distance with a stopwatch.

Here are the results:

distance = 30 m and time = 3 s

You can calculate speed using this formula:

$$speed = \frac{distance}{time}$$

$$metres\ per\ second\ (m/s) = \frac{metres\ (m)}{seconds\ (s)}$$

So, by using the equation $speed = \dfrac{distance}{time}$

the speed of the car $= \dfrac{30\,m}{3\,s} = 10\,m/s$

▲ *Measuring distances with a trundle wheel*

b A train travels 140 km from Liverpool to Birmingham in 2 hours. Calculate the speed of the train in km/h.

The speed of this train is measured in km/h. We measure speeds in units that are sensible. A snail will probably not move a kilometre in its lifetime. In a sprint on a good day, it may move 2 mm in 1 second. Sensible units for speeding snails may be mm/s.

Moving object	Sensible units
Train	km/h
Car on a road	km/h or miles per hour (mph)
Toy car in laboratory	m/s
Snail	mm/s
Earth's tectonic plates	cm/year

Speed cameras

The next time you see a **speed camera**, look at the white lines on the road. When a car that is travelling too fast passes a speed camera, the camera flashes as the car reaches the start of the white lines. The camera then flashes again, by which time the car will have passed more white lines. The two flashes are a certain time apart and the white lines are a certain distance apart so

the speed of the car can be calculated. The photographs also record the registration number of the car.

c Explain how speed cameras help the police to work out the speed of a car.

Distance–time graphs

You can use **distance–time graphs** to show if something is moving fast or slowly on a journey. You can also use your graphs to calculate speeds accurately.

The graph shows a distance–time graph for a toy car. We can use the graph to describe how the car moves on its journey.

Part A   The car moves 20 m in 10 s at a steady speed.

$$speed = \frac{distance}{time}$$

so the speed of the car $= \frac{20\,m}{10\,s} = 2\,m/s$

Part B   It is stationary (zero speed) for 20 s.

This tells us some important information about distance–time graphs:

- sloping straight lines show steady speeds
- horizontal straight lines show zero speed.

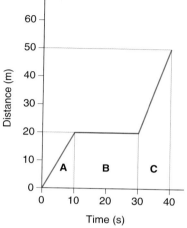
▲ Distance–time graph for a toy car

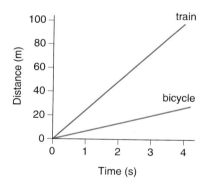
◄ Distance–time graphs for a bicycle and a train

Look at the distance–time graphs for the bicycle and the train. What do you notice about them? A train travels much faster than a bicycle and the **gradient** of the line is steeper. This means that on a distance–time graph, the steeper the gradient, the higher the speed.

Keywords

distance–time graph • gradient • speed • speed camera

 d Look at the distance–time graph for the wind-up toy. Describe its journey.

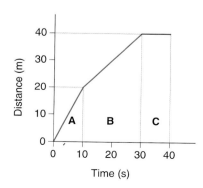
◄ Distance–time graph for a wind-up toy

Getting there

Questions

1. Calculate the speed of each car in m/s.

2. The speed limit is 12.5 m/s. Which car(s) are speeding?

3. Draw one distance–time graph to compare the speeds of all the cars for the 2 seconds they travel through the speed camera. What does the gradient of the graphs tell you about the speeds of the cars?

4. People caught speeding face fines and having points put on their driving licence. If they get too many points they can lose their licence to drive. Do you think this is fair? Explain your answer.

5. Suggest why, in some European countries, the speed limit on housing estates and near schools is about 15 miles per hour. Do you think this is a sensible limit?

John Lindsey is a traffic police officer. One of his jobs is to catch speeding motorists.

There is a big music festival in a nearby town and people are keen to get a good place. John explains how the police are going to handle the drivers.

'Some people leave it a little too late to get there safely and some of the people drive much too fast! The main route to the festival goes through a housing estate and safety is very important.

'We usually have a patrol out on the road, but the cars also travel past a speed camera on the way to the festival. This will help us catch any cars that are speeding.'

Here is some data that the speed camera near the festival has already collected.

Car registration number	Distance moved (m)	Time between flashes (s)	Speed of car (m/s)
G293 EUJ	10	2	
Y165 PUJ	20	2	
W293 VAW	15	2	
Y20 TUJ	25	2	
X112 TAW	30	2	

High acceleration

In this item you will find out

- what acceleration is

- how to calculate acceleration

- how to use speed–time graphs to describe and understand how things move

Dragster cars change their speed very quickly indeed.

The car in the photograph starts and accelerates from 0 to 60 mph in 2 seconds. The driver will need a very strong seat and headrest! Many family road cars accelerate from 0 to 60 mph in about 10 seconds. This is five times less **acceleration** than the dragster.

In some parts of normal driving, having high acceleration is important. It allows higher speeds to be reached more quickly, which means some manoeuvres, like overtaking, can be carried out safely.

 Suggest how high accelerations could cause problems for road safety.

Acceleration happens when the speed of an object changes. The speed can change to become faster or slower. When an object speeds up it has positive acceleration. When it slows down it has negative acceleration or deceleration.

Acceleration depends on two things:

- how much the speed of the object changes
- how long the change in speed takes.

The acceleration of cars is calculated by measuring how many seconds it takes to increase speed from 0 to 60 mph. In science lessons we do not carry out experiments with objects moving at 60 mph. It would be too dangerous. So, we usually define acceleration as how much the speed of an object changes in one second, and its units are metres per second squared, m/s^2.

Amazing fact

Although the Space Shuttle never accelerates at more than $30 \, m/s^2$ during its ascent, after 8 minutes it enters orbit doing 8 000 m/s.

Calculating acceleration

You can calculate acceleration using this formula:

$$\text{acceleration} = \frac{\text{change in speed}}{\text{time}}$$

$$\text{metres per second squared (m/s}^2) = \frac{\text{metres per second (m/s)}}{\text{seconds (s)}}$$

For example, a school bus accelerates from 10 m/s to 30 m/s in 10 s. To calculate the acceleration of the bus in m/s², we first find out the change in speed.

This is 30 m/s – 10 m/s = 20 m/s.

Using $\text{acceleration} = \dfrac{\text{change in speed}}{\text{time}}$

the acceleration $= \dfrac{20\,\text{m/s}}{10\,\text{s}} = 2\,\text{m/s}^2$

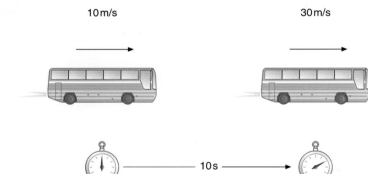

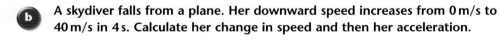

▶ *School bus accelerating*

b A skydiver falls from a plane. Her downward speed increases from 0 m/s to 40 m/s in 4 s. Calculate her change in speed and then her acceleration.

Speed–time graphs

Speed–time graphs can help us to understand acceleration. At a glance they can show us how the speed changes. If you look at them carefully you can work out exact speeds, times and accelerations.

Look at the speed–time graph for the sprinter. You can use the graph to describe the race of the sprinter.

Part A The sprinter accelerates from 0 to 5 m/s in 10 s.

$$\text{acceleration} = \frac{5\,\text{m/s}}{10\,\text{s}} = 0.5\,\text{m/s}^2$$

Part B The sprinter has a steady speed of 5 m/s for 20 s.

$\text{acceleration} = 0\,\text{m/s}^2$ as there is no change in speed

Part C The sprinter accelerates from 5 m/s to 15 m/s in 10 s.

$$\text{acceleration} = \frac{10\,\text{m/s}}{10\,\text{s}} = 1.0\,\text{m/s}^2$$

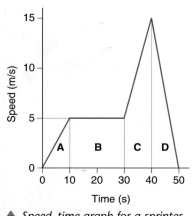

▲ *Speed–time graph for a sprinter*

Quick revision guide for English paper 1 – Tuesday June 2nd

There are three questions – you must answer them all:

Question 1 – remember that the question/s here only ask you to summarise what you have read.
(If possible, use 2 paragraphs when you write your summary – 250 words)
There is no need to quote or analyse in Question 1

Question 2 - remember that this question does ask you to analyse – you are looking at how the creator of the text has used language and presentation to make the message clear - PALL

Question 3 – Writing to inform, explain, describe – remember to write clearly and with as wide a range of vocabulary and accurate punctuation as you can. Remember to think about who the reader is and why/what you are writing for them.

Good luck and remember to come to the focus day on Wednesday for Paper 2

Part D The sprinter decelerates from 15 m/s to 0 m/s in 10 s.

$$\text{acceleration} = \frac{-15\,\text{m/s}}{10\,\text{s}} = -1.5\,\text{m/s}^2$$

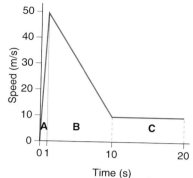
▲ Speed–time graph for a paper aeroplane

c A paper aeroplane is launched and flies across the room. Look at the graph of the speed of the paper aeroplane.

(i) Part A is when it is on the aeroplane launcher. It takes 1 s to reach its maximum speed of 50 m/s. Calculate its acceleration.

(ii) What happens to its speed in part B? Calculate the deceleration in part B.

(iii) Describe the speed and acceleration in part C.

Calculating distance

You can see how we calculated the different accelerations of a sprinter from his speed–time graph. We can also use this type of graph to calculate the average speed and the distance travelled.

You can calculate the distance something has travelled using speed–time graphs by working out the area underneath the graph.

Look at the graph of the sprinter. The area under Part B is 5 m/s × 20 s = 100 m. So the sprinter has travelled 100 m.

You can get the same answer by using a formula and not a graph:

distance = average speed (5 m/s) × time (20 s) = 100 m.

Gradient of a speed–time graph

Have another look at the speed–time graph for the sprinter. The slope or gradient of the graph shows the acceleration.

In Part A, the sprinter's speed is increasing. This is shown by a straight line with a *positive* gradient. In Part B, the sprinter's speed is constant. This is shown by a *horizontal* line. In Part C, the sprinter's speed increases again. The acceleration in Part C is greater than the acceleration in Part A so the gradient of the graph is steeper. In Part D, the sprinter's speed is decreasing and this is shown by a straight line with a *negative* gradient.

▼ A racing cyclist

d Look at the speed–time graph for a bicycle. Describe the speeds and accelerations for each part of the journey.

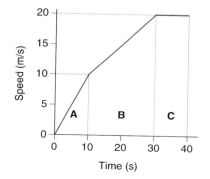
◄ Speed–time graph for a bicycle

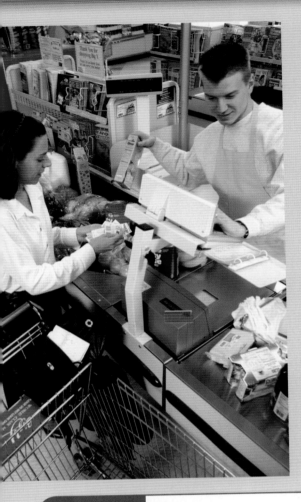

Getting to work

Rochelle, Andy, Sarah, Irene and Kamal all work in a supermarket and they all drive to work.

To get to work, they all travel through two tunnels underneath the city. Both tunnels are the same length.

The table shows the time each of their cars took to go through each tunnel.

Car	Time taken to travel through first tunnel (s)	Time taken to travel through second tunnel (s)
Audi	5	6
BMW	7	7
Citroen	4	6
Ford	5	4
Skoda	4	2

One member of staff, James, uses a motorbike. Here is a speed–time graph for his journey to work.

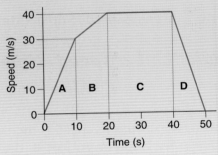

▲ *Speed–time graph of James' motorbike*

Questions

1 Which car is the fastest going through both tunnels?

2 Which two cars go through the second tunnel at increased speed?

3 Assuming that each of these cars increases speed steadily between the two tunnels, which has the highest acceleration?

4 Which two cars go through the second tunnel at reduced speed?

5 Which car has the same speed in both tunnels?

6 Look at the speed–time graph for the motorbike.

   (a) Which part has the highest acceleration (= getting faster more quickly)?
   (b) Which part has a steady speed?
   (c) Describe in detail the journey of the motorbike.

7 Lucy is another worker who also drives to work. Her car starts from rest and accelerates at 2 m/s^2 for 10 s. It travels at a steady speed of 20 m/s for 20 s. It then decelerates (slows down) at 1 m/s^2 for 20 s and comes to rest.

   Draw a speed–time graph for Lucy's car.

Stopping safely

In this item you will find out

- about using forces to make things move faster or slower

- about stopping distances of cars

Before taking your driving test you need to pass a theory test. Part of this involves an understanding of driving safely and a knowledge of car **stopping distances**.

Driving fast may be tempting but stopping safely is more important.

▲ When you are driving you have to be prepared to stop at any time

Our roads are very crowded and we need to be aware of stopping distances and speeds. When we cross the road we need to know if we have enough time to cross before the next car comes. This needs an understanding of speeds. Knowing how quickly cars can stop is also important to all road users – drivers and pedestrians.

When cars move they have lots of energy. When cars brake the energy is absorbed in the brakes and turned into heat energy. The brakes get hot and the car stops safely.

When you drive a car it is easy to get up to speed. However, before you do this it is important to know how to stop. Stopping safely in an emergency is one of the most important skills in driving.

When you need to stop, a small amount of time passes between you deciding to step on the brakes and actually doing it. The car travels several metres in this time. This is called the **thinking distance**.

After you put a foot on the brake the car slows down but it continues to travel until it stops. This is called the **braking distance**.

a Oil tankers only travel about 20 mph. Even at this speed they take a long time and distance to stop. Suggest why.

b It is obviously important for drivers to know about stopping distances. But it is also important for pedestrians too. Explain why.

Amazing fact

The world's largest ship is an oil tanker. At 564 763 tonnes, it takes nearly 10 km to stop!

Examiner's tip

Be clear about what thinking, braking and stopping distances mean.

Stopping distances

As we have already seen, the thinking distance is the distance the car moves while the driver is reacting and the braking distance is the distance the car moves with its brakes on until it comes to a stop.

The stopping distance for a car is the thinking distance + the braking distance.

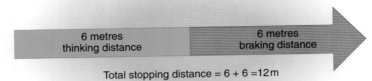

| 6 metres thinking distance | 6 metres braking distance |

Total stopping distance = 6 + 6 = 12 m

▶ *Stopping distance of a car at 8 m/s (18 mph)*

The table shows the stopping distances for cars travelling at other speeds.

Speed of car		Thinking distance (m)	Braking distance (m)	Total stopping distance (m)
(m/s)	(mph)			
8	18	6	6	12
16	36	12	24	36
32	72	24	96	120

As you can see, the faster a car is travelling, the further it goes before the driver applies the brakes, and the further it travels while the driver is braking.

 Explain why thinking, braking and stopping distance increase with speed.

Can't stop!

People who drive while they are tired take longer to react to an emergency than people who are not tired. This means their thinking distance increases and they travel further before they stop.

Thinking distance also increases when drivers have drunk alcohol or if they have taken some types of drugs.

Driving faster does not affect your thinking time but it does increase your thinking distance. This is because a faster car moves further in this time. Thinking distance can also be increased if you are not concentrating or if you have distractions, such as small children, in the car with you.

Different road conditions will affect how long a car takes to stop once the brakes have been applied. Braking distance increases the faster you are driving, when the road is slippery, wet or icy. It also increases if your brakes are not working properly or if your tyres are bald.

Apart from speeding and poor road conditions, a major cause of accidents is driving too close to the vehicle ahead. On some motorways there are chevrons painted on the road. Drivers should keep two chevrons behind the car in front.

d **How do you think motorway chevrons can help drivers reduce the risk of accidents?**

Forces

Forces can speed things up (accelerate) or slow things down (decelerate). How much acceleration or deceleration you get depends on two things:

- the mass of the object
- the size of the force acting upon it.

If an object of a certain mass has a greater force acting on it, it will have more acceleration than if a smaller force is acting on it. So if you hit a golf ball with more force it will accelerate more.

In the same way, for a given force, an object with a bigger mass will have less acceleration than an object with a smaller mass. So if you use your golf club to hit a golf ball or a football, the same force would give the football a much lower acceleration.

You can calculate the force needed to accelerate an object using this equation:

force = mass × acceleration

$kg\,m/s^2$ or newtons (N) = kilograms (kg) × metres per second squared (m/s^2)

▲ *Chevrons are arrowheads on a motorway*

For example, if a car has a mass of 1 000 kg and an acceleration of 5 m/s then we can calculate the force on the car:

force = mass × acceleration

force = 1 000 kg × 5 m/s

force = 5 000 kg m/s² or 5 000 N

e **Use the information in the table to calculate the forces. One has been done for you.**

Object	Mass (kg)	Acceleration (m/s²)	Force (N)
Skateboard	0.5	100	50
Bicycle and rider	80	2.5	
Sprinter	50	4	
Diver	50	10	
Skydiver and parachute	100	10	

Keywords

braking distance • stopping distance • thinking distance

Fast cars

1 What do we mean by the term 'acceleration from 0 to 60 mph in seconds'?

2 Which car has the highest acceleration? Suggest why.

3 Which car has the lowest acceleration? Suggest why.

4 Look at the table. How is the acceleration related to the mass?

5 Calculate the driving force for each car in the table. (Use $F = m \times a$ where m = mass in kg and a = acceleration in m/s^2.)

6 Some people think that high acceleration on the roads can be dangerous. Others think it is safer. Suggest some advantages and disadvantages of high acceleration.

7 The Spirit C3 has the highest driving force of 2550 N. The other cars have different driving forces. Suggest a reason why.

Acceleration is important to Anita. She is buying a sports car but is unsure which one to choose. She does some research on the Internet.

There is a huge amount of information available. She thinks there is too much information so she filters out what she thinks is important to help her make an informed decision.

Look at the information about the cars. They all have the same engine. Manufacturers often quote the 'acceleration' as the shortest time taken to go from stationary to 60 mph. This is shown in the third column.

She also notices that the cars have different masses and she wonders what effect this will have on their accelerations.

Car	Mass (kg)	Acceleration 0 to 60 (mph/s)	Acceleration (m/s^2)
Tulip ZN400	1160	13.4	1.99
Tiger 3900	1200	14.5	1.84
Moda ZX	1400	14.9	1.79
Spirit C3	1500	15.7	1.70

Powerful stuff!

In this item you will find out

- about work and the energy needed to do it
- how to calculate work done and power
- about fuel consumption

What do lifting weights, climbing stairs, pulling a sledge and pushing a shopping trolley have in common? They all involve **work**.

When a force moves an object, work is done and **energy** is transferred.

Buying a car is one thing, paying insurance is another, and putting fuel in it tends to be expensive too. Using cars also has a cost to people and their environment. We drive our cars forgetting that they pump out carbon dioxide gas into the atmosphere. This can add to global warming.

All cars use **energy** but some cars use energy faster than others. These cars are generally more powerful so they will also use more fuel.

People produce a little carbon dioxide too. We do work when we lift weights and we develop high **power** when we do press-ups. These things can keep us fit and they all involve using energy.

Amazing fact

Air travel produces:
- 19 times more greenhouse gases than trains
- 190 times more greenhouse gases than a ship.

Doing work

Work done depends on two things:

- the size of the force (measured in newtons)
- the distance the object moves (measured in metres).

You can calculate the work done using this equation:

work done = force × distance

joules (J) = newtons (N) × metres (m)

Work and energy are both measured in joules (J).

Look at the diagram of a moving car below. A 200 N force moves the car. We can calculate the work done when it moves 5 m.

work done = force × distance

work done = 200 N × 5 m

work done = 1 000 J

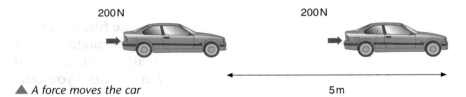

▲ A force moves the car

5 m

a Look at the diagram of the bicycle below. Calculate the work done on the bicycle.

▲ Work is done on this bicycle

20 m

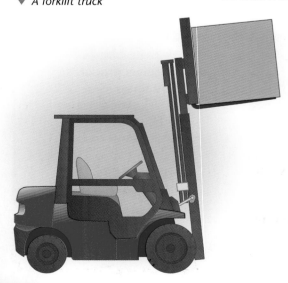

▼ A forklift truck

Power

Power is a measure of how quickly work is being done or how quickly the necessary energy is being used. Power is measured in watts (W) and is:

- how much work is done in one second or
- how much energy is transferred in one second.

We can use this equation to calculate power:

$$power = \frac{work\ done}{time}$$

$$watts\ (W) = \frac{joules\ (J)}{seconds\ (s)}$$

For example, the forklift truck in the diagram on the previous page does 40 000 J of work lifting the box and it takes 5 s. So, we can calculate the power developed.

$$\text{power} = \frac{\text{work done}}{\text{time}}$$

$$\text{power} = \frac{40\,000\,\text{J}}{5\,\text{s}}$$

power = 8 000 W

b The forklift truck then does 50 000 J of work lifting a crate. It takes 10 s. Calculate the power developed.

Cars and energy

It is necessary for work to be done to make cars move. This work uses energy and this energy comes from the fuel that is used. Some cars use energy faster than others. These cars are generally more powerful. They also use more fuel.

When people are thinking about buying a car, the cost of the fuel the car uses is an important factor. Car manufacturers have to give accurate and fair data on **fuel consumption**. This helps people make sensible choices about which car to buy. The fuel consumption tells you how many miles you can drive on one gallon (about five litres) of fuel.

The table on the right shows the fuel consumption for four cars.

c Which car has the best fuel consumption?

d Car C has 10 gallons of fuel in its tank. Estimate how far it can travel before running out of fuel.

If you put 1 gallon of fuel in Car A it will travel about 52 miles. It is impossible to say exactly how far it would go because there will be variables such as different drivers, loads or road conditions.

Car	Fuel consumption (miles per gallon)
Car A	52
Car B	48
Car C	43
Car D	51

Speed (mph)	Fuel consumption (miles per gallon)
30	70
50	66
70	38

The table above shows that a car travels further on one gallon of fuel when going at 30 mph than it does travelling at 70 mph. So the best fuel consumption is at 30 mph and the worst is at 70 mph.

e There was a shortage of fuel in the UK some years ago. The government lowered the speed limit to 50 mph on motorways. Suggest why.

Keywords

energy • fuel consumption • power • work

Energy and the environment

Vehicles produce pollution

More powerful cars use more fuel. This not only costs more money but it creates more pollution. Fumes from vehicles are unpleasant. In cities and towns these fumes can be a serious problem. Asthma sufferers are particularly affected by fumes and there is some evidence to suggest that they can encourage asthma attacks. Other respiratory illnesses have also been linked to this sort of pollution.

When fuels burn they make carbon dioxide and water. Carbon dioxide is a greenhouse gas which adds to global warming. This may lead to more extreme weather and sea levels may rise.

The table shows data for two cars. One car is a small car while the other is a large 4 × 4.

Car	Fuel consumption (miles per gallon)
Small car	53
4 × 4	22

Questions

1 Which car uses more fuel per mile?

2 Which car do you think pumps out more carbon dioxide into the atmosphere per mile?

3 Suggest why people would choose to drive a 4 × 4 instead of a small car.

4 Many cities are planning schemes to encourage fewer people to use their cars. Suggest how the following schemes can help to protect the environment:
(a) congestion charging
(b) expensive car parking
(c) park-and-ride schemes
(d) car sharing.

The cost of transport

In this item you will find out

- about kinetic energy
- about alternatives to petrol and diesel fuels

▲ *Most buses run on diesel*

We all use transport to get around. This can be buses, bicycles, cars, trams, trains or walking.

All these need a source of energy that is changed into movement, giving the object **kinetic energy**.

Most road transport such as cars, buses and lorries run on **diesel** or **petrol** and these are made from **fossil fuels**. Fossil fuels are precious because they cannot be renewed. This means that one day in the future they will become scarce and very expensive. They may even run out altogether.

Some types of vehicles use more fossil fuels than others. This means that they are more expensive to run, use up resources more quickly and cause more pollution in our cities.

But there are alternatives to using fossil fuels in vehicles. We can make oil from plants. We usually use it to cook with but we can also turn it into biofuel, which can then be burnt in engines.

Linseed oil comes from plants and has been used to power buses. Because it is a plant it can be grown again and so this energy is renewable. This protects the reserves of fossil fuels.

The idea of biofuels is used in some countries. Brazil produces lots of sugar. This sugar can be fermented to make alcohol. Alcohol is a fuel that can be mixed with fossil fuels to run cars.

 In Brazil the amount of fuel used is not reduced. The use of sugar helps the environment and energy reserves. Explain how.

Electric transport

Electric vehicles have been around for a long time.

▶ An old electric milk float

A milk float delivers milk and is powered by electricity. It is a very 'clean' vehicle and makes no fumes. This means that, unlike fossil fuel vehicles, it does not pollute the atmosphere when you use it.

Each evening, after the milk is delivered, the milk float is plugged into the mains electricity supply so the batteries can be recharged. This stores enough energy for a journey of about 35km.

But the electrical energy supplied by the mains is produced at a power station, and most power stations burn fossil fuels which does cause pollution.

b   The electric milk float is supposed to be a very 'clean' vehicle. It can also be described as a 'polluting' vehicle. Explain both of these points of view.

Electric vehicles are becoming more common. They are especially useful when we cannot get around too easily. They are very convenient and can even be used indoors, such as in shopping centres.

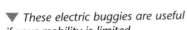

▼ These electric buggies are useful if your mobility is limited

But there is a limit to how far electric vehicles can go between being charged at the mains. Most electric vehicles at the moment have a range of less than 100 miles before they need to be charged. This range will be even smaller if you:

- drive uphill a lot
- carry a large load
- drive at higher speeds.

If we only drove electric vehicles on short local journeys, to go to the shops or the station, this lack of range would not be a problem. But we would need to plan longer journeys carefully so that we could get home again!

Fuel consumption

The fuel consumption of a vehicle depends on the speed the vehicle is being driven at, the style of driving and different driving conditions.

The table shows some data on different vehicles and their fuel consumption. Liquid petroleum gas (LPG) is also a fossil fuel and produces carbon dioxide gas.

Vehicle	Petrol fuel consumption (miles per gallon)	Diesel fuel consumption (miles per gallon)	LPG fuel consumption (miles per gallon)
Family car	43	57	61
People carrier	23	42	LPG version not available
Sports car	27	Diesel version not available	LPG version not available
Van	21	34	LPG version not available

c Which version of the family car has the best fuel consumption – petrol, diesel or LPG?

d Which vehicle has the worst petrol consumption?

How much kinetic energy?

When a mass is stationary it has no kinetic (movement) energy at all. It is only when masses move that they have kinetic energy. Lots of objects around us have kinetic energy: a flying bird, a galloping horse or a speeding car. However, all the kinetic energy is transferred to other forms of energy when they stop. When a car stops, most of its kinetic energy is transferred to heat energy in its brakes.

When a bicycle moves it has kinetic energy. The amount of kinetic energy depends on two things: speed and mass.

> **Keywords**
>
> diesel • fossil fuel • kinetic energy • petrol

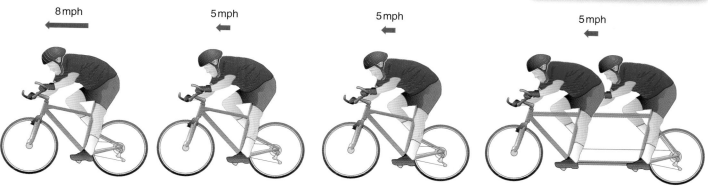

8 mph	5 mph	5 mph	5 mph
high kinetic energy	low kinetic energy	low kinetic energy	high kinetic energy

▲ Kinetic energy depends on speed and mass

As you can see from the diagram above , an object has greater kinetic energy if it is travelling at a higher speed or if it has a greater mass.

Solar-powered vehicles

Solar cells can produce small amounts of electricity from sunlight. This electricity can then be used to provide energy to run things. A solar cell may be used to produce electricity for your calculator. Solar cells can only produce small amounts of energy for their size. They are mostly used to help run low-power devices such as calculators and measuring instruments. If you need more output then you need more solar cells. This can be very expensive.

Solar cell design has improved so that the latest cells can produce more power than the first cells that were developed. Some solar cells charge up batteries during the day to provide electricity for lighting during the night. How realistic are solar-powered cars though? Could solar cells produce enough power to run a family car?

New solar-powered cars are still at the research stage. They are usually small, light and specially shaped to reduce the energy needed to propel them. They are not yet suitable for family cars. Improvements in motor design have developed very efficient electric motors. There have also been improvements in battery design.

Questions

1 Suggest the advantages of using solar-powered cars?

2 What do you think are the disadvantages of using solar-powered cars?

3 Lots of research is done on solar-powered cars. Suggest why.

4 Suggest why it is important to increase the efficiency of electric motors, batteries and solar cells for solar-powered cars.

5 Some designers are thinking about cars that can run on fuel and/or solar power. Suggest why this may be a good idea.

Crash protection

In this item you will find out

- about absorbing energy safely

- about safety features of cars

Each year in Britain about 3 200 people are killed in road accidents. This means about nine people are killed every day.

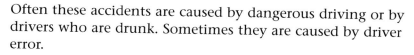

▲ *Testing the safety of a car*

Often these accidents are caused by dangerous driving or by drivers who are drunk. Sometimes they are caused by driver error.

We can get advice on how to drive safely from the Highway Code, driving instructors, TV and the Internet. But no matter how carefully you drive someone else can always run into you.

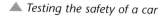

▼ *A skateboarder performs a trick*

Cars are fitted with many safety features. They help reduce injuries in a crash. They are also designed to reduce injury to pedestrians. If you choose to walk, ride or drive, then vehicle safety is important and it could save your life.

Crash protection is not new. We have used the science of collision protection for years. Some crash protection needs to be carried by us, especially when we do some sports.

Skateboarders need protection when they fall. The vulnerable parts of the body need protection because they are likely to hit hard surfaces such as the floor. They need to wear their protective gear as they skate around. A gymnast rarely uses body protection. Instead they perform on a crash mat, which is soft.

a Suggest why the skateboarder's head, knees and elbows need to be protected.

Amazing fact

The padding in the safety pit that a pole vaulter falls into after his jump has to be 1 m deep to fully absorb his kinetic energy.

Absorbing energy

When cars move they have kinetic energy. When cars stop this kinetic energy needs to be absorbed.

If it is absorbed safely by parts of the car, instead of being transferred to the human body, then injuries can be reduced. The brakes on a car absorb energy. The brake pads grip the wheel and stop the car. Forces cause a heating effect and the kinetic energy is absorbed mainly by the brakes.

The **crumple zones** in cars collapse in a crash. They help reduce injuries by changing shape and absorbing energy.

▶ *Crumple zones in a car*

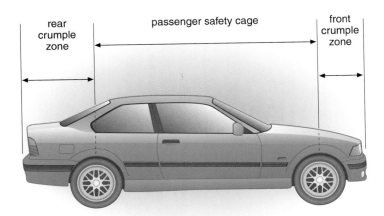

rear crumple zone   passenger safety cage   front crumple zone

Other safety features in cars absorb energy too. Air bags and seat belts help to reduce injuries by changing shape. Seat belts stretch slightly in a crash and need to be replaced afterwards. This is because they may not be able to stretch again in another crash. This would mean that your energy could not be absorbed and your injuries would be much worse.

 If air bags inflate during a crash, they must then be replaced. Suggest why.

Passive safety features

Designers develop cars with many more safety features. Some of these are called **passive safety** features. To us they may seem like luxuries but they also help to prevent injuries.

Electric windows are a luxury but they can be a safety feature. Winding down a window can be distracting. It can mean taking one hand off the steering wheel. That means you are less in control of your car.

Many cars have **paddle shift controls** around the steering wheel, for example for gears or for stereo controls. So, without taking a hand off the steering wheel, you can change gear or control the CD player. This can help you to concentrate on your driving and make you safer.

Making drivers more comfortable is important. Air conditioning keeps the inside of the car at a comfortable temperature. Adjustable seats reduce aches, pains and distractions.

Cruise control helps cars keep to a steady speed. This means the driver does not need to use the pedals. This can reduce tiredness and so improve concentration. If there is a hazard ahead, then the driver brakes and the cruise control is cancelled.

c Explain how electric windows can help to prevent car accidents.

Active safety features

Other features are called **active safety** features.

An **anti-lock braking system (ABS)** help you stop without skidding. They prevent the wheels from locking so that you can stop sooner. They are especially important on a wet road when braking hard. Avoiding skids reduces braking distances.

Traction control can increase or decrease forces to each wheel. This is really helpful on icy or muddy surfaces as it increases friction and grip. It also works on normal roads and reduces the chance of sliding out of control.

The **safety cage** is made of hardened steel. It keeps its shape in a crash. This protects the passengers.

d Explain why traction control is a safety feature.

> **Keywords**
>
> active safety • anti-lock braking system (ABS) • cruise control • crumple zone • paddle shift control • passive safety • safety cage • traction control

▼ Cars are built around safety cages

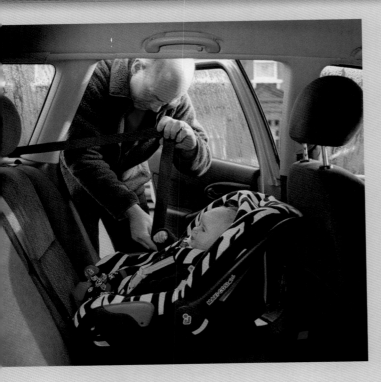

Keeping Ellie safe

Andy and Sarah are the proud parents of a baby girl called Ellie. They are keen to get baby Ellie home from the hospital.

When they leave the nurse checks that the car has a good baby seat. The nurse is pleased that the baby seat faces backwards but there is a problem. Although the seat is a safe one, it is in the front seat next to where Sarah will be driving. The nurse says that because there are air bags in the front, Ellie must have her baby seat in the back of the car.

Andy fits the seat in the back of the car and makes sure that any loose items, such as bags, are put in the boot.

When Ellie gets older she will sit in her brother Robin's front-facing car seat. He can't use it any longer because his mass is more than 32 kg. It has wide straps that stretch a little in a crash. This seat is rigid and well padded with foam and spongy materials. Its size can be adjusted as Ellie grows.

Questions

1   Why do you think it is a good idea for baby seats to face backwards?

2   Explain why Ellie's baby seat should be put in the rear of the car?

3   Andy puts the bags in the boot. Suggest reasons why it can be dangerous to leave them loose in the car.

4   Why do you think there is a mass limit and not an age limit on Robin's car seat?

5   Robin's car seat belt has wide straps that stretch a little in a crash. Suggest reasons why.

6   Why do you think it is not a good idea to buy a second-hand child's car seat?

What a drag!

When you drop an object on Earth it always falls downwards. This is because the force on the object due to gravity (the object's weight) pulls the object towards the centre of the Earth.

Objects accelerate as they fall so they get faster. But **drag** from the air in the Earth's atmosphere provides a force in the opposite direction. This slows the object down.

The Moon is the only natural body away from the Earth that people have visited. It has gravity so things fall downwards, but the force of gravity is less than on Earth.

There is no atmosphere on the Moon to provide any resistance so a dropped object would get faster and faster. There would be no limit to its speed, until it hit the Moon! The same can happen in outer space where there is no atmosphere either.

We often forget about gravity because we are always under its influence here on Earth. But we can clearly see its effect when people jump out of aeroplanes and then fall safely to Earth using parachutes. Skydivers need to understand forces to keep them safe and increase their fun.

a If skydivers jumped from a greater height would they be able to go faster than 200 km/h? Explain your answer.

Amazing fact

Skydivers can reach speeds of up to 200 km/h.

▲ Gravity in action

▲ On the Moon, the hammer and the feather fall at the same speed because there is no atmosphere to cause drag

drag

weight

▲ Forces on a parachute

▲ A shuttlecock

What is drag?

If a person jumps out of an aeroplane and opens a parachute, the parachute pushes air particles out of the way. This causes an upward **frictional force** called air resistance or drag. This slows the parachute down. Drag and other frictional forces always act against the movement of an object.

A fast-moving parachute pushes more air particles out of the way. A wide parachute also pushes more particles out of the way. The drag forces increase with speed and with the surface area of the parachute.

Players of some sports use drag to help them defeat their opponents. In badminton the shuttlecock has a shape that causes a lot of drag. The shuttlecock moves quickly at first then slows down.

 Suggest another sport where drag is an advantage.

Terminal speed

When objects fall through the Earth's atmosphere they get faster and faster until they reach a speed where the forces of drag and weight are equal. This is called the **terminal speed**.

Look at the diagram of the skydiver. Her weight is always the same. Her changing speed changes the drag forces.

At the start of the dive, her speed is 10 m/s and is increasing because her weight is more than the drag. When she gets faster her drag force increases.

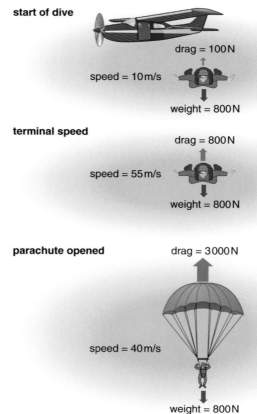

start of dive

drag = 100 N

speed = 10 m/s

weight = 800 N

terminal speed

drag = 800 N

speed = 55 m/s

weight = 800 N

parachute opened

drag = 3000 N

speed = 40 m/s

weight = 800 N

▶ Forces on a skydiver

When her drag and weight forces are equal she moves at a steady speed and stops accelerating. Her terminal speed is 55 m/s.

When she opens her parachute her drag is much larger than her weight so she slows down to 40 m/s. As she continues to slow down the drag force is reduced until it equals her weight again. She then moves at a slower steady speed.

Free fall

A spaceship accelerates towards the surface of the Moon. The table shows how much the speed of the object changes each second.

Time (s)	0	2	4	6	8	10	12	14	16
Speed (m/s)	0	3.2	6.4	9.6	12.8	16.0	19.2	22.4	25.6

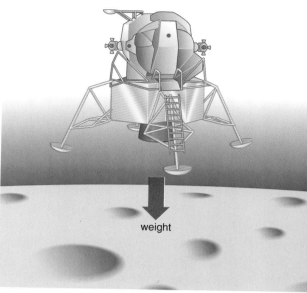

▲ *Falling spaceship*

The falling spaceship has only one force on it. That is the downward force of weight. There is no drag force as the Moon has no atmosphere. The speed increases steadily and the acceleration is constant. This is known as **free-fall** acceleration.

c Why do you think a spaceship would not use a parachute when landing on the Moon?

d Suggest how a spaceship could reduce its speed.

Unwanted drag

Drag can be useful if you are trying to slow down, but it can also be a nuisance when you are trying to go faster.

Racing cars need to be able to go as fast as possible to win, so they have a shape which allows air particles to flow more easily around them so the drag or air resistance is reduced.

Some high-speed sports find drag and friction a nuisance. A downhill skier reduces the drag of the air by wearing a tight smooth suit. He can also put wax on his skis. This wax lubricates the ski and reduces friction.

Lorries and caravans are not very streamlined so they can be slowed down a lot by drag. Some have deflectors to help the air flow over them. This helps reduce fuel costs.

e Suggest how the roof box on top of a car can reduce its top speed.

Keywords

drag • free fall • frictional force • terminal speed

▼ *Racing cars need to reduce drag*

▲ A skydiver

All fall down

Karen is investigating falling objects. She is interested in why some things fall quicker than others. She knows that when a ball falls it accelerates because its weight pulls it down.

She wonders though what would happen if there were no drag to slow it down. She predicts what would happen and the table shows her predictions of the speed of the ball after each second.

Time (s)	0	1	2	3	4	5	6
Speed (m/s)	0	10	20	30	40	50	60

Karen also collects some data from the Internet on the speed of skydivers when they are affected by air resistance or drag.

The table shows the downward speed of a skydiver as she falls.

Time (s)	0	2	4	6	8	10	12	14	16	18	20	24	26	28
Speed (m/s)	0	19	34	45	52	55	55	55	55	20	5	5	5	0

Questions

1 Look at the first table with Karen's predictions. Draw these results on graph paper with the vertical axis from 0 to 60 m/s and the horizontal axis from 0 to 30 s.

2 How much does the speed increase each second?

3 What is the acceleration of the ball in m/s²?

4 Look at the table of the falling skydiver. Draw these results on graph paper.

5 What was the skydiver's highest speed in m/s?

6 At what time do you think the skydiver opened her parachute?

7 What was the skydiver's speed in m/s when she reached the ground?

8 When was her deceleration highest? (When did the speed change most quickly?)

The science of fun

In this item you will find out

- about gravitational potential energy and what affects it

- how gravitational potential energy is converted to kinetic energy

- how energy is used in theme rides

▲ Having fun with kinetic and potential energy

Theme ride designers make use of your kinetic and potential energy. You gain potential energy when the ride goes uphill. You gain kinetic energy as the ride falls towards Earth. Designers have a scientific understanding about the forces on you and how they can affect and scare you. They are experts on how far they can go safely. Most people are not experts on forces and so they can be scared.

Do not fear the science of fun – enjoy the ride because you are in safe hands!

When we stretch a catapult we are doing work against the elastic force. This energy can be stored until you want to fire the stone. The energy stored in the catapult is called **elastic potential energy**. This is the energy stored in the elastic force field.

When the elastic is released the potential energy quickly changes to kinetic energy, and is transferred to the stone which then speeds away.

a A catapult uses stored elastic energy which is converted into kinetic energy. Name three other things that change stored elastic energy into kinetic energy.

> **Amazing fact**
>
> **Some of the world's roller coasters are higher than 130 m, longer than 2 km and move you at speeds up to 120 mph.**

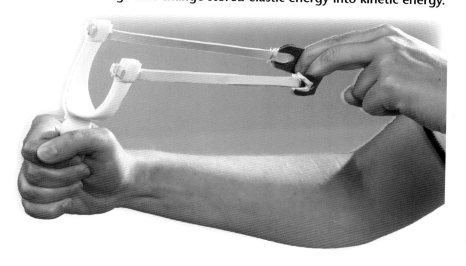
◄ Elastic potential energy

Gravitational potential energy

On Earth we are always being acted upon by the force of gravity.

When a baggage handler lifts a case off the ground, the case has potential, or stored, energy due to gravity. This is called **gravitational potential energy**. If the baggage handler drops the case, gravity pulls it back towards the Earth.

The amount of gravitational potential energy objects have depends on their mass and position in the Earth's gravitational field. The more mass an object has, the greater its gravitational potential energy. The higher an object is, the greater its gravitational potential energy.

UNCLAIMED BAGGAGE

◀ The baggage handler is giving the cases gravitational potential energy

b Look at the diagram of the baggage handler lifting three cases.

(i) Which case has the least gravitational potential energy?

(ii) Which case has the most gravitational potential energy?

The baggage handler gives potential energy to the bags when he lifts them. This work can be tiring. Any object lifted up gains potential energy: a flying helicopter, a ball thrown into the sky or a person climbing a diving board. Sometimes this energy is useful. The diver uses the potential energy she has at the top on the diving board to change to kinetic energy as she falls into the pool.

The gravitational potential energy of an object also increases when the force of gravity (gravitational field strength (g)) increases. On Jupiter gravity is about three times stronger than on the Earth. This means if objects of the same mass were lifted the same height on the Earth and Jupiter, the object on Jupiter would have greater gravitational potential energy.

Kinetic energy

When objects move they have kinetic energy.

The table shows the kinetic energy of two remote-controlled cars at different speeds. One car is twice the mass of the other.

Speed of car (m/s)	Kinetic energy of small car (mass = 1 kg (J))	Kinetic energy of large car (mass = 2 kg (J))
0	0	0
1	0.5	1.0
2	2.0	4.0
3	4.5	9.0
4	8.0	16.0
5	12.5	25.0
6	18.0	36.0

▼ Hydroelectric power station

As you can see from the table, the kinetic energy of the larger car is twice the kinetic energy of the smaller car. So doubling the mass doubles the kinetic energy.

The cars have a lot more kinetic energy when they move faster. If the speed doubles the kinetic energy quadruples.

Converting energy

A hydroelectric power station exploits gravitational potential energy. Water is held high up in a reservoir behind a dam. When the water is released, the gravitational potential energy of the water changes to kinetic energy as the water falls. The kinetic energy drives a turbine which turns a generator and creates electricity.

 High-energy output hydroelectric power stations have reservoirs with a large mass of water very high up in the mountains. Explain why.

On the roller coaster

Roller coaster rides usually start with the highest climb. The cars are pulled up by a chain which is powered by an electric motor. Once you have reached the top you have maximum gravitational potential energy.

As you start to go down, this energy is changed into kinetic energy and you go faster. Sometimes the energy is changed back to gravitational potential energy as you climb another hill. This may be repeated several times. But it cannot continue for ever. Kinetic energy is also transferred to heat energy due to friction and air resistance so you eventually come to rest.

Keywords

elastic potential energy •
gravitational potential energy

Try the log flume – if you dare!

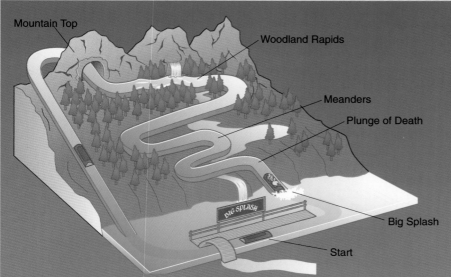

Mountain Top
Woodland Rapids
Meanders
Plunge of Death
Big Splash
Start
BIG SPLASH

The log flume is one of our most popular rides in the park. It is not our fastest ride but it is our wettest!

Enjoy the steep climb at the start which lifts you to the highest part of the ride –'Mountain Top'. Wait at the top until the pumped water sweeps you down. Enjoy the 'Woodland Rapids' where you quickly cruise through the forest. Then relax as you slowly travel the 'Meanders'.

The Meanders will give you a rest before entering the 'Plunge of Death.' Be prepared for the terror as you look over the steepest slope on the ride. This is the fastest part of the ride until you hit the 'Big Splash'.

When you hit the water we can promise you three things:

◆ your deceleration will be the highest on the ride
◆ you will feel the biggest forces on the ride
◆ you will be without doubt at your wettest.

Questions

1 Why does the 'Mountain Top' have to be the highest part of the ride?

2 How does the water get its gravitational potential energy?

3 Which part has the steeper slope? 'Woodland Rapids' or the 'Meanders'. Explain your answer.

4 Why is the 'Plunge of Death' the fastest part of the ride?

5 The log flume hits the water in the 'Big Splash'.

   (a) Why is the deceleration here the largest on the ride?
   (b) What has happened to the energy of the log flume?

P3a

1 Ifzal wants to check the speed of cars outside his school.

  a What two measurements should he take? [2]
  b What equipment does he need to take these two measurements? [2]
  c What units do we use for the two measurements we need to calculate speed? [2]

2 A toy moves 10 m in 5 s. It then stays still for 2 s.

  a Calculate its speed for the first 5 s. [3]
  b Sketch a distance–time graph describing how the toy moves. [1]

3 A speed camera is placed near white lines painted on a road. The speed camera takes two photographs of a speeding car. Explain how the speed of the car can be found out. [3]

4 On motorways during roadworks, there are often signs which state Maximum average speed 40 mph.

  a How are the average speeds of cars measured?
  b Why is this better than installing one speed camera in the road works area?

5 The distance by train from London to Stoke-on-Trent is 160 miles. The journey time is 1 hour 45 minutes.

  a What is the average speed of the train is mph?
  b What would be the time of the journey if the average speed was 100 mph?

P3b

1 Look at the speed–time graph.

  a Which part of the graph shows constant speed? [1]
  b Which part of the graph shows increasing speed? [1]
  c Which part of the graph shows decreasing speed? [1]
  d What does 'acceleration' mean? [1]
  e Which units do we use for acceleration? [1]

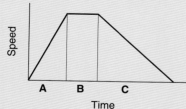

2 Look at the speed–time graph.

  a Which part of the graph shows the highest acceleration? [1]
  b Which part of the graph shows the lowest acceleration? [1]

c In part A of the graph the speed increases from 0 m/s to 10 m/s in 5 s. Calculate the acceleration. [3]

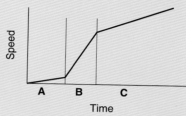

3 Describe experiments you coud do to measure the accleration of a:

  a mountain bike [3]
  b car. [3]

4 What is the correct unit of acceleration?

  A m/s/s
  B m/s
  C m/s^2
  D m

5 What name is given to negative acceleration ?

P3c

1 Look at the diagram of stopping distances for a car.

| 12 metres thinking distance | 24 metres braking distance |

  a What does thinking distance mean? [2]
  b What does braking distance mean? [1]
  c Calculate the total stopping distance for the car. [1]

2 **a** Write down three factors that can increase thinking distance. [3]
  b Write down three factors that can increase braking distance. [3]

3 A car accelerates at 2 m/s^2. Its mass is 1500 kg. Calculate the driving force.
Use force = mass × acceleration. [3]

4 Two objects have masses of 1000 kg and 2000 kg. They are both accelerated by the same driving force. How would their accelerations differ?

5 A driving force of 1000N is applied to an object and the acceleration is 0.5 m/s^2. What is the mass of the object?

P3d

1 Dale does some work carrying furniture up a flight of stairs.

   a He does more work when he climbs two flights of stairs. Suggest why. [1]

   b He does more work when he lifts heavier furniture upstairs. Suggest why. [1]

   c Which units do we use to measure work? Choose from:

     joules   newtons   metres   watts [1]

   d Dale runs upstairs and produces lots of power. Which units do we use to measure power? Choose from:

     joules   newtons   metres   watts [1]

2 Heidi pulls the sledge a distance of 30 m with a 200 N force.

   a Calculate the work done on the sledge. [3]

   b Heidi then pulls her friend on the sledge. She now does 20 000 J of work in 40 s. Calculate the power she needs to do this. [3]

3 Cars burn petrol or diesel in their engines. Some cars use more fuel than others. List and explain the problems this causes. [6]

4 Joe takes part in a cycle race. He applies a constant force of 60 N throughout the race and travels 100 m. His time for the race is 5 s.

50N   50N

100m

   a What is his average speed? (Look back to P3a)

   b How much work has he done?

   c What is his power during the race?

5 Which of the following are units of power?

   A joule

   B joule per second

   C newton per second

   D watt

P3e

1 **a** Which are the two most common fuels used in cars? Choose from:

     alcohol   diesel   LPG   petrol   coal [2]

   b Look at the table. It shows the fuel consumption of different cars.

Car	Fuel consumption/miles per gallon
A	25
B	38
C	42
D	30
E	21

     i Which car has the best fuel consumption? [1]

     ii Which car has the worst fuel consumption? [1]

2 **a** Electric cars are encouraged in cities. Suggest a reason why. [1]

   b Explain how they collect and use their energy. [2]

   c Electric cars can cause pollution. Explain how. [2]

3 Look at the list of moving objects. They all have different amounts of kinetic energy.

   A Bicycle and rider moving at 25 km/hr

   B Bird flying at 50 km/hr

   C Bus moving at 50 km/hr

   D Car moving at 50 km/hr

   E Motorbike moving at 50 km/hr

   F Wasp flying at 25 km/hr

Arrange them in order of amounts of kinetic energy. Put the highest one first. [6]

4 Which of the following affect the kinetic energy of a car?

The speed it is travelling at
The type of fuel it uses
The mass of the car
Its acceleration

5 A Toyota Prius is a hybrid car with a petrol engine and an electric battery.

It does not have to have the battery recharged overnight like an electric milk float.

Suggest why.

P3f

1 Cars have many features. Look at the list.

air bags   cruise control   crumple zones electric windows

a Which two are active safety features? [2]
b Which two are passive safety features? [2]

2 a Seat belts reduce injuries in a crash. Explain how they do this. [2]
b How can ABS brakes make driving safer? [2]
c How can electric windows help make driving safer? [1]
d How does an air bag help reduce injuries in a crash? [1]
e Seat belts must be replaced after a crash. Suggest why. [1]

3 Aisha makes some paper crumple zones for model cars. Describe an experiment she could do to test these crumple zones. [3]

4 Cars eighty years ago did not have the safety features we find in modern cars today. Suggest reasons why they would not be as necessary as they are today.

5 Active safety features tend to be fitted to even the cheaper cars but passive safety features are often fitted to only the most expensive models. Suggest why.

P3g

1 A skydiver falls from a plane.

a What happens to his speed for the first few seconds? [1]
b What is the name of the force that pulls him down? [1]
c A force tries to slow him down.
  i What is the name of this force? [1]
  ii In which direction does this force act on the skydiver? [1]
  iii This force does not act on spaceships in outer space or near the Moon's surface. Explain why? [2]

2 Ellie drops a closed parachute in the laboratory. It increases speed at first. The parachute then opens and slows down. It eventually reaches a terminal speed.

In the following three questions use the ideas of forces in your answers.

a Why does the speed of the closed parachute increase? [2]
b Why does the open parachute slow down? [2]
c Why does the parachute reach a terminal speed? [1]

3 Describe an experiment to work out the terminal speed of a falling shuttlecock in badminton. [4]

4 a What name is given to the maximum speed that an object can fall at?
b Explain why the object remains at this constant speed and does not accelerate further

P3h

1 Look at the list of objects. They all have energy.

A hot air balloon rising through the clouds
B lorry rolling down hill
C electric train speeding along a level track
D an apple hanging from a tree

a Which one has only gravitational potential energy? [1]
b Which one has only kinetic energy? [1]
c Which two have kinetic and gravitational potential energy? [2]
d Which one is gaining gravitational potential energy? [1]
e Which one is losing gravitational potential energy? [1]

2 A roller coaster starts off at the highest point of the ride. It accelerates downhill to the bottom of the slope. It then climbs up to another high point before accelerating and travelling downhill again to the lowest point on the ride.

a Why do you think the start of the ride is the highest point? [1]
b What happens to the kinetic and gravitational potential energy when the roller coaster is travelling downhill? [1]
c What happens to the kinetic and gravitational potential energy when the roller coaster is climbing uphill? [1]
d The lowest point of the ride is the fastest. Explain why. [2]

3 A 4 × 4 car has a mass of 2000 kg. It moves at 40 km/hr.

a What happens to its KE if its speed is doubled to 80 km/hr? [1]
b The car pulls a trailer. The trailer has a mass of 2000 kg. the car pulls the trailer at 40 km/hr. What happens to its KE? [1]

4 A rubber ball is dropped from a height of 1 metre onto a concrete surface. It bounces up to a height of 80cm.

a Describe the energy changes that take place.
b What is the efficiency?

P4 Radiation for life

- A paramedic can electrocute you safely. If you suffer a heart attack, the paramedic will give you a huge electric shock to restart your heart. In hospitals radiographers inject radioactive liquid into people or make the patients swallow radioactive liquids. This sounds dangerous. So why are these people happy to have radioactive substances in their bodies?

- Many people want renewable energy and there are thousands of wind farms being built in the UK. Some environmental groups don't like wind power because it removes energy from the wind and harms birdlife. But what is the alternative? Some people see nuclear power as the cleanest way to generate electricity but others complain about the dangerous nuclear waste. Can scientists make nuclear waste safe?

Nuclear power should be banned. It's too dangerous.

Nuclear power is cleaner than any other way of generating electricity.

I don't see how radiation can generate electricity.

What you need to know

- What electrical conductors, insulators and resistors do.

- What alpha, beta and gamma radiation are.

- What an atom is made of.

Static electricity can kill

In this item you will find out

- why synthetic clothing can cling to you

- why you can get an electric shock when you are shopping

- how static electricity can be dangerous

When your clothes cling to you it can be very annoying. When you walk around a shop then get a shock when you touch the clothes rail, it can be painful. These effects are caused by **static electricity**

There are two types of electrostatic charge. There is **positive charge** and **negative charge**. Everything contains both positive and negative charge.

When you rub a balloon on your jumper there is friction. The friction tears tiny particles called **electrons** off the balloon and they stick to your jumper. Electrons have a negative charge. The jumper gets extra electrons so it becomes negatively charged. The balloon now has fewer electrons so it becomes positively charged.

When you put the balloon against the wall it will be attracted and stick to the wall because of the electrons in the wall. This is because positive charge **attracts** negative charge. If you rub together two materials that are **insulators**, like the balloon and jumper, they will often become charged.

So why do your clothes cling to you? If your clothes are made of synthetic materials instead of natural fibres like cotton or wool, they will get an electrostatic charge on them as you walk along because of friction as they rub together. Unlike charges attract each other so your clothes will attract and cling to each other. If you use anti-static fabric conditioner, it should stop your clothes getting an electrostatic charge on them, so they won't cling.

a Why should you choose natural fabrics for your clothes if you don't want them to cling?

▲ Static electricity makes your clothes cling

▼ Electrostatic charge makes the balloons stick to the wall

▲ *Combing your hair can be a hair-raising experience*

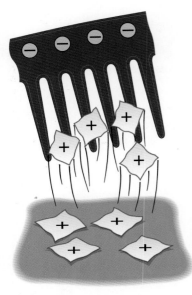

▲ *Unlike charges attract*

Charging a head

Comb clean hair and you might find your hair will stand on end. Friction makes your hair get a positive charge. At the same time your plastic comb gets a negative charge

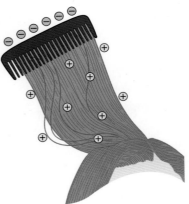

Repelled

Your hair will stand on end because each hair is positively charged. Charges that are the same, such as two positive or two negative, will **repel** each other because like charges repel.

b Explain why after you have combed your hair with a plastic comb your hair will be attracted to the comb.

Attracted

Put the comb near to tiny pieces of paper or cork and they will jump up onto the comb. This is because different (unlike) charges attract each other and the negatively charged comb attracts the paper or cork because of the positive charge in them.

c Suggest why the end of a long piece of Sellotape seems to drift towards the paper before you stick it down.

Exploding custard

Electrostatic charges can cause explosions in food factories. Sometimes flour, sugar or custard powder gets an electrostatic charge on it. The powder is so light it floats in the air. Workers can cause a spark from their clothing as their clothes rub together. The spark can set fire to the powder. If there's plenty of oxygen to help things burn, the powder can explode, like gunpowder.

Exploding ships

Oil tankers can explode too. The oil vapour droplets in an empty tanker will float around in the air. If the droplets with positive charge on get separated from the droplets with negative charge on, there can be a spark between the charged particles and this can make the oil vapour ignite and blow the ship apart.

d Explain how an electrostatic charge can cause explosions in custard factories or flour mills.

◀ *Electrostatic charge can cause explosions*

Can you die of shock?

You can die of shock – especially if it is an **electric shock**. You are a good conductor of electricity. Touch something that has a large electrostatic charge on it and the charge will flow through you. You get an electric shock because the charge flowing through you makes your muscles contract. It can even stop your heart beating.

Shocking shopping

Shopping can be shocking. You can get an electric shock when you are out shopping. As you walk across a carpet or plastic laminate flooring, the friction between your shoes and the carpet or flooring will generate an electrostatic charge on your body. This is because the carpet or flooring is an insulator. When you touch a metal object like a clothes rail or a water pipe, the charge will jump from you onto the metal object. You feel a slight electric shock.

▼ *When electric charge flows through your body you get an electric shock*

e Why do you think you can get a shock in shops with carpets but not in shops with wooden floors?

Static nuisance

Often you will notice much more dust on a TV screen than on a radiator. This is because the TV screen is an insulator and the metal radiator is a conductor. Dust particles have electrostatic charge on them so when they land on a TV they will stick to it – the charge cannot flow away because the screen is an insulator.

f Explain why dust doesn't stick to radiators as much as to TV screens.

Keywords

attract • electric shock • electron • insulator • negative charge • positive charge • repel • static electricity

Electrostatic dusters make cleaning easier by trapping dust among the fibres

Making a profit

Some companies who manufacture household products are making money out of electrostatics. Should we believe what they say in their adverts?

Dust particles are mainly made of dead human skin. Often the dust has an electrostatic charge on it.

When the dust particles land on a plastic container or TV screen, they stick to it because plastic is an insulator and the electrostatic charges cannot be discharged (flow away).

Now manufacturers are using special fibres called electret fibres to make dusters. Electret fibres have an electrostatic charge on them.

By making dusters and dusting brushes that are electrostatically charged, these manufacturers are making sure that the dusters attract the dust instead of flicking it around the room.

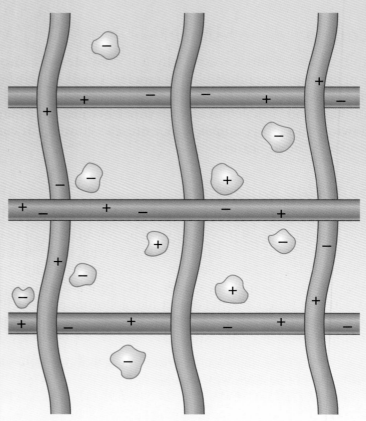

The dust is trapped because unlike charges attract each other

Questions

1 Why is there usually far more dust in your bedroom than in the kitchen or the living room?

2 Why does dust stick to plastic things more than it sticks to metal things?

3 What is the name of the special fibres that manufacturers are using to make dusters?

4 What is special about these fibres that they are using to make dusters?

5 Why do electrostatic dusters work better than normal dusters?

6 Do you think we should believe the claims that manufacturers of these dusters make for their products? Explain your reasons.

Hearts, chimneys and paint!

In this item you will find out

- how paramedics use electrostatics to save heart attack victims
- how electrostatics can clean smoke from chimneys
- why putting electrostatic charge on spray paints is a good idea

▲ Lightning can destroy buildings

Lightning kills more people every year than snow, hurricanes or tornadoes. In the UK about 30–60 people are struck by lightning every year and on average three people die. A lightning strike is a huge bolt of electricity.

However, a paramedic in a hospital can use a huge bolt of electricity to save a heart attack victim. They have to be careful to send the electricity through the body in the correct way. They use a **defibrillator** and place the large paddles onto each side of the patient's chest. It is important to remove the patient's clothes to get good contact with the skin.

▼ An electric shock can stop the heart and kill you or, in the hands of a trained paramedic, it can start the heart and save your life

The paddles are charged up and then the charge flows through the patient. The charge will make the patient's heart contract strongly, which should start it beating again. It is important that the operator does not get a shock as this would be painful and may be dangerous. This is why they tell any doctors or nurses near the patient to 'stand clear'.

Apart from saving patients' lives, there are many other places where electrostatic charges are used to make life easier:
- cleaning up the smoke that comes out of factory or power station chimneys
- printing documents with photocopiers and laser printers
- paint spraying.

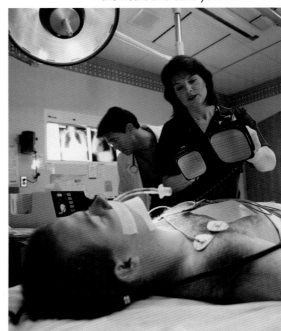

Amazing fact

A defibrillator pumps 360 J of energy into a patient's body. This is the same as the energy consumed by an electric light bulb in four seconds. However, the shock to the heart is delivered in only a fraction of a second.

▲ Didcot power station burns coal to produce electricity

Removing pollution

The ash from coal-fired power stations contains more radioactivity than is allowed in the low-level nuclear waste released from nuclear power stations. Didcot power station in Oxfordshire produces about 3 420 tonnes of ash per day. 80% of this ash flies up the huge chimneys in smoke where **electrostatic dust precipitators** remove 99.9% of it.

a How many tonnes of ash go up the chimneys of Didcot power station every day?

b How much is removed by the electrostatic dust precipitators?

Charges suck

In a simple electrostatic dust precipitator, opposite high voltages or potential differences (pds – plus and minus) are put on two grids in the chimneys. The ash is carried up the chimney by the hot air rising. The positive grid makes the dust particles positive by tearing the electrons off it. The negative grid attracts the dust, because unlike charges attract.

The dust particles clump together to form larger particles that eventually become heavy enough to fall back down the chimney into containers.

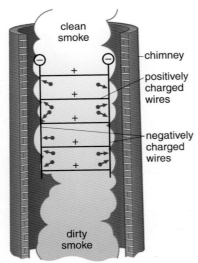

clean smoke

chimney

positively charged wires

negatively charged wires

dirty smoke

↘ positively charged dust particles attracted to plates

▲ The ash particles are charged positive as they pass the positive grid and then they are attracted to the negative grid

▲ Ash from the chimneys is collected and made into building materials

Charging paint

Paint spraying a car is much faster than painting by hand. But a lot of paint is wasted as it sticks to everything, and not just to the car. One way to save paint (and money) is to charge up the spray gun so that the paint droplets pick up electrostatic charge. This means all the particles have the same type of charge and so they repel each other. This makes the droplets of paint spread out and become a fine spray.

The car is charged opposite to the spray and so the spray is attracted to the car and gives an even coating. This is because unlike charges attract. The whole process is much less wasteful and more effective and the spray will find its way into cracks and crevices that the operator could not see.

◄ *Charging the spray means that the car attracts the paint*

c Explain why charging paint gives a fine, spread-out spray.

d Why does the paint stick well to the car?

Copying... copying... copying

Photocopiers use static electricity to make copies. There is a huge round drum in the copier made of a material that can be charged up. Inside the copier a bright light reflects off the paper you want to copy onto the drum. The white bits on the page reflect lots of light onto the drum and the drum loses its electrostatic charge.

The black bits do not reflect the light so those parts of the drum stay charged. The ink (toner) sticks to the parts of the drum that are charged. As the drum goes round it sticks the toner onto the paper and a heater warms up the paper to make it stick permanently.

A laser printer is similar. In a laser printer the laser writes the page and discharges the drum, leaving the background with a positive charge and the written areas with a negative charge. The toner is positive so sticks to the letters and not to the background.

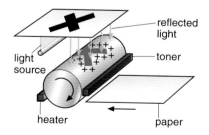

▲ *Electrostatic charge sticks the ink to the drum in a photocopier*

Keywords

defibrillator • electrostatic
dust precipitator •
photocopier

How candles help kill bacteria

People do not usually expect scientists to be experimenting on candles, but Dr Lindsey Gaunt at the University of Southampton is working on a project that can explain why candles made with essential oils can be very good at killing harmful bacteria.

Q: How did you get into working with candles?
Lindsey: We knew that essential oils like orange oil, thyme oil and citronella oil are all good at killing different bacteria. We needed to heat the oil to get it into the air. We were surprised that, when we used a candle to heat them, more bacteria were killed than when we just heated the oils in a pot.

Q: So why was the candle better than heating the oil in a pot?
Lindsey: Candle flames make ions in the air. Ions are particles with an electrostatic charge. Ions can kill bacteria as they make the bacteria cell wall weaker.

Q: So where does the essential oil come in?
Lindsey: Once the cell wall has been made weaker, the essential oil can then get in and this kills bacteria more quickly than the ions on their own.

Q: How do you know it was the ions that made the difference?
Lindsey: We did another experiment where we put a metal grid over the bacteria so that fewer ions could get in. This time more bacteria survived.

Questions

1 What are the essential oils that Lindsey says can kill bacteria?

2 Why did they need to heat the oils?

3 How did they heat the oils?

4 How did Lindsey work out that using a candle was better than heating the oil in a pot?

5 What is an ion?

Keeping safe

In this item you will find out

- how an electric circuit works
- what is inside a 3-pin plug
- why you need fuses and circuit breakers to be safe

All new appliances have to have a 3-pin plug fitted when you buy them. Older appliances may need their plugs replacing if, for example, the casing cracks. It is essential to do this correctly if you want to use the appliance safely.

Every plug has two or three coloured wires.

Colour	Name	Function
brown	**live wire**	carries high voltage
blue	**neutral wire**	completes the circuit
yellow and green (if present)	**earth wire**	safety wire to prevent the casing of the appliance becoming live

The green and yellow earth wire is connected to the metal casing of the appliance (which is a conductor) so that the casing can never become live. This means it can never get an electric charge on it because the electric charge will flow away along the earth wire. When this happens, a correctly rated fuse or circuit breaker will blow or trip.

Some plugs do not have an earth wire. This is because the appliance has a plastic case. A plastic case can never get a charge on it (become live) because it is an insulator. This means there is no need for the earth wire to take the electric charge away. Appliances like this are called **double insulated**.

a What colour is the live wire in a 3-pin plug?

b Which wire is sometimes missing from a 3-pin plug?

c In a double insulated appliance, what is the casing made of?

▲ *Plugs are safer when intact*

▼ *Damaged plugs must be replaced*

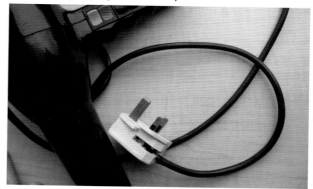

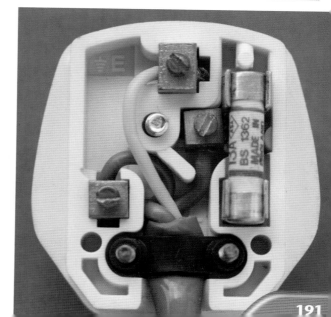

▶ *A safely-wired 3-pin plug*

On the move

Static electricity is charge that does not move. As soon as the charge moves, it is an electric current. Charge can only flow through an electrical conductor such as metals or carbon. It cannot flow through insulators such as rubber and most plastics. To make a working electric **circuit**, you have to have a complete loop for the current to flow round.

Controlling your circuit

If you want a large current to flow in the circuit you can use a large **potential difference** (pd) or voltage to drive it, or you can keep the **resistance** small which means the current finds it easier to pass through the circuit.

	Cause	Effect
For given resistor	higher pd	higher current
	lower pd	lower current
For given pd	higher resistance	lower current
	lower resistance	higher current

d If in a circuit the pd remains at 12V but the resistance is doubled, what effect would you expect this to have on the current?

e If in a circuit the resistance remains the same but the pd is halved, what effect do you expect this to have on the current?

Your resistance is low

If you want to change the current in a circuit you can use a variable resistor called a **rheostat**. You can see one in the photograph below. You slide the handle along to change its resistance and control the current.

▶ *Moving the sliding handle changes the resistance of the rheostat*

Working it out

For most circuits kept at a steady temperature you can work out the resistance you need to get a certain current.

$$\text{resistance} = \frac{\text{voltage}}{\text{current}}$$

resistance is in ohms

voltage is in volts (symbol V)

current is in amps (symbol A)

For example, if the voltage of the circuit is 12 volts, and the current you require is 0.5 amps, then you can calculate the resistance you have to put into the circuit:

$$\text{resistance} = \frac{\text{voltage}}{\text{current}}$$

$$\text{resistance} = \frac{12\,\text{V}}{0.5\,\text{A}}$$

resistance = 24 ohms

f Work out the resistance in the circuit if the pd is 220 volts and the current you want is 10 amps.

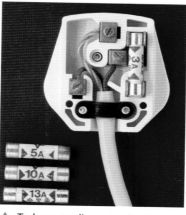

▲ To keep appliances safe, the correct fuse should be put into the plug

When the fuse blows

If an appliance develops a fault, a very high current might flow through the wires. This might melt the wires and cause a fire. If the plug has the correct **fuse** in it, this high current will melt the fuse and break the circuit. This stops the current flowing before any damage can be done.

If the wrong fuse is in the plug, it may not melt in time and so the high current keeps on flowing and this is how electrical fires start.

g Explain how a fuse can make you safer.

Resetting... resetting... resetting

When the fuse in a plug blows it often causes the fuse in a fuse box to blow as an extra precaution. Older fuse boxes contain strips of metal fuse wire that melt.

More modern fuse boxes contain resettable **circuit breakers** that trip (switch off), so they are often called trip switches. These can be reset but it is sensible to check what tripped it in the first place to make sure no one is in danger. Lawn mowers often have a special plug with a circuit breaker in it.

h Why is it important to check why a resettable fuse tripped before you reset it?

▲ These fuses 'trip' if there is a problem

Keywords

circuit • circuit breaker • double insulated • earth wire • fuse • live wire • neutral wire • potential difference • resistance • rheostat

▲ *A qualified electrician rewiring a socket*

Qualified electricians only

A new law makes it illegal to do electrical wiring in the kitchen, bathroom or garden unless you are a qualified electrician or you can prove that you can satisfy safety regulations. On average 10 people die and 750 are seriously injured each year because of faulty electrical wiring.

Kitchens, bathrooms and gardens have taps or water features. If you touch a faulty electrical installation with wet hands you are very likely to get an electric shock, which could kill or injure you. This is because wet hands make a very good electrical connection for the current to flow through.

The new law means that anyone who does wiring work but who isn't qualified may be fined £5 000. And if you do work in your own house you may not be able to sell the house because it will be unsafe.

But you are still not completely safe in your living room or bedroom. A girl aged 10 was killed when she stood on the gas pipe and reached up to switch on the Christmas tree lights. She touched the metal part of the empty bulb holder in a lamp where her father had connected the wires from the Christmas tree lights. The current flowed straight through her to the metal gas pipe and she died instantly.

Questions

1 What does the new law stop you doing if you are not a qualified electrician?

2 How many people died in the last 10 years because of faulty electrical installations?

3 Why is it more dangerous to have a faulty electrical installation in the kitchen than in the living room?

4 How many people are injured every year by faulty installations?

5 Explain why the electric current flowed through the girl who was killed.

Ultrasound is important

In this item you will find out

- about the ultrasound scan you received before you were born

- that shock waves from ultrasound can shatter kidney stones in your body

- that ultrasound can measure your blood flowing in your body

Mice make squeaks that we cannot hear, but a cat can hear. These squeaks are very high pitch sound called **ultrasound**. Dogs and bats can also hear ultrasound

▲ ▼ *Bats, cats and mice can hear ultrasound*

The highest pitch sound that a human can hear is called the **upper threshold of human hearing**. For most people this is about 20 000 vibrations per second (written as 20 000 Hz) when they are very young, but this gets lower as they get older. Ultrasound is sound above about 22 000 Hz.

When you are about 15 your upper threshold of hearing may be down as low as 15 000 Hz, depending on how much loud music you have been listening to. Older adults have even lower limits and often can't hear a bell ringing.

If you start to hear a ringing in your ears you are suffering from tinnitus and it is a sign your range of hearing is getting worse. Once your hearing is damaged there is no treatment and the only way to improve things is to wear a hearing aid.

a What is the threshold of human hearing for most people?

b What could cause your threshold of hearing to get lower than it should be?

Amazing fact

Mice can squeak at 70 000 Hz but cats can hear sounds above 90 000 Hz. That's evolution!

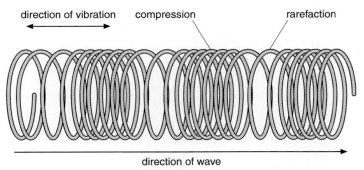

direction of vibration — *compression* — *rarefaction*

direction of wave

▲ *Longitudinal wave with areas of compression and rarefaction*

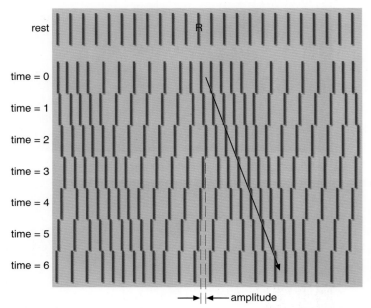

rest

time = 0

time = 1

time = 2

time = 3

time = 4

time = 5

time = 6

amplitude

▲ *The amplitude is the distance, in metres, travelled by molecules from their normal position*

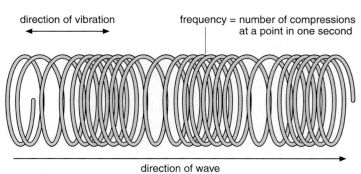

direction of vibration — *frequency = number of compressions at a point in one second*

direction of wave

▲ *The number of waves per second is the frequency*

Longitudinal waves

All sound waves, including ultrasound, are **longitudinal waves**. The waves travelling along a slinky spring are also longitudinal waves. This means that the wave is made of little areas where the particles are closer together, called a **compression**, and little areas where the particles are further apart called a **rarefaction**. All the particles are moving back and forth *along* the same direction as the wave is going which is where the name 'longitudinal wave' comes from

Amplifying the meaning

When you turn up an amplifier to make the sound louder, you are giving the sound wave a larger **amplitude**. This means that, in a loud sound, the air molecules will move further back and forth. They hit your eardrum faster and harder and you will hear a louder sound.

On the right wavelength

The distance between one compression and the next is called the **wavelength**. We measure the wavelength in metres.

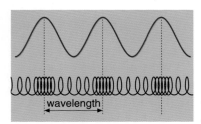

wavelength

◄ *Longitudinal wave showing one wavelength*

Frequency

If you count the number of waves hitting your ear drum each second, this is the **frequency** measured in waves per second (or hertz – Hz). A high pitch sound has a high frequency.

 Make a table of words with their meanings for the words: amplitude, frequency, wavelength, compression, rarefaction.

Babies and ultrasound

All sound can reflect off objects – an echo is the best example.

Ultrasound can reflect off soft tissue in our bodies. In hospitals they use ultrasound waves to take pictures of the developing baby inside the mother's womb.

The ultrasound used has frequencies of about 1 000 000 waves per second (1 MHz) which reflect off the baby and are turned into an image by a computer.

The ultrasound waves are very low energy (very small amplitude) so they do not cause any damage to the fetus or to the mother.

Bodies and ultrasound

Hospitals use ultrasound to look inside bodies to see problems such as tumours or kidney stones. Ultrasound images can show soft tissue such as your organs but X-rays can only show hard tissue such as bones.

Ultrasound also shows the speed that your blood flows round your body. The ultrasound wave reflects off the blood in different ways depending on how fast the blood is flowing. This is useful to see whether you have any blockages or very narrow arteries where a blood clot might stop your blood flowing.

Smashing time

Ultrasound is safe for babies but it can also be used to smash stones inside a patient's body. Some people develop hard stones in their kidneys or gall bladders. Years ago the only treatment was to open up the patient and take out the stones. Now a strong pulse of ultrasound is aimed at the spot where the stone is lying.

This shock wave causes the stone to break up so it can pass out of the body naturally. The treatment takes about 1 hour and the patient will receive about 8 000 high intensity shock waves in this time.

d Explain how ultrasound is used to break up stones in the body.

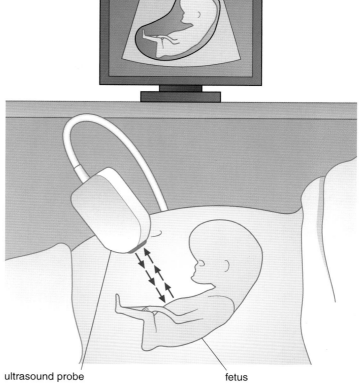

ultrasound probe   fetus

▲ ▼ *Uses of ultrasound*

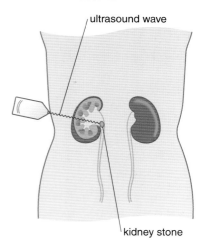

ultrasound wave

kidney stone

Keywords

amplitude • compression • frequency • longitudinal wave • rarefaction • ultrasound • upper threshold of human hearing • wavelength

Wendy's baby

Wendy Taylor is expecting her second baby on October 12th. She describes what it was like to have an ultrasound scan.

▶ *Wendy's baby at 20 weeks*

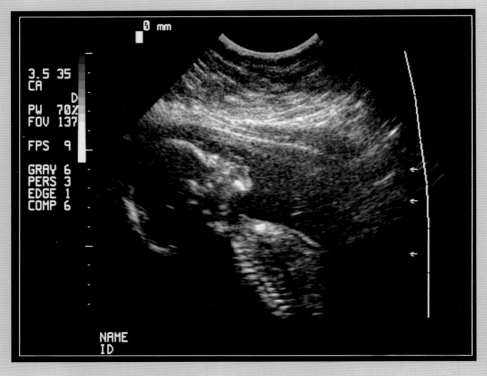

'An hour before you go in you have to drink a pint of water so that you will have a full bladder when they do the scan. This is because the ultrasound pictures are clearer if you have a full bladder.

'You lie on a bed and the ultrasound operator puts a transparent jelly all over your tummy. The operator rolls the detector about over your tummy. It looks like a little hammer. If the baby isn't in a good position to get a clear picture, the nurse will push hard on the side of your tummy to move the baby. This can be a bit uncomfortable.

'They freeze the picture on the screen so that they can take measurements. They measure the leg length and the head diameter to check that the baby is growing properly. They also look at the chambers of the heart to see if there is a hole in the heart and to check that it is beating properly.

'Then they look at the spinal cord to see if the skin has closed over it. If it doesn't close properly the baby is suffering from spina bifida which leaves it disabled.

'For me the scan was the first time I realised there really was something inside me growing. You can see the hands and feet and face, and you start to get to know the baby. It really looks like a little person and that brings you closer to the baby. '

Questions

1 Why does the mother need to drink water before the ultrasound scan?

2 What does the operator measure during the scan?

3 Why does the operator take these measurements?

4 What problems might the operator see during the scan?

5 Why did Wendy like having the scan?

Radiation can kill or cure

In this item you will find out

- how we use nuclear radiation in hospitals
- the difference between X-rays and gamma rays

Many years ago we used **X-rays** to check that children's shoes were fitting correctly. Now we are more careful about how many X-rays we aim at people because we know that too many X-rays can damage our cells.

Long ago, radioactive materials that gave out **gamma rays** were popular in people's pillows to help them sleep. Now we would not sleep on a radioactive material because we know it would be dangerous as gamma rays can also damage our cells.

But we do know that gamma rays and X-rays can be very helpful in hospitals. For example, gamma rays are used a lot in hospitals:

- for treating cancer patients
- for sterilising hospital equipment
- as tracers to see how the blood is flowing round the body.

X-rays are used in hospitals for:

- looking at broken bones
- finding things people have swallowed or pushed into their ear by accident.

A **radiographer** is the person who takes the X-rays in a hospital.

Gamma rays are only one type of radiation that comes out of the nucleus of a radioactive atom. The others are alpha radiation and **beta radiation**. Gamma rays and beta particles can travel through skin, but **alpha particles** cannot because they are too big and move too slowly.

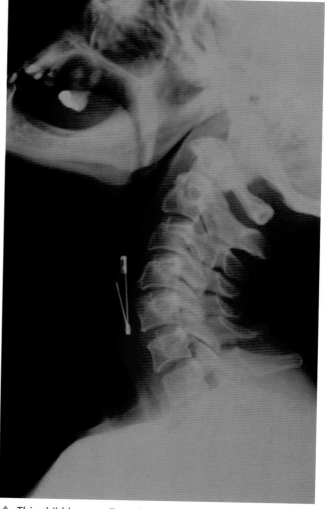

▲ This child has swallowed a safety pin

a Where in an atom does gamma radiation come from?

b What can gamma and beta radiation do that alpha radiation cannot do?

Amazing fact

The wavelength of a gamma ray is about 0.000 000 000 1 m. This means that 10 000 000 gamma waves fit into one millimetre.

X-rays v gamma rays

Gamma rays and X-rays are often confused with each other because they have many things in common. They are both electromagnetic waves so they travel through the air at the speed of light (300 000 000 m/s),

They are produced in different ways. Gamma rays naturally come out of the nucleus of a radioactive atom – you cannot make them artificially. X-rays are made by firing electrons at a metal – they do not come out of the nucleus of the atom.

Gamma rays	X-rays
naturally emitted from the nucleus of a radioactive material	made by firing electrons at a metal target – the X-rays come out of the metal
are electromagnetic waves	are electromagnetic waves
similar wavelength to X-rays	similar wavelength to gamma rays
can travel through human skin	can travel through human skin
can damage or kill living cells	can damage or kill living cells
used to treat cancer as they kill tumour cells	used by radiographers to create X-ray images because X-rays are stopped by bones
used as a **tracer** to show progress of drug around body	
used to sterilise hospital equipment as they kill bacteria	

c What is the main difference between X-rays and gamma rays?

d Make a list of the ways in which X-rays and gamma rays are the same.

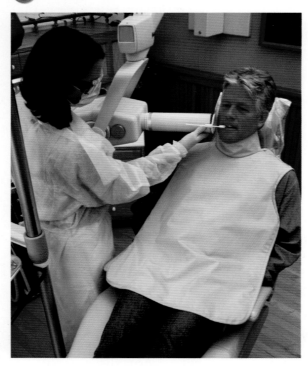

▶ A dentist uses X-rays to check the roots of our teeth

Gamma rays – a real killer

Gamma radiation is good for treating cancer because it can kill the cancer cells in the patient's body. It can also kill bacteria cells so it is a good way to sterilise hospital equipment. You can even sterilise equipment while it is inside the packet as the gamma radiation can go through the plastic wrapping.

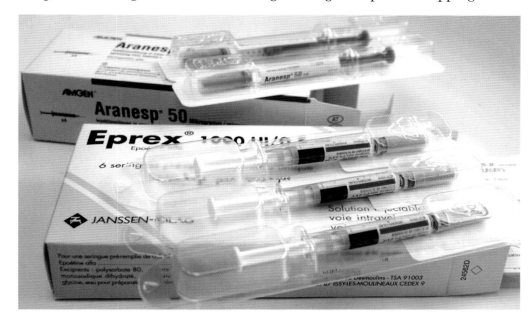

◀ Gamma radiation can sterilise this equipment while it is still in the wrapper

Now you see it... now you don't

Nuclear radiation is also a good way to diagnose a wide range of medical conditions. Medical physicists in hospitals can look inside patients without cutting them open by using gamma rays or beta particles that can get through human skin. These materials are called radioactive **tracers**.

Sometimes medical physicists feed a radioactive drink to a patient and then use a radiation detector called a gamma camera outside the patient to track the gamma radiation as it passes through the patient's digestive system.

▼ The radioactive tracer flows round the body and the medical physicists use the gamma camera to see where it gets to

If there is a blockage in the patient's digestive system, the radioactive material will not get through. If there is a leak the radiation will start coming from unexpected areas. The medical physicists call gamma radiation or beta radiation used in this way tracers. Without medical physicists and radiographers, the doctors would not be able to work out what was wrong with lots of their patients.

Radioactive tracers can also be radioactive gases that the patient breathes so that the doctors can look at their lungs or tracers can be a radioactive liquid injected into the patient's veins to look at the blood circulation.

e **Would a medical physicist use a radioactive liquid tracer or a radioactive gas tracer if they wanted to show how the blood was flowing round a patient's body? Explain why.**

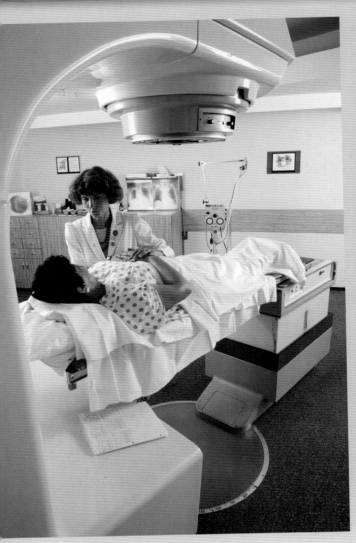

▲ A radiographer at work

Being a radiographer

With a starting salary of about £17000 per year it may not be the best paid job in the world, but radiographers can quickly get promoted and end up with a top salary of £35000 per year or more. And radiographers will tell you it is a very interesting job with plenty of chance to meet and help new people every day.

There are two types of radiographer. The diagnostic radiographer will take X-rays to diagnose a broken bone or will feed radioactive tracers that give out gamma or beta radiation to a patient to see what is wrong with their digestive system. They will also have the most satisfying job of showing a pregnant mother the ultrasound image of her unborn baby. Ultrasound is good for looking at soft tissue but X-rays can only make images of hard tissue like bones and may damage the unborn baby.

A therapeutic radiographer will work with doctors and nurses to give patients their treatment. For example if a patient has cancer, the therapeutic radiographer will treat the patient's tumour with gamma rays. There is also an assistant radiographer who will help and support the patients during their treatments.

Without radiographers, it would be impossible to diagnose and treat many different health problems and injuries. It is an important job and you have to be reliable and good with people. To be an assistant radiographer you need four GCSEs and you will be trained in the hospital. To start towards being a qualified radiographer you might have Advanced GCE or a vocational qualification.

Questions

1 What is the difference between a diagnostic radiographer and a therapeutic radiographer?

2 Why do you think that radiographers say that their job is interesting?

3 Why does a radiographer use ultrasound and not X-rays to show a pregnant woman her baby?

4 What does the radiographer use X-rays for?

5 What two type of radiation does the radiographer use for making tracers?

Is radioactivity really dangerous?

In this item you will find out

- that radioactive substances give out nuclear radiation from their nucleus

- that the radioactivity from a substance decreases with time

- what alpha and beta radiation are

▲ *This sign shows that there is radioactive material near by*

A lot of people are frightened by the word **radioactivity**. They think that radioactivity is like the most dangerous poison and that it will kill them if they come into contact with it.

They do not realise that we are surrounded by radioactivity. There are lots of natural things that are radioactive including food such as coffee beans and even the soil and rocks.

This means that there are radioactive atoms all around us that are waiting to give out their radiation. Some atoms have been waiting for 4 000 million years, since the Earth formed, and still have not decayed yet. We and all other animals have evolved to live and grow surrounded by this low level radiation.

a Why are people frightened of radioactivity?

b Do you think they should be frightened of radioactivity?

▲ *Edinburgh Castle is built on radioactive granite*

What is radioactivity?

There are huge numbers of natural substances around us that are radioactive. To be radioactive the material has to **decay** or break apart to give out alpha radiation, beta radiation or gamma radiation. This radioactivity comes from the nucleus of the atom that is unstable. It has nothing to do with the electrons that go round the nucleus of an atom.

The number of radioactive particles or rays a substance gives out every second is called its radioactivity. All radioactive substances give out less radiation as they get older because there are fewer radioactive atoms left in the substance. This means their radioactivity gets less.

▲ *Measuring radioactivity in the environment*

c Where does the radioactivity come from in the atom?

d Does radioactivity increase or decrease as radioactive substances get older? Why does this happen?

Alpha radiation

When a radioactive material decays, it might give out an **alpha particle**. An alpha particle is really two protons and two neutrons stuck together. This means it is just like the nucleus of a helium atom – though it has not come out of a helium atom.

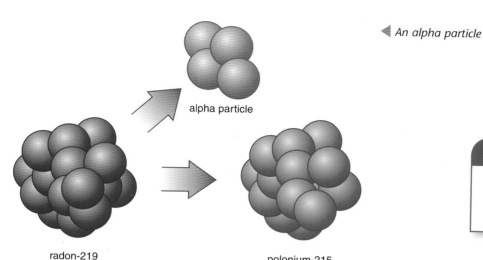

alpha particle

◄ *An alpha particle*

radon-219

polonium-215

Examiner's tip

Know the difference between alpha, beta and gamma radiation.

Beta radiation

A different material may decay by giving out a **beta particle**. A beta particle is a very fast moving electron that has come straight out of the atom's nucleus.

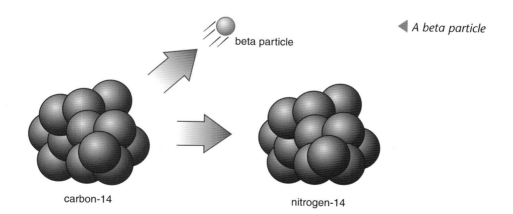

beta particle

◄ *A beta particle*

carbon-14

nitrogen-14

Gamma radiation

Gamma radiation also comes out of the nucleus of the atom but it isn't a particle like the other two, alpha and beta. Instead it is high-energy electromagnetic radiation (like a flash of light) that we cannot see but that can go straight through us.

e Make a table to show the differences between an alpha particle, a beta particle and a gamma ray.

Keywords

alpha particle • beta particle • decay • radiation

Marie Curie

▲ *Marie Curie (on the left) and Marguerite Perey*

Marie Curie is famous for her work with radioactivity in the nineteenth century. Her friend Henri Becquerel had found that uranium gave out rays that made photographic film turn black. The rays seemed to be like the rays that Wilhelm Roentgen had discovered a few months earlier. He called them X-rays because he could not think of a better name. But Marie's waves were weaker.

Marie wanted to know what was causing these 'uranium rays'. The first thing she realised was that she got more rays if there was more of the material. This makes sense to us now as we know that the nucleus of every atom can give out a gamma ray so the more atoms you have, the more rays you get.

But she wanted to know exactly what the new material was that was causing the rays. She worked for years to separate the material and in the end she found two new elements. She named them polonium and radium. She could only find tiny amounts of these new materials but she knew they were extremely radioactive.

When she measured their activity, she got extremely high measurements – but the measurements got lower and lower each time she measured it. This seemed very odd to her but for us it is obvious that the activity of a radioactive substance goes down as each nucleus gives out its gamma ray in turn.

For a long time the activity of radioactive materials was measured in 'Curie' named after Marie. Now we measure activity in Becquerel. One Becquerel is one decay per second.

Questions

1 What are the names of the two radioactive materials that Marie Curie discovered?

2 Marie was surprised by two things that happened. What surprised her?

3 The activity of radioactive materials was measured in Curie. Now we use a different measurement. What is it called?

4 If we measure 120 alpha particles coming out of a substance in 1 minute, what is the radioactivity in decays per second?

5 Explain why, when we measure the radioactivity of the same substance later in the month, we get a lower number.

Detecting, tracing and dating

▲ Some of the rocks in Cornwall are very radioactive

In this item you will find out

- how we use tracers to track waste and find blockages in underground pipes

- how we use alpha radiation to detect smoke from fires

- how we can work out the age of materials using radioactivity

There are many natural materials in rocks and soil that give out alpha, beta or gamma radiation. The rocks and soil of Cornwall and Edinburgh may be tens or hundreds of times more radioactive than rocks in the rest of the UK.

This is called **background radiation** and it is in the environment all the time. The radiation from rocks helps us to work out how old the rocks are and how old the Earth is.

Some of the background radiation comes from artificial sources such as radioactive waste from hospitals or the luminous paint on very old alarm clocks or watches. Even the air we breathe contains radioactive carbon in the carbon dioxide. We cannot escape.

Luckily we are quite safe so long as the background radiation levels are quite low. If the levels of background radiation get very high then people may start to develop diseases such as cancer.

We are also bombarded all the time by radiation such as gamma rays from outer space – called **cosmic rays**. This is also background radiation. Pilots in fighter jets fly so high and so often that they have to make sure they don't get a high dose of cosmic rays because this could be dangerous for them. If they do get too high a dose, they are grounded for several weeks.

a Suggest why background radiation is called background radiation.

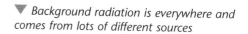

▼ Background radiation is everywhere and comes from lots of different sources

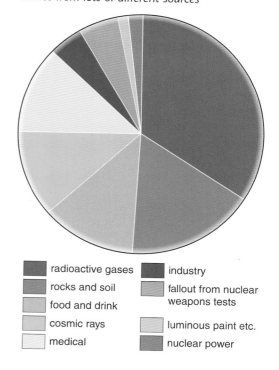

- radioactive gases
- rocks and soil
- food and drink
- cosmic rays
- medical
- industry
- fallout from nuclear weapons tests
- luminous paint etc.
- nuclear power

Dating an Egyptian

If archaeologists want to know when an Egyptian mummy died they use carbon dating. Some of the carbon in the carbon dioxide in the air we breathe is radioactive carbon. This means this carbon decays, emits radiation and changes to a different element.

When someone dies, they stop breathing in air. The radioactive carbon in their body decays. By knowing how fast the radioactive carbon decays we can work out a reasonably accurate date for when the Egyptian mummy died. They can use this technique for anything that died over 500 years ago including trees. They can't use it for objects that haven't lived, such as pottery or rocks.

b Why can't we use carbon dating to work out the age of an ancient sword?

Smoking you out

There should be at least one piece of radioactive material in your home if you want to keep safe from fire. **Smoke detectors** have a tiny piece of radioactive substance (americium) inside them that gives out alpha particles. The alpha particles collide with atoms in the air and ionise them (knock off electrons). The electrons are then attracted to a positive electrode while the positive ions go to a negative electrode. A sensor detects this tiny electric current. If smoke gets in the way the electrons will not get through so the sensor detects that there is no current and the smoke alarm goes off.

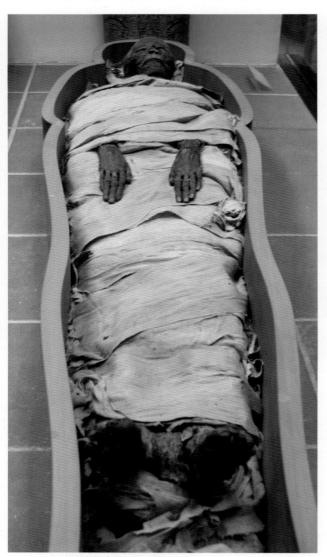

▲ We can use radioactive carbon to work out when this Egyptian mummy died

▶ The current cannot flow in the smoke detector if there is smoke in the way, so the alarm will go off

c What type of radiation does the americium in a smoke detector give out?

d What happens inside the smoke detector if there is a fire?

Going underground

Radioactive tracers are used in industry as well as in hospitals. Oil companies lose huge amounts of money if oil leaks out of their pipelines. Digging up the whole pipeline to find the leak costs too much. Instead they use a radioactive tracer (similar to the tracers used in hospitals). They add a radioactive material to the oil and use radiation detectors above ground to see how it flows along the pipe.

They have to use gamma radiation because alpha and beta radiation cannot get to the surface. As soon as they see that there is no radioactivity they know that the substance must have leaked out. Then they only have to dig up the leaking part of the pipe.

Where's that pipe?

Workers can also find where underground pipes go using radioactive tracers. They put a radioactive material into the pipe. Then they use radiation detectors to follow it along the pipe. They walk along above ground and when they get a reading on the radiation detector they know that is where the pipe is.

Where's the waste?

Companies often have to get rid of lots of chemical waste. Inspectors will track the waste along pipes and out into the sea to check that it is being dispersed properly and not polluting rivers or the sea. They add radioactive substances to the waste then track it with radiation detectors.

e Explain how radioactive tracers can be used to find blockages in pipes.

▲ Where there is a leak the radioactive fluid leaks out and radiation is not detected further along the pipe

Keywords

background radiation • cosmic ray • smoke detector

▼ Chemical waste can pollute rivers

When carbon dating goes wrong

William Libby was the first person to suggest we could work out the age of long-dead objects using the amount of radioactive carbon in them.

He tested his idea on a wood sample from the tomb of the Egyptian pharaoh Djoser. He got the right answer so it seemed his idea worked.

But other scientists used this method and found they got the wrong answers. Sometimes they were hundreds of years out. Perhaps the method did not work after all.

In fact you have to know how much radioactive carbon was in the atmosphere when the object was alive before you can work out its age. There are now many laboratories around the world where archaeologists can send their finds for dating.

But there is still a problem with the famous Turin Shroud. This shroud has the image of a crucified man on it. Some say it is the image of Jesus Christ, others say it is a medieval forgery. In 1988 it was dated, using radioactive carbon, by scientists in three different laboratories and they all agreed it dated to around 1300 AD.

But there are many people who still believe it is 2000 years old. One man from the USA says that the piece they tested was only a medieval patch, which is why they got the date of 1300 AD. He claims he has proved the rest is much older using a different technique. So far he has not explained in detail what his technique is.

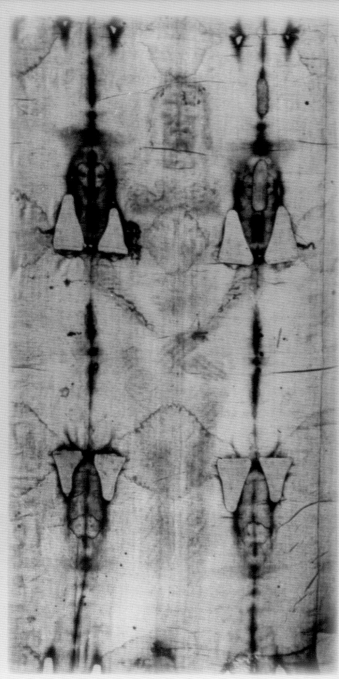
▲ Turin Shroud

Questions

1 Who first had the idea of using radioactive carbon to work out the age of historic objects?

2 How did he test if his idea worked?

3 Some scientists used this method and kept getting the wrong dates. What do you have to know to make sure your answer is right?

4 Which famous shroud was dated using radioactive carbon?

5 When do the scientists think it was made?

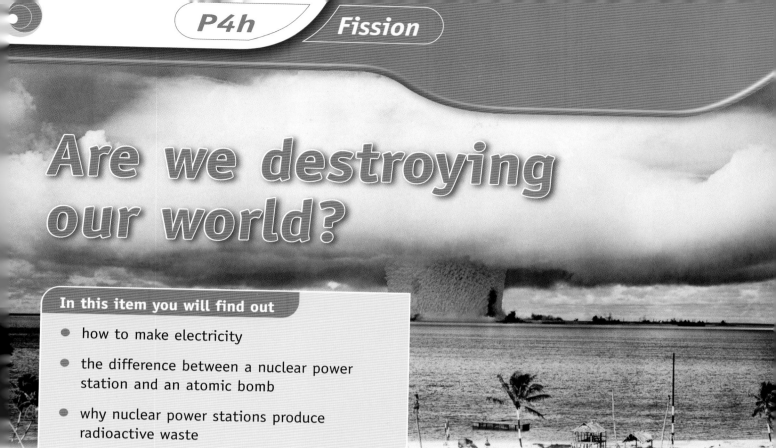

Are we destroying our world?

In this item you will find out

- how to make electricity

- the difference between a nuclear power station and an atomic bomb

- why nuclear power stations produce radioactive waste

▲ Atomic bomb exploding

Many people are frightened of **nuclear power** stations because they have seen images of the terrible destruction caused by the atomic bombs dropped on Japan at the end of the Second World War. They think that nuclear power stations are the same as atomic bombs. However, nuclear power stations are very different from bombs, and soon we might find that using nuclear power stations to generate electricity is the only way to reduce pollution.

Coal and gas fired power stations produce tonnes of carbon dioxide every day. Some scientists believe that this is making the planet too warm. This is called global warming. If we don't reduce the amount of carbon dioxide in the atmosphere we risk destroying the planet.

Nuclear power does not produce carbon dioxide. Some people believe the only way to stop global warming is to build new nuclear power stations and close all the old coal and gas power stations.

Other people are worried that more nuclear power stations will produce lots more nuclear waste which they think is dangerous for living things. It seems we can't win!

For some years people believed that wind power would be the answer. We now realise though that wind power cannot solve the problem of global warming because we cannot build enough wind turbines in the countryside and it is too unreliable anyway.

a Why are we now looking for new ways to generate electricity?

Amazing fact

To replace a single nuclear power station with a wind farm you would have to build one new wind turbine every day for 10 years.

▶ Wind farms need over 3 000 turbines to replace one normal power station

211

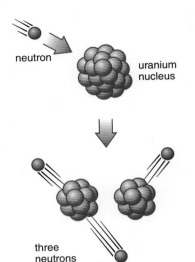

▲ *Firing a neutron at a uranium atom makes it split apart and get very hot*

neutron

uranium nucleus

three neutrons

Uranium – the new coal

Uranium is a very dense metal. It has a very special property. If neutrons are fired at the nucleus of a uranium atom at very high speed, they will get into the atom's nucleus. This nucleus becomes too heavy and cannot hold itself together. It splits into two unequal parts making two new atoms (two different elements) as well as firing out a few spare neutrons.

The process of splitting apart is called **nuclear fission**. The fission process generates a lot of heat energy – and this is why it is useful. This heat can be used to generate electricity.

Making electricity

To make electricity in a power station all you need is water, a **turbine** and a **generator**.

Then you need to:

- burn a fuel to create heat
- heat the water to make steam
- feed the steam into a huge turbine (like a water wheel)
- drive the turbine round and rotate a generator.

The rotating generator will create electric current in wires that is then fed into the national grid to supply our houses when we need it.

The only difference between power stations that work in this way is how the water is heated in the first place. In some power stations the fuel, such as coal or oil or gas, is burned. In nuclear power stations, nuclear fission generates heat energy. (Scientists talk about burning nuclear fuel but there are no flames involved!)

▼ *How electricity is made in a coal-fired power station*

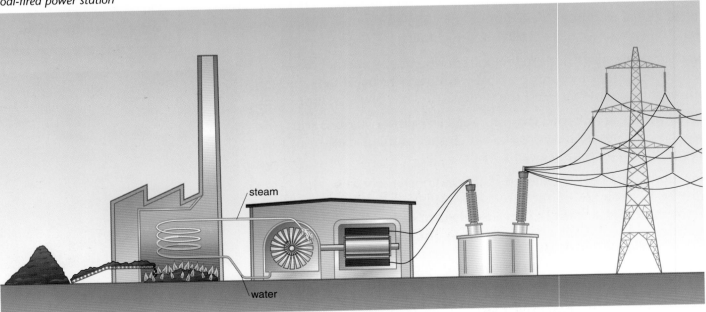

steam

water

coal burnt to make steam

steam drives turbine

turbine rotates generator

electricity from generator fed to national grid

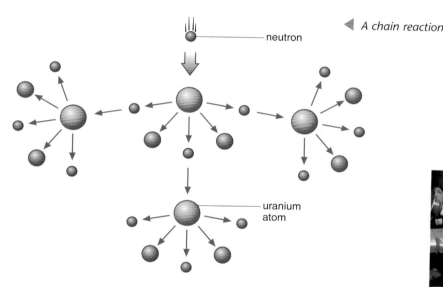

b What are the different ways of heating water in a power station?

c Explain how electricity is generated from steam.

Is the power station just a bomb?

In a nuclear power station, uranium decays by nuclear fission. After a nuclear fission reaction there are spare neutrons left over. If one of these neutrons hits another uranium atom, you get a **chain reaction** so that each fission reaction makes another atom split apart and so on. If this chain reaction goes out of control so that two or three or more neutrons hit uranium atoms each time, you get an atomic bomb. Nuclear power stations are built so that this cannot happen. There are special materials in the reactor that absorb the spare neutrons so that they can't find a uranium atom to hit.

neutron

◀ *A chain reaction*

uranium atom

Amazing fact

The instant you flick a switch the electricity that you use has just been made. The sort of electricity we use from the mains can't be stored.

Keywords

chain reaction • generator • nuclear fission • nuclear power • radioactive waste • turbine • uranium

Nuclear waste can be safe

In the nuclear reactor, when each uranium atom splits apart you get new materials that are often radioactive. This forms **radioactive waste**. In fact other parts of the nuclear reactor absorb some of the neutrons and this makes them radioactive too. These materials are also called radioactive waste. We have to store the waste and make sure no one touches it until it is safe. Some of the most dangerous materials will last for millions of years so we need to find ways to deal with the waste so that no one touches it while it is still toxic and dangerous.

d What is nuclear (radioactive) waste made from?

e Why is nuclear waste dangerous?

▶ *Storing nuclear waste*

Nuclear power in the future

▲ *A nuclear power station*

For years organisations like Greenpeace were keen to remove all nuclear power stations. Now things are different and some scientists think that the polluting gases in the atmosphere are acting like a blanket around the Earth and causing it to heat up. These gases are called greenhouses gases. All of our coal and gas power stations pump tonnes of these greenhouse gases into the atmosphere every day.

The latest idea is that nuclear power is the only way to reduce our greenhouse gases and stop the Earth getting any warmer.

The main reason people do not like the idea of nuclear power is because the nuclear waste is dangerous for such a long time. But scientists are already inventing new ways to deal with this waste. The best idea is to make the radioactive elements change into new elements that are only dangerous for a very short time. This is called 'transmuting'.

Other people say that nuclear power stations are dangerous and that, if there were an accident, thousands of people could die. But very few people have died or become ill from nuclear power station accidents. Only 56 people died in total because of the famous Chernobyl accident in Russia in 1986.

Twenty eight people died within four months from radiation or thermal burns, 19 have died since, and there have been around nine deaths from thyroid cancer apparently due to the accident. This is far fewer than in many mining accidents and fewer than have died in building wind turbines.

An authoritative UN report in 2000 concluded that there is no scientific evidence of any significant radiation-related health effects to most people exposed. This was confirmed in a very thorough study in 2005.

Questions

1 What is global warming?

2 Why are some people keen to get rid of nuclear power stations?

3 What is the problem with coal, oil or gas power stations? What are scientists doing to solve the problems of nuclear power?

4 How many people died as a result of the Chernobyl accident in 1986?

5 What fraction of these people died from thyroid cancer?

P4a

1 A company has decided to manufacture a spray polish that is electrostatically charged. How will this be better than normal spray polish? [2]

2 Cars often have devices hanging off the back of the rear bumper that claim to stop you getting an electric shock when you get out of the car. They are supposed to discharge the car after it stops.

a Explain why this device won't work if it is attached to a plastic bumper. [1]
b Explain why the car might need a device like this. [1]

3 What are the two types of electrostatic charge? [2]

4 Describe what will happen if you rub a plastic ruler on your jumper and put it close to tiny pieces of paper on the desk. [2]

5 If you rub a balloon on your jumper, it becomes charged. Explain how the balloon gains a positive charge and work out what charge the jumper gains. [3]

6 Static electricity can be a nuisance. Explain how this is true by describing two different situations when static electricity causes problems. [2]

P4b

1 If a defibrillator sends a charge through you which carries 360 joules of energy in 0.01 seconds, how much energy would there be in a second? [1]

2 If there are eight coal fired power stations in an area of the UK each producing 3500 tonnes of ash each day:

a How much ash is produced in total in this area of the UK each day? [1]

If $\frac{1}{5}$th of the ash remains at the bottom of the chimney and $\frac{4}{5}$th flies up the chimney:

b How much ash flies up the chimneys of one power station on average per day? [1]
c How much ash flies up all the chimneys in the area per day? [1]

3 Describe how electrostatics can be useful in a hospital for saving someone suffering a heart attack. [2]

4 Describe how electrostatics is useful in an office. [2]

5 Explain how high voltages are useful for cleaning up the smoke from the chimneys in a power station. [2]

6 Describe how a paramedic uses a defibrillator to restart a heart when it has stopped. [4]

7 In a car factory the paint and the car are often charged. This is to make spraying the car bodies more efficient. Explain how this works. [4]

P4c

1

Current (amps)	Voltage (volts)	Resistance (ohms)
0.2	4	
0.4	8	
0.6	12	
0.8	16	
1.0	20	
1.5	30	
2.0	40	
3.0	60	
5.0	100	

This table shows the current and voltage measured for a small motor.

a Copy out this table and complete the final column to find its resistance. [1]
b Plot a line graph of the current on the x-axis and the voltage on the y-axis and work out the gradient of the line. [1]
c What do you notice about the value of the gradient? [1]

2 In a 3-pin plug, the three wires are different colours. What colour is the:

a earth wire? [1]
b live wire? [1]
c neutral wire? [1]

3 Some appliances do not need earthing. Complete these two sentences.

a An appliance that does not need earthing is called double _____ . [1]
b An appliance that does not need earthing has a casing made of _____ . [1]

4 Why do we have to have a fuse in a plug? [2]

5 In a 3-pin plug describe what these parts do.

a the live wire [1]
b the neutral wire [1]
c the earth wire [1]
d the fuse [1]

6 For a given resistor:

a if you increase the potential difference (pd), what happens to the current? [1]
b if you increase the resistance what happens to the current? [1]

7 Explain why a double insulated appliance does not need an earth wire. [2]

P4d

1

Sound	Frequency (Hz)
Ultrasound scan in hospital	1 000 000
Upper threshold of cats' hearing	90 000
Mouse squeaking	70 000
Lowest level of ultrasound	22 000
Upper threshold of human hearing	20 000
Upper threshold of human hearing for older person	15 000
High pitched note on guitar	10 000
High pitch voice	1 000
Low pitch voice	100
Bass drum	20

Make a frequency line to show these frequencies. [3]

2 Sound waves are often used to work out how deep the sea is by sending a sound to the sea bed and waiting for the echo. This is called sonar. If the sound travels at 1 500 m/s in water and the echo takes 0.6 seconds to return to the ship, how deep is the water? [2]

3 List three things that ultrasound waves can be used for. [3]

4 From the list of words below, choose the correct one for each meaning:

amplitude   wavelength   frequency
compression   rarefaction

  a The number of waves per second measured in hertz. [1]
  b The area in a wave where the particles are closest together. [1]
  c The area in a wave where the particles are furthest apart. [1]
  d The distance between two compressions. [1]

5 Explain what 'the upper threshold of human hearing' means. [1]

6 Explain why ultrasound is safe to use on an unborn baby. [1]

7 Explain how ultrasound can break up a kidney stone. [2]

P4e

1 You need to find where there is a blockage in an underground pipe that carries waste water out to sea.

  a What form of radioactivity would you choose if the pipe is made of plastic and is buried 1 metre below ground? Explain your answer. [2]
  b Why would it be impossible to find the blockage if the pipes were made of lead? [1]

2 You need to treat a patient to find out whether they have swallowed a marble and whether it is stuck in their gut and blocking their digestive system.

  a What would you do to see if there is a marble in their digestive system? [1]
  b What would you do to see if the marble was blocking their digestive system so that no food could get through? [1]

3 Select the correct phrase to complete this sentence.

X-rays and gamma rays are both _____ .
A longitudinal waves
B electromagnetic waves
C radioactive particles [1]

4 Why do we have to be careful not to give someone a high dose of radiation? [1]

5 What is the name of someone who takes X-rays in a hospital? [1]

6 Which types of radiation can get through human skin? [2]

7 X-rays and gamma rays have similar wavelengths. Describe one difference between them. [1]

8 Substances that emit beta or gamma radiation can be used as tracers in hospitals.

  a Explain what happens to a patient if they are treated with a tracer. [2]
  b Why do the radiographers use beta or gamma radiation but not alpha radiation? [1]

P4f

1 An experiment measured the radioactivity of protactinium.

Time (s)	Counts in 10 s	Time (s)	Counts in 10 s
0	68	80	17
10	63	90	15
20	48	100	12
30	40	110	10
40	38	120	9
50	29	130	7
60	25	140	6
70	19		

  a Plot these data as a line graph with the time on the x-axis and the counts on the y-axis. [3]
  b Why does the radioactivity go down gradually? [1]
  c Why do some of the points not lie neatly on the line if the experiment was done very carefully? [1]

2 When we measure the radioactivity of a substance, what are we measuring?

A the number of nuclear decays emitted each second
B the number of nuclear decays emitted each minute
C the number of nuclear decays emitted until the substance has finished emitting radioactivity [1]

3 What happens to the radioactivity of a substance if you keep measuring it over a long time?

A it stays the same
B it goes up
C it goes down [1]

4 If a radioactive substance decays, it can give out three different types of nuclear radiation.

a What are the three types called? [3]
b Which two of these are particles and what are they? [4]

5 Why is radiation often called 'nuclear radiation'? [1]

6 Which type of radiation cannot get through a piece of paper? [1]

P4g

1 In a factory that manufactures aluminium foil (kitchen foil) radioactive materials can be used to monitor how thick the foil is as it is rolled out. The radioactive material is placed above the foil and the detector is below the foil. If too little radiation gets through it means the foil is too thick.

a Would you choose alpha, beta or gamma radiation to monitor the thickness of the foil? [1]
b Explain why this form of radiation is suitable and the other two are not. [2]

2 Which of these items, that you should have in your home, has an alpha source in it?

A a hair drier
B a microwave oven
C a smoke detector [1]

3 Radiation is all around us. It comes from rocks and soil. What do we call this radiation?

A background radiation
B environmental radiation
C general radiation [1]

4 Radiation can be used in hospitals and in industry as 'tracers'. What three things might a waste treatment company use radiation to do? [3]

5 Explain what 'carbon dating' is and what it is used for. [2]

7 Where does background radiation come from? [3]

8 From the list of ancient objects below, state which items can be dated using radioactivity. Of these, which can be dated using carbon dating?

A ancient cooking pot   B skeleton
C meteorite   D clothing [4]

P4h

1 Put these into the correct order to show how electricity is generated.

A Fuel is burnt
B Turbines turn and make generators turn to generate electricity
C Electricity is sent out to consumers
D Steam causes the turbines to turn
E Water is heated to make steam [4]

2

Fuel	Reserves	Pollution
Coal	200 years	Carbon dioxide and sulfur dioxide
Oil	40 years	Carbon dioxide and sulfur dioxide
Gas	50 years	Carbon dioxide
Wind	Renewable	None
Uranium	1000+ years	Nuclear waste produced

Carbon dioxide is one of the main gases that cause the greenhouse effect which seems to be making the temperature of the earth increase (global warming). Sulfur dioxide causes acid rain.

a Which of these fuels is a fossil fuel? [1]
b Why is the wind described as renewable? [1]
c What is the advantage of burning gas compared with coal? [1]
d What is the disadvantage of burning gas? [1]
e What is the advantage of nuclear power over fossil fuels? [1]
f What is the disadvantage of wind power? [1]

3 What is the name of the metal used as fuel in a nuclear power station?

A carbon   B uranium   C gas   D oil [1]

4 A nuclear power station works because of a chain reaction. Explain what a chain reaction is. [2]

5 Describe how electricity is generated in a nuclear power station. [4]

6 Explain what 'fission' means. [2]

7 How can materials become radioactive when they absorb extra neutrons? [2]

8 Apart from uranium in nuclear reactors, what other fuels are used to heat water to generate electricity? [3]

Research Study

What do scientists do?

Why do people become scientists?

Do the things that scientists believe change?

What good do scientists do to benefit everybody?

To help you answer these questions, and as part of your GCSE Additional Science course, you have to carry out at least one Research Study. If you do more than one Research Study your best mark will count.

Scientists at work

The Research Study is about the work of scientists. It could be the work of scientists today trying to find a cure for a disease such as AIDS, or developing an alternative fuel for petrol. Or, it could be about the work of scientists in the past showing how ideas have changed over time, for example, how ideas of the structure of the atom have changed.

In some ways the Research Study is like the Science in the News you did for GCSE Core Science. But, Science in the News required you to give your opinions. The Research Study requires you to do a little research to answer five or six specific questions.

The questions in the Research Study are graded:

- The first couple of questions will be straightforward and use the information you are given. You should not find them difficult.
- The next couple of questions will be more difficult. You might have to look up some information in a book or CD-ROM or on the Internet before you can answer them. You might have to complete charts or graphs at this stage.
- The last one or two questions will be difficult. Often they have no single straightforward answer. You should not worry if you cannot answer them. You can still get a good mark without doing them.

Important things to remember when doing research

- You don't have to do lots of research. Two suitable references are enough.
- Don't print out large amounts of material from the Internet. You won't need it and you won't have time to use it.
- You should carefully reference where the information has come from, for example:
  1 www.webelements.com
  2 Heinemann Gateway Science: OCR Science for GCSE, Foundation text book pages 75–77.

Attempting the Research Study

Your teacher will give you the Research Study and explain it to you in one lesson. They may then give you time in class or at home to collect some data. They will not help you to answer the questions.

In a later lesson you will be asked to write a report answering the questions. You can use the notes you have made. Your teacher may collect them in, but will not mark the notes.

Read each question carefully. Be clear in your mind what the question is asking. After you have answered the question, read your answer again to make sure you have answered all of it. Only when you are sure that you have, move onto the next question.

How your Research Study is marked

Your teacher will mark your Research Study and a Moderator for OCR will check a sample to ensure that the marking is fair.

Your teacher is looking for four things only in your report. Each is marked on a scale of 0–6 marks. The total for the Research Study is 24 marks. It represents about 13% of the marks available for GCSE Additional Science.

What your teacher is looking for	Advice to you
What relevant information have you collected?	You should try to collect information from at least two sources. If you do no research you will lose 6 marks here.
How have you used the information?	You should show how you have used the information to answer the questions.
How do you show an understanding of how scientific ideas develop?	You should show how the information helps to explain how scientific ideas change.
How well written is your report?	You should be careful with your spelling, punctuation and grammar. Try to use correct scientific words. Read it through carefully before you finish.

Scientists do have responsibility to use their science to benefit people. Fritz Haber, the German scientist, developed the Haber Process to make ammonia. This process has enabled large amounts of fertiliser to be made to feed the world. But, the same man was responsible for the development and use of poison gases in the First World War by the Germans.

Nuclear power stations may provide the electricity needed by people without emitting carbon dioxide. However, the same science can produce the atomic bomb that can kill millions of people.

Science is not a set of known facts that must be learned and passed on to future generations. Science is a living subject that is likely to change as we find out more. Scientists have a responsibility to use this information for the good of everybody.

Good luck with your Research Study.

Data Task

What is a Data Task?

During your GCSE Additional Science course you will do a task that involves analysing and evaluating some real data from an experiment. This is called a Data Task. You will also then do some planning of a further experiment.

Your teacher will have a number of Data Tasks they can give you to do. You only need to do one. If you do more than one, your best mark will count.

An example of a Data Task is:

Is there a link between the height the ball is dropped from and the height to which it bounces? This links with the science in P3e Energy on the move.

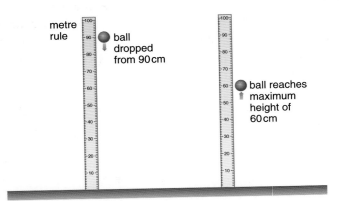

Carrying it out

You will be given some instructions to follow to do a simple experiment. You can do this individually or as part of a group, or you can watch your teacher do a demonstration, or get some data from a computer simulation.

You need to collect some results and record them in a table.

There are no marks for collecting the results, but later on you are going to suggest improvements to the experiment. You cannot really do this unless you understand what was done in the first place.

Your results should be collected in by your teacher to keep them safe for the next lesson. If you didn't get any results, your teacher can give you a set of results. In the next lesson, your teacher will give you back your results and another sheet of instructions.

You can write your answers in the spaces given on the separate sheet given to you by your teacher, or you can write your answers on lined paper. If you use lined paper, number the parts of your answer to match the tasks on the second sheet.

Writing up

The instruction sheet will usually tell you to:

1 Average your results.

2 Draw a graph to display your results. Remember your graph should fill at least half the grid. Make sure you choose a suitable scale for each axis and label each axis clearly. If you are finding this difficult to do ask your teacher for advice.

3 Look for any pattern in these results.

4 Make some comments about the accuracy and reliability of your results. Look back at your table. Are the results the most accurate results you could get with the apparatus? For example:

- If you are using a hand-held stopwatch it might show the time to the nearest one hundredth of a second, e.g. 10.17 s. But you would be better recording this as 10.2 s because you cannot use it more accurately. There is a delay when you turn the stopwatch on and off and this makes a reading to more than 0.1 s wrong. When electronic timing is used, for example in the Olympic Games, there is not this delay because the turning on and off is done automatically by a computer. So times can be given accurately to 0.01 s.
- If you are using a burette to the nearest 1 cm^3, you are not using it to the maximum accuracy. You should be able to read to the nearest 0.1 cm^3. If you have three very similar results, e.g. 32.5, 32.4 and 32.5, this indicates that your results are reliable.
- Also, if you look at the graph you have drawn, are all the points you have plotted either on or close to the line or curve? Again, this suggests reliability. Any points that are away from the graph are called anomalous results. You should be able to identify anomalous results. You should show these clearly on the graph or in your writing. Remember that if the results you collected are, for example, 32, 33 and 154, 154 is an anomalous result and you should not include it. Instead you should ignore the 154 and average 32 and 33.
- Finally, you may be given the opportunity of suggesting what you could do to improve the experiment or get better results. This is called evaluation. Comments like 'take more readings' or 'do the experiment more carefully' are not worth credit. Take more readings might be worthwhile if you can qualify it, e.g. take more readings between 10°C and 30°C.

5 At this stage, you should try to use some science to explain the pattern in the results you have found. In the bouncing ball example, you should know that when the ball is dropped it has potential energy and as it falls it transfers potential energy into kinetic energy. When the ball bounces it loses some kinetic energy. As the ball bounces up, the kinetic energy is converted back into potential energy. As it lost some energy when it bounced, it cannot reach the same height as before.

6 Finally, you will be asked to do some planning for a further experiment. This may be either to improve the experiment you have done or to extend the experiment to investigate another variable, e.g., 'How does changing temperature affect the height a ball bounces to?' You will not be expected to do this practically. The best way to do this is probably a series of bullet points. For the bouncing ball experiment this could be:

- Bounce the ball from the same height each time. Choose a height near the top of the range in your original experiment.
- Heat a large beaker of water (or better, a thermostatic water bath) and put a thermometer in the water. Turn off the heat and put the ball into the water.
- After 10 minutes, when the ball has reached the temperature of the water, read the temperature of the water and take the ball out of the water.
- Bounce the ball and measure the height it bounces to.
- Put the ball back into the water and repeat.
- Do the same thing again at five temperatures, spread between room temperature and 70°C.

Marking your work

Your teacher will mark your Data Task against a set of criteria. Your teacher may give you a set of 'student speak' criteria. There are five things to be assessed by your teacher on a scale of 0–6. This makes the total for the Data Task a mark out of 30. This represents nearly 17% of the marks for the GCSE Additional Science award.

Interpreting your data	Can you draw a bar chart or, better, a line graph to display your results?		
Analysing the data	Can you see a pattern? This should be expressed as, for example, As _____ increases,		_____ increases.
Evaluating your data	Can you comment on the quality of the data and suggest any limitations with the method used?		
Justifying your conclusions	Can you link your conclusions with science and understanding?		
Ideas for further work	Can you give a plan which is detailed so another person can follow it up?		

Unlike the written papers, if you do Foundation there is no limit to the mark you can achieve. It is possible, if you do the Skills Assessment well, to boost your overall grade above C even if you do Foundation papers. A sample of the Data Tasks from your school or college will be sent to a Moderator from OCR to confirm the marking.

Good luck with your Data Task.

Assessment of your Practical Skills

During your GCSE Additional Science course your teacher will have you make an overall assessment of your practical work. This is not based on any one practical activity, but it is a general view of your practical work throughout the course.

There are two things your teacher will be asked to look for:

How safely and accurately you carry out practical activities in science.

How you collect data from an experiment, either individually or in a group:

They are asked to use a scale of 0–6 and are given some help to do this. They are told what is required for 2, 4 and 6 marks. They can give 1, 3 or 5 on their own judgements. If you have done no worthwhile practical work you may get 0.

The table summarises what is required for 2, 4 and 6 marks.

Number of marks	What is required?
2	You carry out practical work safely and accurately, but you need a lot of help doing the work
4	You carry out practical work safely and accurately, but you need some help doing the work
6	You carry out practical work safely and accurately, and you do not need any help doing the work. Also you are aware of possible risks and take this into account

This assessment is worth about 3.3% of the marks available for GCSE Additional Science.

Don't worry about asking for help thinking it might cause you to be marked down. The most important thing is that you are able to complete the activity safely.

Enjoy the practical work in science. It is this that makes science different from other subjects you do.

Good luck.

Periodic Table

Key

relative atomic mass
atomic symbol
name
atomic (proton) number

1	2											3	4	5	6	7	8
																	4 **He** helium 2
7 **Li** lithium 3	9 **Be** beryllium 4					1 **H** hydrogen 1						11 **B** boron 5	12 **C** carbon 6	14 **N** nitrogen 7	16 **O** oxygen 8	19 **F** fluorine 9	20 **Ne** neon 10
23 **Na** sodium 11	24 **Mg** magnesium 12											27 **Al** aluminium 13	28 **Si** silicon 14	31 **P** phosphorous 15	32 **S** sulfur 16	35.5 **Cl** chlorine 17	40 **Ar** argon 18
39 **K** potassium 19	40 **Ca** calcium 20	45 **Sc** scandium 21	48 **Ti** titanium 22	51 **V** vanadium 23	52 **Cr** chromium 24	55 **Mn** manganese 25	56 **Fe** iron 26	59 **Co** cobalt 27	59 **Ni** nickel 28	64 **Cu** copper 29	65 **Zn** zinc 30	70 **Ga** gallium 31	73 **Ge** germanium 32	75 **As** arsenic 33	79 **Se** selenium 34	80 **Br** bromine 35	84 **Kr** krypton 36
85 **Rb** rubidium 37	88 **Sr** strontium 38	89 **Y** yttrium 39	91 **Zr** zirconium 40	93 **Nb** niobium 41	96 **Mo** molybdenum 42	[98] **Tc** technetium 43	101 **Ru** ruthenium 44	103 **Rh** rhodium 45	106 **Pd** palladium 46	108 **Ag** silver 47	112 **Cd** cadmium 48	115 **In** indium 49	119 **Sn** tin 50	122 **Sb** antimony 51	128 **Te** tellurium 52	127 **I** iodine 53	131 **Xe** xenon 54
133 **Cs** caesium 55	137 **Ba** barium 56	139 **La*** lanthanum 57	178 **Hf** hafnium 72	181 **Ta** tantalum 73	184 **W** tungsten 74	186 **Re** rhenium 75	190 **Os** osmium 76	192 **Ir** iridium 77	195 **Pt** platinum 78	197 **Au** gold 79	201 **Hg** mercury 80	204 **Tl** thallium 81	207 **Pb** lead 82	209 **Bi** bismuth 83	[209] **Po** polonium 84	[210] **At** astatine 85	[222] **Rn** radon 86
[223] **Fr** francium 87	[226] **Ra** radium 88	[227] **Ac*** actinium 89	[261] **Rf** rutherfordium 104	[262] **Db** dubnium 105	[266] **Sg** seaborgium 106	[264] **Bh** bohrium 107	[267] **Hs** hassium 108	[268] **mt** meitnerium 109	[271] **Ds** darmstadtium 110	[272] **Rg** roentgenium 111							

Elements with atomic numbers 112–116 have been reported but not fully authenticated

* The lanthanoids (atomic numbers 58–71) and the actinoids (atomic numbers 90–103) have been omitted.

Glossary

acceleration rate of increase of velocity (= (change in speed)/time)

acrosome a structure in the head of the sperm that contains enzymes to digest a pathway into the egg

active safety features in a car that act to make it safer, for example, anti-lock braking and traction control

actual yield the amount of product obtained in a chemical reaction

alkali metal element in Group I of the Periodic Table

alpha particle particle made of two protons and two neutrons that is emitted when certain radioactive nuclei decay (resembles a helium nucleus)

alveolus small air sac found in the lungs (plural = alveoli)

amplitude the maximum displacement of a wave from its rest position

anion ion with a negative charge

anode positive electrode

anti-lock braking system (ABS) prevents the wheels of a car locking when it is braking so preventing a skid

aorta the main artery that carries blood from the heart, out to the body

aquifer rock containing water

artery blood vessel that carries blood away from the heart

artificially inseminate sperm are collected from the testes of the male and inserted into the vagina of the female using a syringe. Sperm from one male can be used to fertilise the ova in thousands of females

asexual reproduction the production of genetically identical offspring from one parent

atom smallest particle of an element

atomic number the number of protons in an atom of an element

atria the left and right atria are the two upper muscular chambers of the heart. They pump blood into the ventricles

attract when two objects move towards each other, such as opposite poles of a magnet or objects with opposite charge

automation process not under direct human control

auxin a plant hormone that is produced in the growing points. It stimulates the growth of a shoot

background radiation radioactivity that is always present around us

base a metal oxide which reacts with an acid to form a salt and water only

batch process non-continuous chemical process to produce a small quantity of product

battery farming keeping animals in controlled conditions indoors

beta particle a high-speed electron emitted when certain radioactive nuclei decay; it can pass through skin

beta radiation radioactive emission comprising high-speed electrons

bicuspid a valve between the left atrium and left ventricle in the heart

biological control the use of a living organism to control a pest population

biomass the mass of living material

bleach a solution containing chloride ions (Cl^-) and chlorate(I) ions (ClO^-) made by dissolving chlorine in sodium hydroxide solution. Bleach will decolourise dyes by oxidising them

braking distance distance moved by a car in stopping after the brakes have been applied

bulk chemical a chemical produced in large quantities

capillaries tiny blood vessels that carry blood to the tissues of the body. A human being has thousands of miles of capillaries

cathode negative electrode

cation ion with a positive charge

cell membrane a thin structure, made of protein and fat, that surrounds every cell

cell wall a tough protective structure made of cellulose that surrounds the cell membrane in plant cells

chain reaction process that occurs when the neutrons emitted from one atom hit other similar atoms causing them to decay and emit further neutrons that collide with other atoms, and so on

chlorination treatment with chlorine

chlorophyll a green pigment produced by plants that is used to trap light energy for the process of photosynthesis

chloroplast a plant cell organelle that contains chlorophyll and is the site of photosynthesis

circuit (electrical) closed pathway connecting different electrical components

circuit breaker automatic switch which 'trips' (turns off) if the current exceeds a specified value; it can be reset by turning the switch back on

clone two or more organisms that are genetically identical

compost a natural fertiliser made from decayed dead organisms and waste materials

compound substance made from two or more elements chemically joined

compression part of a longitudinal wave where the particles are closer together than normal

consumer an organism that needs to take in food ready made

continuous process chemical process that produces product all of the time

225

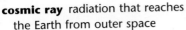

cosmic ray radiation that reaches the Earth from outer space

covalent bond a type of bond involving the sharing of one or more pairs of electrons. The electrons are provided by the atoms that are combining

cross-breeding breeding from a male and female of different lineage

cruise control keeps a car travelling at a constant speed making it less tiring for the driver

crumple zone the parts of a car that collapse and absorb energy in a crash, usually the front and rear parts

cuticle a waxy layer mainly on the top surface of leaves that reduces water loss

cuttings an artificial way of making genetically identical copies of plants by removing and planting sections of stems or roots

cytoplasm contents of a cell outside the nucleus, made up mainly of water with dissolved chemicals, and organelles

decay (radioactive) the splitting of a radioactive nucleus with the emission of ionising radiation

decomposer organism that feeds on dead organic remains by secreting enzymes onto them and taking up the semi-digested food

defibrillator electrical device used following a heart attack to restore a normal rhythm to the heart

deficiency a lack of one or more minerals resulting in a lack of healthy growth

detergent chemical that has a cleaning effect

detritivore animals that feed on pieces of dead organic material

detritus loose fragments or grains that have been worn away from rock

dicotyledonous a flowering plant with two embryonic seed leaves or cotyledons that usually appear at germination

diesel a fossil fuel used in cars, lorries and buses

differentiation the process by which cells become specialised for different functions

diffusion net passive movement of particles from an area of high concentration to an area of low concentration

diploid when the chromosomes in a cell occur in pairs

displacement in chemistry, replacement of one atom or ions with another

distance–time graph graph showing distance moved by an object plotted against time; the gradient of the line at any point on the line gives the velocity of the object at that time

DNA the molecule that codes for all the instructions needed to make an organism, and is also capable of replication

DNA fingerprinting a photograph of bands produced from sections of DNA that can be used to identify an individual

dormancy the state in seeds or buds where development or growth is occurring very slowly

double helix the shape of a DNA molecule consisting of two chains twisted into a spiral

double insulated electrical device with plastic casing which does not require an earth wire as the casing can never become live

drag frictional force opposing the motion of an object through a fluid, for example, air

earth wire part of household wiring that only carries a current if there is a fault, breaking the fuse

egestion discharging undigested or waste material from a cell or organism

elastic potential energy the energy stored in the elastic, for example, when an elastic band or a spring is stretched

electric shock symptoms resulting from the passage of an electric current through a body

electrode an electrical connection from the power supply to a conductor such as an electrolyte

electrolysis the decomposition of a compound by the passage of electricity

electrolyte the liquid or solution used in electrolysis

electron negatively charged sub-atomic particle which exists outside the nucleus

electrostatic dust precipitator device fitted to the chimneys of power stations and factories to reduce pollution

element smallest part that a compound can be broken down into

energy the ability to do work

enzyme organic catalysts that speed up the rate of a reaction

essential element element that is needed by a living organism, e.g. plant

fertilisation the fusion of male and female sex cells

fertiliser compound or mixture of compounds designed to give plants essential minerals

fetus an embryo that has developed to the point where it contains all the necessary structures needed to grow into a new individual

fish farm tanks or ponds in which fish are raised for food

flame test test carried out by placing a chemical in a Bunsen flame to determine the identity of the metal it contains

food preservation keeping food in conditions that stop it decaying

fossil fuel fuel produced by the slow decay of dead things

free fall when an object is falling under constant acceleration

frequency the number of complete waves passing a point in one second

frictional force contact force opposing the motion of one object sliding past another

fuel consumption the distance you can travel using a certain amount of fuel, usually measured in miles per gallon

fullerene form of carbon discovered in 1985; fullerenes are made of ball-shaped molecules containing many carbon atoms

fungicide a chemical that kills fungi

fuse thin piece of wire which melts if the current through it is too high, breaking a circuit

gamete a cell involved in reproduction, such as an ovum or a sperm

gamma ray most energetic and penetrating electromagnetic radiation, emitted when certain radioactive nuclei decay

gene a section of DNA that codes for one specific instruction

generator device that uses mechanical energy to produce electricity

genetic engineering the moving of genes from one organism to another

genetic modification any alteration of genetic material to make it capable of producing new substances or performing new functions

geotropism a growth response in plants either towards or away from gravity

gestation period the period of time between fertilisation and birth

gradient measure of steepness; often related to graphs – taking two points that lie on the line, it is the difference in the y-coordinates divided by the difference in the x-coordinates

graphite one form of the element carbon. The carbon atoms are present in layers. These layers are only weakly held to each other

gravitational potential energy the energy something has when it is lifted up against gravity

group vertical column in the Periodic Table

guard cell two cells that control the opening and closing of a stoma

Haber Process process to manufacture ammonia, invented by Fritz Haber

haemoglobin a red protein containing an iron atom that can combine reversibly with oxygen

halide a compound containing the ions of a halogen (any element in Group 7 of the Periodic Table)

halogen element in Group 7 of the Periodic Table

haploid when each cell only has one copy of a chromosome from each pair

herbicide a chemical that kills plants

hydroponics growing plants without soil, usually in water

insecticide a chemical that kills insects

insoluble description of a chemical that will not dissolve in a solvent

insulator (electrical) material that does not allow an electric current to pass through it

intensive farming trying to produce as much food as possible from a certain area of land

ion positively or negatively charged particles formed when an atom or group of atoms loses or gains electrons

ionic bond type of chemical bond involving the complete transfer of one or more electrons from a metal atom to a non-metal atom. Ions are formed

isotopes atoms of the same element and therefore with the same proton number, but with a different number of neutrons and therefore a different mass number

kinetic energy the energy possessed by a moving object

live wire a high voltage wire, with brown insulation, that carries electric current to mains appliances

longitudinal wave a wave whose vibrations are parallel to its direction of travel

lower epidermis the bottom layer of cells in a leaf

lustrous with a shiny but not brilliant appearance

mass number sum of the number of protons and neutrons in an atom

medicine chemical administered to cure illness

meiosis cell division that occurs when gametes are produced. It reduces the number of chromosomes from 46 to 23 by half, e.g. in humans

metallic bonding the forces that keep atoms together in a metal

mineral a compound containing essential elements needed by plants for their growth (and obtained from soil and fertiliser)

mitochondria microscopic organelles found in the cytoplasm of plant and animal cells. They are the site of many of the reactions of respiration (singular = mitochondrion)

mitosis cell division that produces identical copies of cells

molecule particle with two or more atoms joined together.

multicellular made up of many cells

mutation a change in the structure of a gene or DNA, caused by such things as chemicals, X-rays or radiation.

nanochemistry the chemistry of very small particles

nanoparticle a very small particle (about one-millionth of a metre in diameter)

nanotube very small particles arranged in a tube shape

negative charge the charge on an electron; the charge on a substance that has gained electrons

neutral wire wire, with blue insulation, kept at $0\,V$, which provides the return path for mains electricity

neutralisation reaction in which an acid reacts with a base or alkali

neutron neutral sub-atomic particles which exist inside the nucleus

NPK the ratio of nitrogen:phosphorous:potassium in a fertiliser

nuclear fission the splitting of unstable nuclei to release energy

nuclear power the use of nuclear energy (from fission) to produce electricity

nucleon number sum of the number of protons and neutrons in an atom

nucleus the area of a cell that contains the genetic material and so controls the processes occurring in the cell

nucleus the central part of an atom. It contains protons and neutrons

optical brightener chemicals added to washing powders to reflect light and so make clothes look whiter or brighter

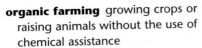

organic farming growing crops or raising animals without the use of chemical assistance

osmosis the movement of water molecules from a dilute solution to a concentrated solution, through a partially permeable membrane

paddle shift control control positioned on, or close to, the steering wheel which the driver can operate without letting go of the steering wheel

palisade mesophyll large rectangular cells in the leaf that are the main site of photosynthesis

partially permeable allowing certain molecules through but not others

passive safety features that make a car safe but do not actively affect how the car is driven, for example, cruise control and paddle shift controls

period horizontal row of elements in the Periodic Table

pesticide a chemical that will kill a pest on crops

petrol a fossil fuel used in cars, lorries and buses

pH scale numbers from 0 to 14 to show how acidic or alkaline a solution is

pharmaceutical drug a chemical that is made to be used as a medicine

phloem plant tissue that transports dissolved food around the plant

photocopier device that uses electrostatics to print a copy of a document

phototropism movement of an organism in response to light

placenta a structure produced by the embryo that grows into the wall of the uterus to absorb nutrients for the growing baby

plant hormone a substance that stimulates growth in plants

plasma a pale-yellow liquid that forms the fluid part of the blood

platelets small fragments of cells found in the blood and involved in blood clotting

positive charge the charge on a proton or the charge on a substance that has lost electrons

potential difference voltage in an electric circuit

power the rate of transfer of energy

precipitate solid that appears when two solutions are mixed together

precipitation the separation of a solid from a solution. The solid usually settles out

predicted yield the maximum amount of product that could be made during a chemical reaction, calculated using the equation and relative atomic masses

producer an organism that can make its own food from simple inorganic chemicals

protein made up of chains of amino acids, proteins are one of the many substances found in food such as meat, cheese, fish or eggs, that are necessary for the body to grow and be strong

proton positively charged sub-atomic particle which exists inside the nucleus

proton number the number of protons in an atom

pulmonary artery A large artery that conducts venous blood from the heart to the lungs of tetrapods

pulmonary vein A large vein that conducts oxygenated blood from the lungs to the heart in tetrapods

pyramid of biomass a diagram that represents the total mass at each trophic level of a food chain

pyramid of numbers a diagram showing the relative numbers of organisms at each trophic level of a food chain

radiation how heat energy is transfered by infrared waves

radioactive waste unwanted material resulting from radioactive decay

radiographer the person who takes X-rays in a hospital

radioisotope an isotope of an element that decays by emitting radiation

rarefaction part of a longitudinal wave where the particles are further apart than normal

recycling returning used material to the production chain

red blood cells blood cells that contain the red pigment haemoglobin, which carries oxygen from the lungs around the body

relative atomic mass the mass of an atom measured on a scale where one atom of the isotope carbon-12 is exactly 12 units

relative formula mass the mass obtained by adding together the relative atomic masses of all the atoms shown in the formula of a compound

repel when two objects move away from each other, such as like poles of a magnet or objects with like charge

reservoir a place where large quantities of water are stored

resistance opposition of a circuit component to the flow of electricity (= voltage/current)

reversible reaction a chemical reaction that can move in either direction, forwards or backwards

rheostat electrical device that allows you to change its resistance and control the current in the circuit

rooting powder a treatment containing plant growth substances that is used to encourage cuttings to produce roots

safety cage the passenger compartment of a car which stays rigid in a crash to reduce crushing injuries

sedimentation settling of solid particles out of a suspension

selective breeding a way of improving stock by selecting and breeding from those animals and plants that have the desired characteristics

selective weedkiller artificial plant hormones that kill some plants but not others

semilunar a half-moon-shaped valve at the beginning of each of the arteries leading from the heart

sewage untreated waste materials

sex cells specialised cells that are produced to join with each other to form a zygote

smoke detector device used to detect the presence of smoke

soluble able to dissolve in a solvent

solute material (gas, solid or liquid) that will dissolve in a solvent

solution mixture formed when a solute dissolves in a solvent

solvent liquid in which a solute dissolves

speciality chemical a chemical produced in small quantities for special use, e.g. a medical drug

speed rate of change of distance (= distance/time)

speed camera roadside device that measures the speed of cars as they pass and takes a picture of any car that is going faster than the speed limit

speed–time graph graph showing the velocity of an object plotted against time; the gradient of the line gives the acceleration of the object; the area under the line gives the distance travelled

spongy mesophyll a layer of cells in the leaf with large airspaces between them to allow gases to diffuse

static electricity build up of stationary charge

stem cell a cell that has the capability to become any other type of cell

stomata small pores on the underside of a leaf that regulate the release of water, and allow release of oxygen and the absorption of carbon dioxide (singular = stoma)

stopping distance distance a vehicle travels from the time the driver sees a hazard to when the vehicle comes to rest (= thinking distance + braking distance)

superconductor material that conducts electricity with very little or no resistance

surrogate a woman who bears a child on behalf of another

tensile strength maximum load that can be applied to stretch a material without it breaking

terminal speed the speed of an object where the forces acting on it balance

thermal decomposition breaking down of compounds by the action of heat

thinking distance distance travelled by a vehicle in the time it takes the driver to start braking once he has seen a hazard

tracer a radioisotope introduced into a system so that its path can be followed

traction control increases or decreases the forces to each wheel of a vehicle to reduce the chance of it sliding out of control

transition element element in the central block of the Periodic Table

translocation the movement of sugars and other food materials through the phloem in plants.

transpiration the loss of water from plant leaves

tricuspid a valve between the right atrium and right ventricle in the heart

trophic level a feeding level in a food chain

turbine a device, powered by water or steam, that produces rotation

ultrasound sound of a high frequency – above 20 000 Hz – which cannot be heard by humans

upper epidermis the top layer of cells in a leaf. It does not contain any chloroplasts

upper threshold of human hearing highest frequency of sound that can be heard by the human ear

uranium element that exists as a number of isotopes, some of which are radioactive

vacuole part of a cell that contains fluid enclosed in a membrane

vascular bundle a collection of xylem and phloem vessels that transport food and water around a plant

vein blood vessel that returns blood to the heart

vein one of the vascular bundles in a leaf

vena cava the large vein that returns blood from the body to the heart

ventricles the lower two muscular chambers of the heart. The left ventricle pumps blood around the body; the right ventricle pumps blood to the lungs

water softener chemical added to water to remove the salts that cause water hardness

wavelength the distance between two succesive compressions in a sound wave

white blood cells found in the blood and form part of the body's defence mechanism. They produce antibodies and engulf bacteria

wilt the drooping of a plant when its cells become flaccid

work the energy transferred when a force moves an object (= force × distance)

X-ray high energy, penetrating electromagnetic wave of short wavelength

xylem conductive tissue found in plants that carries water up from the roots to the leaves

yield the quantity of product made during a chemical reaction

zygote the single cell produced when two gametes join

Index

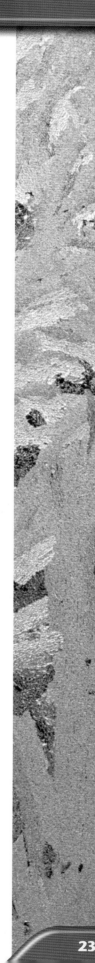

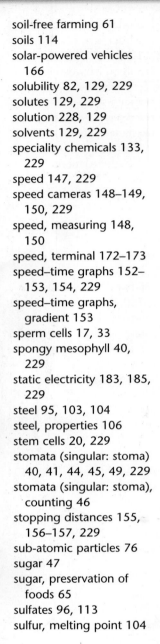